BILLY GRAHAM
Evangelistic Association
Always Good News.

Dear Friend,

I am pleased to send you this copy of my father's classic devotional collection, *Unto the Hills*. I pray its timeless truths, gathered from a lifetime of study and ministry, will inspire and encourage you in your walk with God.

Providing daily food for thought, this book will help you live a joyful and fruitful life even during difficult times. The 366 meditations—one for each day of the year—will remind you to keep your focus on the Source of your strength. As the psalmist said, "My help comes from the Lord." May you experience His help, too, as you lift up your eyes unto the hills.

For nearly 60 years the Billy Graham Evangelistic Association has worked to take the Good News of Jesus Christ throughout the world by every effective means available, and I'm excited about what God will do in the years ahead. If you would like to know more about our ministry, please contact us:

In the U.S.:

Billy Graham Evangelistic Association
1 Billy Graham Parkway
Charlotte, NC 28201-0001
billygraham.org
webmaster@billygraham.org
Toll-free: 1-877-2GRAHAM (1-877-247-2426)

In Canada:

Billy Graham Evangelistic Association of Canada
20 Hopewell Way NE
Calgary, Alberta T3J 5H5
billygraham.ca
Toll-free: 1-888-393-0003

We would appreciate knowing how our ministry has touched your life. May God bless you.

Sincerely,

Franklin Graham
President

STEPS TO PEACE WITH GOD

1. RECOGNIZE GOD'S PLAN—PEACE AND LIFE

The message you have read in this book stresses that God loves you and wants you to experience His peace and life.

The BIBLE says ... For God loved the world so much that He gave His only Son, so that everyone who believes in Him may not die but have eternal life. John 3:16

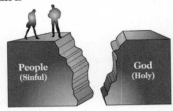

2. REALIZE OUR PROBLEM—SEPARATION FROM GOD

People choose to disobey God and go their own way. This results in separation from God.

The BIBLE says ... Everyone has sinned and is far away from God's saving presence. Romans 3:23

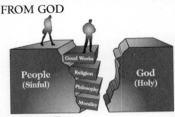

3. RESPOND TO GOD'S REMEDY—CROSS OF CHRIST

God sent His Son to bridge the gap. Christ did this by paying the penalty of our sins when He died on the cross and rose from the grave.

The BIBLE says ... But God has shown us how much He loves us—it was while we were still sinners that Christ died for us! Romans 5:8

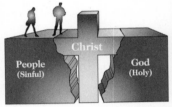

4. RECEIVE GOD'S SON—LORD AND SAVIOR

You cross the bridge into God's family when you ask Christ to come into your life.

The BIBLE says ... Some, however, did receive Him and believed in Him; so He gave them the right to become God's children. John 1:12

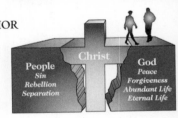

THE INVITATION IS TO:

REPENT (turn from your sins), ASK for God's forgiveness, and by faith RECEIVE Jesus Christ into your heart and life and follow Him in obedience as your Lord and Savior.

PRAYER OF COMMITMENT

"Dear Lord Jesus, I know that I am a sinner, and I ask for Your forgiveness. I believe You died for my sins and rose from the dead. I turn from my sins and invite You to come into my heart and life. I want to trust and follow You as my Lord and Savior. In Your Name, Amen."

If you are committing your life to Christ, please let us know!
Billy Graham Evangelistic Association
1 Billy Graham Parkway, Charlotte, NC 28201-0001
1-877-2GRAHAM (1-877-247-2426)
billygraham.org

Billy Graham

UNTO

the

HILLS

A Daily Devotional

This *Billy Graham Library Selection* is published
with permission from W Publishing Group,
a division of Thomas Nelson, Inc.

W PUBLISHING GROUP™

www.wpublishinggroup.com

A Division of Thomas Nelson, Inc.
www.ThomasNelson.com

Unless otherwise indicated, Scripture quotations in this publication are from the King James Version of the Bible. Other Scripture quotations are from the following sources: The Amplified Bible (AB), Old Testament, ©1962, 1964 by Zondervan Publishing House, and from The Amplified New Testament, ©1958 by the Lockman Foundation (used by permission). The Jerusalem Bible (JB), ©1966 by Darton, Longman & Todd, Ltd. and Doubleday and Company, Inc. Used by permission. The New Testament: a New Translation, ©1964 by James Moffatt, published by Harper & Row, Inc. (MOFFATT). The New American Standard Bible (NASB), ©1960, 1962, 1963, 1968, 1971, 1972, 1973, 1975, 1977 by the Lockman Foundation. Used by permission. The Holy Bible: New International Version (NIV), ©1978 by the New York International Bible Society. Used by permission of Zondervan Bible Publishers. The New King James Version (NKJV), ©1979, 1980, 1982, Thomas Nelson, Inc., Publishers. The Revised Standard Version of the Bible (RSV), ©1946, 1952, 1971, 1973 by the Division of Christian Education of the National Council of the Churches of Christ in the U.S.A. Used by permission. Today's English Version of the Bible (TEV), ©1966, 1971, 1976 by the American Bible Society. Used by permission. The Living Bible (TLB), ©1971 by Tyndale House Publishers, Wheaton, Ill. Used by permission.

The meditations in this book are excerpted from the following publications by Billy Graham: *Angels*, ©1975, 1986; *Approaching Hoofbeats*, ©1983; *The Holy Spirit*, ©1978; *How to Be Born Again*, ©1977; *Peace with God*, ©1953, 1984; *The Secret of Happiness*, ©1955, 1985; *Till Armageddon*, ©1981. Sermon excerpts from *Decision* magazine are copyrighted by the Billy Graham Evangelistic Association, 1 Billy Graham Parkway, Charlotte, NC 28201.

Library of Congress Cataloging in Publication Data
Graham, Billy, 1918–
Unto the hills.
1. Devotional calendars.
1. Title.
BV4811.G62 1986 242'.2 86-24534
PREVIOUS ISBN 0-913367-47-8
ISBN 0-8499-1334-9 (hardcover)

Printed in the United States of America

OUR family has lived for many years in a comfortable log home in the mountains of North Carolina, 3,200 feet above sea level. There is something serene about living in the mountains or on a hill.

When Jesus appointed the twelve apostles, He called them unto the hills and they came to Him (Mark 3:13). Our Lord frequently retreated to the hills or mountains for moments of solitude when the crowds became too great.

But as English devotional writer Oswald Chambers has noted, we were not made for mountaintop experiences alone. We are made for the valley of life. God will sometimes allow us a view from the hills, but only so that we might be refreshed enough to return to the valley—where the action is—that we might be of service to Him. Mountaintops are for views and inspiration, but fruit is grown in the valleys.

As much as my wife, Ruth, and I enjoy our home in the hills of North Carolina, we spend very little time there because God has called us into the valley of life where the lost people are. If we spent all of our time in the hills and on mountaintops, how would we effectively serve God?

I have compiled some thoughts from more than fifty years as a minister of the Gospel of Jesus Christ in hopes of better equipping you as you live for Christ in the valley.

Some of you will read this book as you search for answers to the problems in the valley of life. You have tried everything else and have not found satisfaction. It is you that I am particularly interested in reaching.

Others of you who are already believers still need assurance that, as you walk through the valley of the shadow of death, God has not forgotten you and is, in fact, still with you. I hope this book will be a help to you, as well.

While the hills and mountains are a wonderful place to "get away from it all," we must always remember that our ultimate and certain help comes from the Lord who made the mountains and the valleys. David expressed this beautifully in Psalm 121:

> I will lift up mine eyes unto the hills,
> from whence cometh my help.
> My help cometh from the Lord,
> which made heaven and earth.
>
> (vv. 1–2)

May God bless and direct you as you read *Unto the Hills*.

January

January 1

A CLEAN SLATE

Create in me a clean heart, O God; and renew a right spirit
within me.   Psalm 51:10

DID you ever have the experience in school of erasing an
entire blackboard? When the slate has been wiped clean, it is
as if nothing at all had ever been written on it.

This is what God does for us when we come to Him
confessing our sin. First John 1:9 says, "If we confess our sins,
he is faithful and just to forgive us our sins, and to cleanse us
from all unrighteousness."

How many times in your life have you wished you could
start all over again with a clean slate, with a new life? Resolve
right now to allow God to wipe your slate clean by confessing
your sins and letting Him give you a brand new start.

The apostle Paul did this when he said, "Forgetting what
lies behind and straining forward to what lies ahead, I press
on toward the goal for the prize of the upward call of God in
Christ Jesus" (Philippians 3:13–14, RSV).

January 2

LOST AND FOUND

I am the way, and the truth, and the life; no one comes to the Father, but
by me.   John 14:6, RSV

RECENTLY, while returning to my hotel in a major city, the
driver turned left when he should have turned right, and it
took him awhile to figure out how to get to our destination.
He had to stop and check his road map.

Often in life just one wrong turn, just one wrong decision
can take us where we do not want to go or, more importantly,

can keep us from going where we do want to go.

There is an ancient saying that "all roads lead to Rome." When one is lost on a road to Rome or anywhere else, all that is needed to find the way is a good road map or directions from someone who knows the way.

Not all roads lead to God, as some suggest. There is a roadblock which keeps man from reaching God, no matter what road he takes. That roadblock is sin. But God has provided a map—the Bible—and He has provided One who knows the way and can give directions—Jesus Christ.

Christ said, "No man comes to the Father but by me." Not only does Christ give directions to the Father through Himself, He also gives us daily directions as to His Father's will for our lives. Like directions from a map or a person in our travels, we can follow them and get to our desired destination, or we can ignore them and become lost.

Remember, Jesus did *not* say, "I am one of the ways, or one of the roads you can take to get to the Father." What He said was, "I am *the* way." Determine to follow Christ and never be lost!

January 3

THE ULTIMATE PROTECTION

For he has said, "I will never fail you nor forsake you."
Hence we can confidently say, "The Lord is my helper, I will
not be afraid." Hebrews 13:5–6, RSV

SOME years ago when our son Ned entered a new school, he met some boys from the city who thought they were pretty tough. Ned had never had to confront boys from the streets who had much experience in having to defend themselves and who witnessed fights as a regular occurrence. The boys from the city soon began picking on him.

Another boy, who had befriended Ned, saw that in order for our son to survive he would have to learn to defend himself, so he taught Ned a few basics of karate and some of the other martial arts. After much practice, Ned demonstrated his new skills on one of the boys who had been harassing him, and the bullies stopped picking on him.

God wants to teach us how to defend ourselves against sin. Satan, the ultimate bully, attacks us at our weakest points and wants to defeat us so that we will not be effective for God.

In the Bible God offers us some spiritual "training" which builds us up inside in much the same way as physical exercise and discipline can build us up on the outside. But, like exercise or training in martial arts, we must be consistent in our reading of Scripture and diligent in its application to the situations and circumstances around us. God has not promised to shield us from trouble, but He has promised to protect us in the midst of trouble.

Nothing can touch us apart from God's will. If something does touch us, we can be sure that it is for the purpose of building us up into a stronger and more effective witness so that God can use us to do battle with the evil bully of history, the devil.

Remember, God will never fail you or forsake you!

January 4

THE VALUE OF A MAN

What is man, that thou art mindful of him? Psalm 8:4

A CERTAIN rich man died and the question was asked at his funeral, "How much did he leave?"

"He left it all," came the reply.

Often, I hear someone introduced this way: "This is Bob

and he works for . . . ," as if where a person works determines his or her value. I have noticed that it is usually only the well-to-do or those who are thought of as "successful" who are introduced this way.

Yet God does not judge us by success. He loves each person the same because your value and mine does not come from what we do or have, the clothes we wear, the house in which we live, or the type of car we drive. Our value comes from the fact that God made us and Christ died for us. And so, whether we have things or not, we are just as valuable to God.

God gave all that He had—His Son, the Lord Jesus Christ—because He valued us so highly, even when we did not value Him. Since God thought this much of us, shouldn't we show that we value Him by putting Him first in all that we do—our family life, our business life, our spiritual life?

There is a song which says, "Put Jesus first in your life, let Him handle all the problems that come your way . . . you have searched in vain for something; now you don't want that something you've found. Put Jesus first in your life, and turn your life around."

The actual value of an object is that which is placed on it by the owner or buyer.

God has shown the value He has placed on you by sending His Son to redeem you.

January 5
....
GOD IS A PERSON

It is of the LORD'S mercies that we are not consumed, because his compassions fail not. They are new every morning: great is thy faithfulness. Lamentations 3:22–23

WHEN I was a small boy, I thought of God as an old man

with a long white beard. After all, hadn't Michaelangelo painted Him that way?

Later, as I read the Bible, and after I had accepted Christ as my Savior, I realized that God is a spirit, yet He has the attributes of a person: He thinks, He speaks, He communicates, He loves, He becomes angry, He grieves.

Because God is a person, He feels that which we feel. After all, we are made in His image, so it is to be expected that we would be able to communicate our deepest feelings and emotions to God.

God communicates with us in two ways. First, He communicates with us through His written Word, the Bible. It tells us who God is, who we are, and why we need a Savior so that we might have that relationship with God which sin has broken.

Second, God communicates with us through His Son. Jesus said that no man can come to the Father except through Him. We have that access to Jesus, and thus to God, through salvation.

God is the same yesterday, today, and forever. He never changes.

January 6

FREEDOM OF CHOICE

Choose this day whom you will serve, whether the gods your fathers served in the region beyond the River, or the gods of the Amorites in whose land you dwell; but as for me and my house, we will serve the LORD. Joshua 24:15, RSV

W E hear a lot about "freedom of choice" these days. But think about it. The very word "choice" presupposes at least two alternatives.

When Joshua asked the Israelites to "choose this day

whom you will serve," the choice he gave them was between God and the false god Baal. Before waiting for their reply, Joshua announced his choice, "As for me and my house, we will serve the LORD."

Choices are offered throughout the Bible as they are throughout our lives. Repeatedly throughout Scripture, both God and man made choices.

God commands man to make those choices, but only after providing him with sufficient information so that his choices will be informed ones. Because of truth in lending and truth in labeling laws, one cannot apply for a loan or buy a product in a supermarket without being furnished with certain information.

This information is necessary in making intelligent choices. God has given us information about Himself, including His holiness, man's sinfulness, God's provision for that sin, Jesus Christ, and scores of promises to man about what will happen if he accepts God's promises and what will happen if he does not. Galatians 6:6–8 says, "Let him that is taught in the word communicate unto him that teacheth in all good things. Be not deceived; God is not mocked: for whatsoever a man soweth, that shall he also reap. For he that soweth to his flesh shall of the flesh reap corruption; but he that soweth to the Spirit shall of the Spirit reap life everlasting."

Some time ago there was a television program called "Truth or Consequences." The host of the program used to say to the contestants, "If you don't tell the truth, you will have to pay the consequences." It is the same with choices. If you make the wrong choice, you will have to pay the consequences. But if you make the right choice, you receive all of the benefits. So it is best to choose wisely, as Joshua did, because the choices we make have the potential for affecting our lives for better or for worse.

GOD'S POWER REVEALED THROUGH PRAYER

Pray without ceasing. In every thing give thanks: for this is the will of God in Christ Jesus concerning you. 1 Thessalonians 5:17–18

HOW many times have you heard someone say, "All I can do is pray"?

All I can do is pray?! You might as well say to a starving man, "All I can do is offer you food," or to a sick person, "All I can do is give you medicine that will make you well," or to a poor child, "All I can do is buy the toy you most want for your birthday."

Praying unlocks the doors of heaven and releases the power of God. James 4:2 says, "Ye have not, because ye ask not." And Jesus said, "And all things, whatsoever ye shall ask in prayer, believing, ye shall receive" (Matthew 21:22).

Many of us want to do a work *for* God, but few of us want to spend hours in prayer *to* God. It goes against our natural inclinations to pray, which is precisely why prayer counts so much with God. It is unnatural. It is, in fact, supernatural! And it always gets God's attention.

I am sometimes amused when people tell me, "God answered my prayer." What they mean is that God gave them what they asked for. But if He had not granted their request, He would still have answered their prayer. We forget that "No" and "Wait" are also answers, as is "Yes."

I have answered every request made by my children to me. The answer has not always been what they wanted, but it has always been in accordance with what I have thought was best for them at the time. God is the same way, except that His answers are always right and good and best, while mine may or may not have been.

And remember, whether prayer changes our situation or not, one thing is certain: Prayer will change us!

January 8

THE STORMS OF LIFE

Thou wilt keep him in perfect peace, whose mind is stayed on thee. Isaiah 26:3

ONCE while flying between cities on the African continent, I began to share my faith in Christ with some reporters who were accompanying me. None seemed interested in hearing the Gospel.

Suddenly, the plane entered a very turbulent storm. The plane shook and began to bounce up and down.

After we had successfully come through the storm, one of the reporters approached me and said, "What were you saying about life after death?"

When Jesus was on the Sea of Galilee with some of His disciples, a storm came up and began to toss the boat around. His disciples cried out in fear, but Jesus slept at the stern of the boat, unafraid and unintimidated by the weather.

When they awakened Him, He rebuked them for their lack of faith, and then He rebuked the storm. Both the storm and the disciples were silenced!

There is a wonderful old hymn which says, "He gives us peace in the midst of a storm." In life there are all kinds of storms: storms of unbelief; storms of materialism (mostly brought about by those who want more material things than they have); storms of secularism, moral degeneracy, and international tensions.

Jesus was at peace in the midst of that storm because He and His heavenly Father had a relationship that gave Him peace. It is that type of relationship that God wants to have with us.

Are storms in your life making you afraid? You can have peace despite the storms. Stay close to Jesus Christ. Read God's Word. Pray.

January 9

ANGELS

The angel of the LORD *encamps around those who fear him, and delivers them.* Psalm 34:7, RSV

A FEW years ago there was a television program called "Charlie's Angels." These "angels" were three attractive women who were involved in fighting crime. In the theater, people who finance expensive productions are called "angels" because without them, the shows would never get to the stage. These are modern interpretations of the word "angel," but the idea is correct, nevertheless.

Angels are beings who help other people against evil forces, and they do perform certain duties, without which we could not always be able to achieve a certain goal or station in life.

In the Bible, there are several instances when angels revealed themselves to man. Although these instances occur mostly in the Old Testament, perhaps the most famous appearance occurs in the New Testament, when Mary is visited by an angel and told that she is to bear the Son of God, Jesus Christ.

Mostly, though, angels are invisible. Of course this does not make them any less real than you would be to me if I happened to be blindfolded. Our ability to see angels or not to see them has nothing at all to do with their existence and their role in protecting us from certain harms.

Though we do not pray to angels, and man, for the

moment, is only "a little lower than the angels," they are just one more example of how God cares for and keeps us against the forces of Satan which are constantly trying to defeat us.

Truly, angels are God's "secret agents."

THE FOUNDATION OF MARRIAGE

What therefore God hath joined together, let not man put asunder. Matthew 19:6

WITH the divorce rate hovering around 50 percent, will any homes be left by the end of the century? The impact of divorce on children is staggering and is still to be assessed as the psychological and emotional scars break through to harm some future families.

One of the primary reasons for the breakdown in the home is that we have forgotten the biblical commands relating to marriage and the family, commands which never change. Even some "Christian" writers are publishing books today which reject the Bible's strict teaching on divorce.

The Bible does not allow divorce on grounds of "he doesn't love me" or "she doesn't love me." The Bible says God *hates* divorce. He hates divorce because, as Jesus taught, marriage is a picture of the unity between God the Father, God the Son, and God the Holy Spirit. When people get divorced they are tearing at the very fabric of the unity of God.

From the beginning, Satan has tried to disrupt the unity of the Trinity. First, Satan tried to make himself a part of the Trinity by desiring to be co-equal with God. It was his sin of pride that caused his expulsion from heaven. Second, Satan was successful in tempting our first parents into sin, thereby breaking the unique relationship between man and his

Creator. Third, Satan tried to pry Jesus loose from His relationship to the Father when he tempted Him in the wilderness. Today, Satan is eating away like a large termite at the foundation of marriage and the family.

Satan never changes, but neither does God. God still hates divorce.

There is no marriage that is beyond repair in the sight of God. If we will first submit ourselves to Christ and then our marriage into His care and keeping, nothing is impossible with God. But we must humble ourselves and lay our pride and desire to please ourselves first on His altar. It is only then that God can restore feelings and bring healing to a marriage in trouble.

The first step in healing a marriage is ours. God provides the salve that heals.

January 11

THE FAMILY AND THE WORKPLACE

Children are a gift from God; they are his reward.   Psalm 127:3, TLB

TODAY there are more pressures on the home than perhaps at any time in the history of the human race.

By necessity or by desire, more women are working today than ever before. Many feel guilty about leaving their children in the care of others or having them return to an empty home while they are at work. Many divorced women must work to support themselves and their children, a phenomenon which is becoming more and more common in the age in which we live. But many women (and men, too) devote more time to their working life than they do to their family life. Is it any wonder, then, that so many marriages are in trouble?

To paraphrase the Bible, what shall it profit a man (or a woman) who gains the whole world but loses his (or her) own family? What achievement in life is equal to a happy home and rearing successful children who grow up in praise of their parents? Every material goal, even if it is met, will pass away. But the heritage of children is timeless. Someone has said that our children are our messages to the future. They will tell others who will never know us who we were.

More importantly, our children have been entrusted to us by God, children made in His image and for whom Christ died. Our primary responsibility is not to make sure they have the best clothes and live in the best houses. It is to make sure they grow up in homes where God is present and the love of Christ reigns so that they will come to know God through His Son.

What could be more valuable than successful children and a happy home life?

January 12

WHAT TO DO WITH PROBLEMS

Don't worry about anything; instead, pray about everything; tell God your needs and don't forget to thank him for his answers. Philippians 4:6, TLB

WHAT do you do when you have a problem? Do you worry? Most of us do. But does worrying solve the problem? No, it does not. Then if worry doesn't solve the problem, why worry?

Hezekiah gives us an idea for problem solving: "And Hezekiah received the letter of the hand of the messengers, and read it: and Hezekiah went up into the house of the LORD, and spread it before the LORD. And Hezekiah prayed before the LORD, and said, O LORD God of Israel, which dwellest between the cherubims, thou art the God, even thou alone, of all the kingdoms of the earth; thou hast made heaven and earth. . . ."

Then Hezekiah prayed: "Now therefore, O LORD our God, I beseech thee, save thou us out of his hand, that all the kingdoms of the earth may know that thou art the LORD God, even thou only" (2 Kings 19:14–15, 19).

Hezekiah's unselfish prayer had a purpose, one that God could not ignore.

Hezekiah, who was used to taking his problems directly to God, took the problem that the king of Assyria was about to attack Jerusalem to the Lord. And God answered and miraculously caused this powerful king to be defeated.

Instead of turning to God as a first resource, we so often turn to Him as a last resort. Follow Hezekiah's formula. Turn to God first with your problems, for only He is capable of handling them in a way that will be in your best interest.

January 13

DESPERATE CIRCUMSTANCES

And when he had spent everything . . . he began to be in want. Luke 15:14, RSV

SIGNPOSTS along the highway are there to keep us from getting lost and to keep us safe by regulating our speed and warning us of sharp turns, detours, and other hazards. And when we ignore these signposts, we do so at our own peril.

In the familiar story of the Prodigal Son, the young man ignores every signpost God has erected to keep him from desperate circumstances. Long before the young man reached the pigpen where he finally "came to his senses," he had numerous opportunities to turn around, to repent, and to go home.

His problems began long before he asked his father for his inheritance and then threw it away on "wine, women, and song." He was not satisfied to be in his father's house with all of his needs met. He wanted more. He believed the lie that something more exciting was in store for him away from his father.

Isn't this how we sometimes behave? We think that God is holding out on us, that there is something better than a close relationship with our heavenly Father, that the world has more excitement and fulfillment to offer us than God does. By thinking this way and then by acting as the Prodigal Son did, we create our own desperate circumstances. Then, we turn to God and cry out in the midst of our desperation.

Fortunately, like the Prodigal Son, our Father always hears our cries. But it would be so much better if we would not get into desperate circumstances in the first place. That is why God has erected signposts along life's road—to help keep us out of trouble. They include reading His Word daily, praying "without ceasing," and determining to seek His will for our lives.

Such a path is sure to see us home safely.

January 14

JOY

For the joy of the LORD is your strength. Nehemiah 8:10

WHAT is joy?

Some of us think that joy is a state of perpetual happiness, a bubbling personality, a person who is always smiling and laughing. These can be expressions of joy, but true joy is something far deeper than that.

Joy is produced in our hearts when we know that God loves us, when we have a close relationship with Him through reading His Word, praying, and desiring to honor Him in all that we do, and by serving others.

Joy does not mean that we are never sad, that we never cry. Instead, joy is a quiet confidence, a state of peace in the heart of the believer. Sometimes it manifests itself in an impromptu song while riding alone in a car. Sometimes one is so overwhelmed by the love of God that tears of gratitude form in the eyes. At other times, it is a wonderful feeling of peace in the midst of war and turmoil.

Paul said, "We are troubled on every side, yet not distressed; we are perplexed, but not in despair; persecuted, but not forsaken; cast down, but not destroyed" (2 Corinthians 4:8–9). Paul had joy. So did Jesus, even under the shadow of the cross.

Like happiness, joy cannot be pursued. It comes from within. It is a state of being. It does not depend on circumstances, but triumphs over circumstances. It produces a gentleness of spirit and a magnetic personality.

It is easy to tell who the joyful people are. They are the ones whom others like to be around.

January 15

PREJUDICE

Know ye not that ye are the temple of God, and that the Spirit of God dwelleth in you? 1 Corinthians 3:16

PREJUDICE is a word that so often is used in connection with the race of a person. In this sense, prejudice is always wrong because it judges a person's value by the color of his skin and God has no favorites.

But there is another sense in which the root of the word prejudice is a good thing. To prejudge something is sometimes necessary.

While it is not good to pre-judge a person by appearance, social status, or the lack of education, we can and *should* pre-judge some "entertainment" establishments by what they advertise on the outside and know not to go in.

We can pre-judge drugs, which have become such a terrible problem in our culture. By seeing what drugs have done to others, we can avoid them. Besides, we know that the body is God's temple, and we ought not to cause it to become dirty by doing things to it, like taking drugs, which can cause harm to it.

So, let us avoid prejudice when it comes to a person's race or ethnic background or circumstances over which he or she has no control. But let us correctly prejudge those persons and places God has warned us about avoiding in His Word so that we do not get into trouble.

January 16

HOME SECURITY

Put on the whole armor of God, that ye may be able to stand against the wiles of the devil. Ephesians 6:11

IS your home built on a solid foundation? Is your home secure? Or is it filled with tension? Is it about ready to break up?

The family is the most important institution in the world. It was God's idea in the first place. It was not the idea of sociologists who thought it might be a good way to deliver the mail!

Families existed before cities and governments, before written language, nations, temples, churches.

In the home, character and attitudes are formed; integrity is born; values by which we live are made clear; and goals are set.

These last a lifetime.

Many people today are wringing their hands with fear and

insecurity because far more than what they see happening on Wall Street or in Washington, D.C., is happening to our families and our homes.

The prophet Nehemiah said, "There is much rubbish; so that we are not able to build the wall" (Nehemiah 4:10).

We see rubbish everywhere—rubbish on television and in films and magazines making fun of the home, making fun of marriage, one of the holiest of all institutions. (A well-known woman was asked on a national television program whether she believed in the institution of marriage. "Sure," she said, "but who wants to live in an institution?" This is typical of the ridicule now being heaped on the home and on marriage, particularly by those who are divorced or live together without being married.)

Today, Satan is attacking the family as never before. But what are our defenses against such attacks?

As always, our best defense is the Word of God, referred to by the apostle Paul as the "sword of truth." Put on the whole armor of God. Read the Bible together as a family. Have family devotions. Pray for one another daily by name. And most importantly, commit your marriage to Christ and make Him the center of your home.

January 17

TIME AND ETERNITY

Man that is born of a woman is of few days. . . . His days are determined, the number of his months are with thee, thou hast appointed his bounds that he cannot pass. Job 14:1, 5

LIFE is like a shadow, like a fleeting cloud moving across the face of the sun. David said, "We are strangers before thee, and sojourners, as were all our fathers" (1 Chronicles 29:15). The world is not our permanent home, it is only temporary.

David went on to declare that "our days on the earth are as a shadow, and there is none abiding."

When English patriot Sir William Russell went to the scaffold in 1683, he took his watch out of his pocket and handed it to the physician who attended him in his death. "Would you kindly take my timepiece?" he asked. "I have no use for it. I am now dealing with eternity."

For every one of us time is slipping away.

I had a young friend who went for a ride one day with a friend of his, never dreaming it would be his last ride on earth. He swerved to avoid hitting a car, ran into another car, and was thrown from his vehicle and killed. The newspapers are daily filled with stories of the death of people by accident or by assassination or by war. Those people did not know when they got out of bed that they were beginning their last day on earth.

How different would today be if you knew it would be your last one on earth before meeting God face to face? We should strive to live every day as if it was our last, for one day it will be!

The Bible teaches that God knows the exact moment when each man is to die (Job 14:5). There are appointed bounds beyond which we cannot pass. And I am convinced that when a man is prepared to die, he is also prepared to live. The primary goal in life, therefore, should be to prepare for death. Everything else is secondary.

January 18

A REFUGE IN TIME OF TROUBLE

God is our refuge and strength, a very present help in trouble.
Psalm 46:1

THE one hundredth anniversary of the Statue of Liberty was

a glorious experience and a reminder that America is an immigrant nation. Nearly all of us can trace our roots to another land.

After the Vietnam War, tens of thousands of immigrants came to America as refugees. Many more went to other free countries. The refugees were looking for safe havens for themselves and their families, away from wars and hunger and need. America has provided a safe haven for millions, a place where immigrants can pursue their hopes and dreams.

Like the torch held by the Lady in the harbor, God's light shines to signify that He is a refuge for all who wish to flee from the storms of life, "a helper in the time of storms," as the hymn says.

My wife once heard this story about a poor woman who went up to the foothills in a Chinese town to cut the grass. Her baby was tied to her back and a little child walked beside her. In her hand was a sickle to cut the grass.

Just as she reached the top of a hill, she heard a roar. Frightened, she turned and saw a mother tigress springing at her, followed by her two cubs.

The illiterate Chinese woman had never attended school or church, but a missionary once told her about Jesus, "who is able to help you when you are in trouble." As the tiger's claws tore into her arm, the woman cried out, "O Jesus, help me!" The tiger, instead of attacking again, suddenly turned and ran away.

The Bible says, "He will give his angels charge of you to guard you in all your ways" (Psalm 91:11, RSV).

What "beasts" are attacking you? Chances are you will never be attacked by a wild beast, but you will be attacked by doubts, by fears of other kinds, by worry, by loneliness, by despair.

Cry out to Jesus and He will answer you just as surely as

the Chinese woman's desperate cry was heard and answered.

DEATH AND TAXES

The wicked is driven away in his wickedness: but the righteous hath hope in his death. Proverbs 14:32

SOMEONE once observed that there are only two great equalizers in life: death and taxes. Actually, that person was only half right, because some people manage to avoid paying taxes at all, either because of loopholes in the tax law or because they do not make enough money.

The only true equalizer is death.

Everyone dies.

The writer of Hebrews says, "And as it is appointed unto men once to die, but after this the judgment" (Hebrews 9:27).

Much of the world pretends that death does not exist. We like to speak of the dead as "departed" or persons who have died as having "passed on" or "expired." We do not like the word "death." It seems so final, so irreversible, so hopeless.

But not for the person who has trusted Christ as Savior. Death is only the beginning of the beginning, not the end.

C. S. Lewis once observed that this life is only "shadowlands" compared with the glory that is to come.

There is a wonderful song which says, "It's as though we see through clouded glass, our eyes cannot see past this veil of tears our present pain.

"This world can never comprehend a love that will not end, a life that always will remain. For there, beyond the edge of time, is wisdom so divine, the throne of truth, the shining way. For soon in majesty He'll come to take his people home, and in that bright and glorious day . . . we will see Him as He

is, the Father God so holy, the truth in endless glory; we will
see Him as He is, the wisdom of the ages, the One who died
to save us. We will see Him."

What a glorious thought with which we can comfort
ourselves, no matter what our circumstances. We *will* see
Christ someday if we have put our faith in Him.

January 20

UNTIL DIVORCE US DO PART

*So ought men to love their wives as their own bodies. He that loveth his
wife loveth himself.*   Ephesians 5:28

THOUSANDS of times a day a man and a woman stand
before an American clergyman or magistrate to be united in
marriage. In virtually every ceremony they vow to remain
married "until death us do part."

Tragically, one out of two of these vows will never be
fulfilled because divorce now parts one out of every two
married couples. A recent Census Bureau report found that
for women in their thirties, 60 percent of them can expect to
be divorced. Sixty percent!

There are three elements to a successful marriage, and each
needs to be present if a marriage is to succeed. The first is
love. Unfortunately, love has been redefined by Hollywood
and television to mean something that is only physical, only
feelings. But the apostle Paul defined love beautifully in
1 Corinthians 13. Read it and you will know how God defines
love. Men are to love their wives as Christ loved the Church
and gave Himself for it. What woman could not respond and
submit to such a selfless expression of Christlike love?

Maturity is the second important ingredient in a successful
marriage. Too many are getting a divorce at the first sign of
trouble. God will give you the maturity to handle your

problems even in what seems like a "wrong marriage" if you'll let Him. He will do this because God hates divorce.

Third, faith must be an ingredient for a marriage to be successful. Marriage is difficult enough these days with all of life's pressures, but without Christ at the center of a marriage and a home, it becomes even more difficult.

Determine to put Christ at the center of your individual lives and then at the center of your marriage and it cannot fail. Be faithful in your Bible reading and prayer time . . . together . . . as a family and you will build a fortress around your marriage that can withstand any storm.

January 21

PURITY

Who shall ascend the hill of the LORD? And who shall stand in his holy place? He who has clean hands and a pure heart. Psalm 24:3–4, RSV

PURITY is probably the least appreciated of all the Christian virtues among young people. Yet the Bible teaches there must be total faithfulness within the bonds of matrimony. It also teaches that premarital sex—fornication, the Bible calls it—is to be avoided. In fact, the Bible says that those who commit fornication (and adultery) will have no part in the kingdom of heaven.

We live in the most permissive society since pagan times. Movie marquees, the covers of magazines, and billboards scream sensual messages at us. "If it feels good, do it" has become a national motto.

Yet, if you talk with people who have come to Christ out of deep sin, they will tell you of their regret and of their torment. They will tell you they wish they had never fallen into such deep sin.

Many best-selling Christian books tell of men and women

who committed terrible crimes or were involved in sensual pleasure. We rejoice with them that Christ has redeemed and forgiven them, but the best testimony is never to have fallen into such sin in the first place.

The secret of purity is God. Get a pure heart from God, and you can be supremely happy no matter what the circumstances and no matter what is going on around you.

January 22

TAKING ADVANTAGE OF ADVERSITY

And we know that all things work together for good to them that love God, to them who are called according to his purpose. Romans 8:28

THERE was a popular song not too long ago which contained the lyrics, "I beg your pardon. I never promised you a rose garden."

God, of course, did create for man a beautiful Garden of Eden, a state of perfection in which man could live free of any want. But man sinned against God and God removed him from the Garden. Yet, even now, God has promised to deliver us from all our adversities.

There are two ways to respond to adversity. We can give in and be depressed, or we can triumph over it and be joyful. The problem with giving in and being depressed is that the adversities do not go away and, indeed, seem to grow worse.

One of the best ways to overcome adversity is to praise God in the midst of your turmoil. Begin to sing to God or read the Psalms out loud. Meditate on Scripture, particularly passages like Romans 8:28–39, which includes this wonderful assurance: "For I am persuaded, that neither death, nor life, nor angels, nor principalities, nor powers, nor things present, nor things to come, nor height, nor depth, nor any creature, shall be able to separate us from the love of God, which is in

Christ Jesus our Lord."

Remember that our hope is not based on circumstance. "Our hope is built on nothing less than Jesus' blood and righteousness. . . . On Christ the solid rock I stand, all other ground is sinking sand."

Besides, as another song says, "If I never had a problem, how would I know that God could solve them? How would I know what faith in God could do?"

It is through our adversities that we learn to trust in Jesus and through trusting, to triumph over them.

Look upon adversities as opportunities from God to grow in your faith and to become a stronger servant of His.

January 23

GOD IS OUR STRENGTH

The LORD is my light and my salvation; whom shall I fear? Psalm 27:1

BECAUSE it is a fact that the Lord is my light and my salvation, why should I be afraid? The Scripture reference is a statement of fact followed by a question.

Is the comic strip and movie character Superman afraid of anything? No, because he has superhuman strength. For the Christian, the Lord is our strength (Psalm 28:7), and the Lord fears nothing, so why should we be afraid? The Scripture also declares that God is a "very present help in trouble" (Psalm 46:1).

A friend tells the story of having spoken one evening at a church service inside a prison. It was New Year's Eve, and as he and his wife drove home from the prison at one o'clock in the morning, the car developed engine trouble and stopped.

Despite their efforts, they could not get it going. They were stranded in a remote area with no telephone and the cold wind adding to their distress.

As they wondered what to do, a car came along and stopped. The driver offered to take them to a telephone where they could call for help. The car happened to be a yellow Rolls Royce. God also has a sense of humor!

God is able, indeed He is anxious, to deliver us from all sorts of trouble. He wants to give us strength to overcome the temptation to sin which separates Him from those He loves.

We do not have to sin. God will help us overcome it. But we have to ask for it, and we must stay close to God so that He can give us His strength.

When was the last time you asked God to deliver you from some temptation and then determined, with His help, to succeed?

January 24

STRENGTH THROUGH SUFFERING

Ascribe to the LORD, O heavenly beings, ascribe to the LORD glory and strength. Psalm 29:1, RSV

IN the economy of God there is such a thing as the cloud of suffering. Recently I received a letter from a woman who was suffering on a hospital bed in the last stages of cancer. She did not ask that God would relieve her of suffering or raise her up, but only that we would pray that God's grace would be sufficient through the trial of suffering.

The Bible teaches that human suffering is inescapable. We must accept it as an integral part of life. Job said, "Man that is born of a woman is of few days, and full of trouble" (Job 14:1). Our life has its beginning in suffering. Life's span is marked by pain and tragedy, and our lives end with the enemy called death. The person who expects to escape the pangs of suffering and disappointment simply has no knowledge of the Bible, of history, or of life.

The master musician knows that suffering precedes glory and acclaim. He knows the hours, days, and months of grueling practice and self-sacrifice that precede the one hour of perfect rendition when his efforts are applauded. The master craftsman knows that years of work, sacrifice, and suffering as an apprentice precede his being promoted to the master of his trade. The student knows that years of study, self-denial, and commitment precede the triumphant day of graduation with honors. Astronauts spend years training for a flight that can be as short as a few days.

The Bible teaches that suffering is a part of life in a sinful world. Paul said, "For I reckon that the sufferings of this present time are not worthy to be compared with the glory which shall be revealed in us" (Romans 8:18).

To this dear woman on her hospital bed I would say, "Look toward heaven, look beyond the clouds, and you will see that the sufferings that we are undergoing here are nothing compared to the glory that God has prepared for you yonder."

January 25

A LIFETIME OF FAVOR

For His anger is but for a moment. His favor is for a lifetime. . . .   Psalm 30:5a, NASB

WE may suffer affliction or discipline, yet the psalmist went on to say, "Weeping may last for the night, but a shout of joy comes in the morning" (Psalm 30:5b, NASB).

In order for a tree or any plant to grow and bear fruit, its seed must first be planted in the ground and die. In order for fruit to appear in our lives, we must first be planted in the

Word of God and then die to self. In the face of chastening, adversity, discipline, and affliction, fruit begins to appear.

This process, like steel which has been tempered and made strong by the heat of a furnace, makes us useful to God. But what baby is sent out to fight a battle? The baby must first grow in strength, in size, and in wisdom before he is able to fight. It is the same for those whom God wishes to use.

Joseph would never have been of use to God had he not been sold into slavery by brothers who hated him and wrongly accused by Potiphar, who put him in prison. Even after he had told Pharaoh's cupbearer he would be restored to the king's court and asked him to tell Pharaoh of his unjust imprisonment, Joseph had to wait two more years for release from prison.

All of this was God's preparation for Joseph's ultimate rise to a position of power and authority second only to that of Pharaoh himself, a position he used to feed all of Israel during a famine.

As we wait upon the Lord, God may sometimes seem slow in coming to help us, but He never comes too late. His timing is always perfect. How could it not be so from a God who favors us, as we do our children, for a lifetime?

January 26

THE DYING WORDS OF CHRISTIANS

Into your hands I commit my spirit; redeem me, O LORD, the God of truth. Psalm 31:5, NIV

DEATH for the righteous is distinctly different from what it is for the unbeliever. It is not something to be feared, nor is it to be shunned. It is the shadowed threshold to the palace of God. No wonder Paul declared, "I desire to depart and be with Christ, which is better by far" (Philippians 1:23, NIV).

Most Christians have a triumphant spirit in the way they face death. Some of the statements made and recorded from deathbeds are absolutely thrilling:

"Our God is the God from whom cometh salvation. God is the Lord by whom we escape death"—Martin Luther.

"Live in Christ, die in Christ, and the flesh need not fear death"— John Knox.

"The best of all is, God is with us"—John Wesley.

"I have pain—but I have peace, I have peace"—Richard Baxter.

Augustus Toplady, the composer of "Rock of Ages," was jubilant and triumphant as he lay dying at the age of thirty-eight. "I enjoy heaven already in my soul," he declared. "My prayers are all converted into praises."

When Joseph Everett was dying he said, "Glory! Glory! Glory!" and he continued exclaiming "glory" for over twenty-five minutes.

In my own life I have been privileged to know what some of the dying saints said before they went to heaven. My grandmother sat up in her bed, smiled, and said, "I see Jesus, and He has His hand outstretched to me. And there is Ben, and he has both of his eyes and both of his legs." (Ben, my grandfather, had lost a leg and an eye at Gettysburg.)

There was an old Welsh grocer who lived near us, and my father was at his side when he was dying. He said, "Frank, can you hear that music? I've never heard such music in all my life—the orchestras, the choirs, angels singing"—and then he was gone.

January 27

FORGIVEN SINNERS

Blessed is he whose transgression is forgiven, whose sin is covered. Psalm 32:1

IN England a sensitive boy joined the British army, but when the shot and shell began to fly, he deserted. In time he became a great astronomer and discovered a new planet. He was sent for by King George, but the man realized that his life was forfeit to the king for his desertion. The king knew him too; what would he do? Before the king would see him, the man was requested to open an envelope. It was his royal pardon. The king brought him in and said, "Now we can talk, and you shall come up and live at Windsor Castle." He was Sir William Herschel.

William Herschel was guilty and did not deny it! But King George had mercy upon him and made him a member of the royal household. That is what God promises to do for us. "And he will have mercy upon him . . . for he will abundantly pardon." To all of us poor, lost, wanton sinners the Bible says, "For God sent not his Son into the world to condemn the world; but that the world through him might be saved."

The "Prince of Preachers," Charles Haddon Spurgeon, says of this verse:

> God, who cannot lie—God, who cannot err—tells us what it is to be blessed. Here He declares that "Blessed is he whose transgression is forgiven, whose sin is covered." This is an oracle not to be disputed. Forgiven sin is better than accumulated wealth. The remission of sin is infinitely to be preferred before all the glitter and the glare of this world's prosperity. The gratification of creature passions and earthly desires is illusive—a shadow and a fiction; but the blessedness of the justified, the blessedness of the man to whom God imputeth righteousness is substantial and true.

In Psalm 32:2 David sums it up for me when he says, "Blessed is the man whose sin the LORD does not count against him and in whose spirit is no deceit" (NIV). I'm sure Sir William Herschel would say *Amen!* to that.

January 28

GOD IS LOVE, BUT . . .

God commendeth his love toward us, in that, while we were yet sinners, Christ died for us.   Romans 5:8

THERE is a tendency to focus only on the love of God to the exclusion of the other side of God's nature. Indeed, it is a fearful thing to fall into the hands of the Lord.

God loves, but He also hates. In fact, love would be sentimental were it not for its opposite, hate. We are told in the Scriptures that God hates divorce, that He hates liars, a proud and haughty look, and all other manifestations of sin. God has promised to judge sin with the fierceness of His wrath (see Proverbs 6:16–19).

David said, "I acknowledged my sin unto thee, and mine iniquity have I not hid. I said, I will confess my transgressions unto the Lord; and thou forgavest the iniquity of my sin" (Psalm 32:5). It is easy to see from this verse that God does not take sin lightly.

We live in an age when sin is winked at and where God is treated as one who is indulgent, soft-hearted and understanding, and tolerant of those who break His commandments. People today find it difficult to believe that God hates anything, much less sin.

Dr. Karl Menninger correctly observed the absence of a concept of sin in our contemporary culture when he wrote the book *Whatever Became of Sin?* I will tell you that God has not forgotten about sin, though some men may be pretending it does not exist.

The reason God hates sin is that it is sin which, left unforgiven, sends men and women out into a timeless eternity in hell. God is not willing that any should perish, but that all might come to a knowledge of Him.

What are you doing about sin? Have you confessed your sin to God and received Christ as your Savior? If you are already a Christian, have you let sin creep back into your life so that you are no longer a vessel of honor to God?

Confess your sin today. Don't wait. Receive God's forgiveness and restoration so that you might be of use to Him and enjoy His love.

January 29

WHAT IS FAITH?

Faith is the substance of things hoped for . . . Hebrews 11:1

FAITH must have an object. Faith in faith is meaningless. Telling a person to believe without giving him any evidence or reason for belief is like asking a person to believe that the moon is made of green cheese.

God wants us to know certain facts about Him so that we will have faith in Him and trust Him for the rest.

A child does not repeatedly ask his parents whether he will be taken to a doctor if he becomes ill or whether there will be another meal to eat (at least, not very often in our culture). The reason he does not ask such questions is that his parents have proved to him over and over again that they love him enough to take care of his needs.

It is the same with God. God has proven His love for us in that even while we were yet sinners, He sent Christ to die for us. And He continually proves how much He loves us by providing for our daily needs.

God also wants us to trust that He will continue to provide for us. This is faith. How happy would a parent be if his child constantly questioned him as to whether his needs would be met? The parent would feel frustrated and sad, perhaps angry that the child did not trust him.

There are scores of references to faith about what it can do for us and how much it pleases God. Jesus was amazed that the Roman soldier expressed great faith when he told Jesus just to "say the word" and his servant would be healed. Christ also told a blind man and a sick woman, "Thy faith hath made thee whole."

God values faith, our trust in Him, above every other character quality that a Christian can develop. And how do we develop faith? We do it by spending time in the presence of God through prayer and by applying His Word and His promises to our everyday lives. That way, our faith grows and God is well pleased. And when God is pleased, so are we.

January 30

JOY IN THE MIDST OF TRIALS

Looking unto Jesus, the author and finisher of our faith. . . .   Hebrews 12:2

WHERE did we ever get the idea that the Christian life is to be a carefree life without trials?

When trials come, we sometimes act as if God is out of town on vacation. We question God: Why is this happening to me? What did I do to deserve this? After all, I attend church regularly, give liberally of my tithes and offerings, and have told others about Christ. So why am I going through this difficult circumstance?

Read the promises of Scripture for the answer. Jesus said, "In the world you will have tribulation." He didn't say that you could have tribulation or that if you aren't a good person, tribulation will come your way. Jesus flatly stated that you *will* have tribulation. It is as certain as growing older.

Jesus also said that if He was persecuted, you are going to be persecuted, too, because "no servant is greater than his master." Actually, people are not so much persecuting you as they are persecuting the Christ *in* you.

But the wonderful promise of Christ is that while you will have trials and tribulations, "Be of good cheer. I have overcome the world." So Jesus is saying that while people are persecuting you (or persecuting Jesus in you) don't worry about it. He has already overcome the world, the source of your trials and tribulations.

Have you ever had to worry about a financial debt, only to be told not to worry about it, that someone else would pay the expense? It is a remarkably freeing experience.

That is precisely the experience and attitude God wants us to have in the midst of our trials. God wants us to look to Jesus, the author and finisher of our faith. He has already overcome similar trials and tribulations and will give us the power to do the same. He waits only to be asked.

January 31

TRIUMPH OUT OF TRAGEDY

Every good gift and every perfect gift is from above, and cometh down from the Father of lights, with whom is no variableness, neither shadow of turning. James 1:17

THE playwright William Shakespeare wrote numerous classics, some of which are called "tragedies." *Hamlet, Macbeth,*

King Lear, Julius Caesar, and *Romeo and Juliet* are only some of Shakespeare's more classic tragedies.

Have you ever thought why these plays depict tragedy— indeed, why the stories are, themselves, tragic? It is because in each instance, the characters are victims of their own circumstances and are powerless to free themselves from them.

Not so for the Christian. We have the power to triumph over tragedy, even in situations which might seem hopeless and unredeemable to the world. The key to understanding tragedy is to understand its source.

Death and pain and tragedy came into the world because of sin. Many people blame God for tragedy, but James tells us that "every good and perfect gift comes down from the Father of lights." Tragedy is a result of sin having entered the world.

But Christ has triumphed over tragedy, and He wants us to do the same because in such triumph God is glorified. Indeed, triumphing over tragedy is a form of witness for Christ. When something tragic happens to us—the loss of a loved one, the loss of a job—unbelievers watch us closely to see whether we react differently than they would. If there is no difference, if we despair as unbelievers might, how is God honored? How do we testify of Christ and His power?

Remember, "Now thanks be unto God, which always causeth us to triumph in Christ" (2 Corinthians 2:14).

February

CHRIST IN THE CRISIS

For I can do everything God asks me to with the help of Christ who gives me the strength and power. Philippians 4:13, TLB

A FRIEND told me the story of a nonbelieving friend of his who came to him in the midst of a very troubled day. Knowing that my friend is a Christian, the man asked him, "If I get born again, will all of my problems go away?"

"No," said my friend, "but you will have the power to deal with them."

Think about that. Our problems won't go away, but we will have the power to deal with them. The power to deal with problems produces a muscular Christian who is capable of doing combat with the evil one. If we could dismiss all of our problems with a single stroke, we would be the most shallow of individuals. We would be spiritual "wimps" unable to fight our way out of wet paper bags!

The prayer of Jesus in the Garden of Gethsemane is perhaps the greatest prayer ever uttered. Our Lord asked that this cup of crucifixion, which was about to be thrust upon Him, might be taken away. But then, in the very next breath He said, "Nevertheless not as I will, but as thou wilt" (Matthew 26:39). What a prayer! What strength! What power!

When the apostle Paul asked God to remove his "thorn in the flesh," God did not remove it, saying instead, "My grace is sufficient for thee" (2 Corinthians 12:9). Christ desires to be with you in whatever crisis you may find yourself. Call upon His name. See if He will not do as He promised He would. He will not make your problems go away, but He will give you the power to deal with and overcome them.

A GULL FROM GOD

The angel of the LORD encampeth round about them that fear him, and delivereth them. Psalm 34:7

DURING World War II, Captain Eddie Rickenbacker and the rest of the crew of the B-17 in which he was flying ran out of fuel and "ditched" in the Pacific Ocean. For weeks nothing was heard of him. The newspapers reported his disappearance, and across the country thousands of people prayed. Mayor LaGuardia asked the whole city of New York to pray for him. Then he returned. The Sunday papers headlined the news, and in an article, Captain Rickenbacker himself told what had happened. "And this part I would hesitate to tell," he wrote, "except that there were six witnesses who saw it with me. A gull came out of nowhere, and lighted on my head—I reached up my hand very gently—I killed him and then we divided him equally among us. We ate every bit, even the little bones. Nothing ever tasted so good." This gull saved the lives of Rickenbacker and his companions. Years later I asked him to tell me the story personally, because it was through this experience that he came to know Christ. He said, "I have no explanation except that God sent one of His angels to rescue us."

During my ministry I have heard or read literally thousands of similar stories. Could it be that these were all hallucinations or accidents or fate or luck? Or were real angels sent from God to perform certain tasks? I prefer to believe the latter.

BROKEN HEARTS, MENDED SPIRITS

The LORD is nigh unto them that are of a broken heart and saveth such as be of a contrite spirit. Psalm 34:18

BEFORE I can become wise, I must first realize that I am foolish. Before I can receive power, I must first confess that I am powerless. I must lament my sins before I can rejoice in a Savior. Mourning, in God's sequence, always comes before exultation. Blessed are those who mourn their unworthiness, their helplessness, and their inadequacy.

Isaiah, the mighty prophet of God, knew by experience that one must bow the knee in mourning before one can lift the voice in jubilation. When his sin appeared ugly and venomous in the bright light of God's holiness, he said: "Woe is me! for I am undone; because I am a man of unclean lips: for mine eyes have seen the King, the LORD of hosts" (Isaiah 6:5).

We cannot be satisfied with our goodness after beholding the holiness of God. But our mourning over our unworthiness and sinfulness should be of short duration, for God has said: "I, even I, am he that blotteth out thy transgressions for mine own sake, and will not remember thy sins" (Isaiah 43:25).

Isaiah had to experience the mourning of inadequacy before he could realize the joy of forgiveness. If I have no sense of sorrow for sin, how can I know the need of repentance?

In God's economy, a person must go down into the valley of grief before he or she can scale the heights of spiritual glory. One must become tired and weary of living without Christ before he or she can seek and find His fellowship. One must come to the end of "self" before one can really begin to live.

THE CHRISTIAN'S SECRET OF JOY

My soul shall be joyful in the Lord; it shall rejoice in his salvation. Psalm 35:9

WHEN Jesus Christ is the source of joy, there are no words that can describe it. It is a joy "inexpressible and glorious" (1 Peter 1:8, NIV). Christ is the answer to the sadness and discouragement, the discord and division in our world.

Christ can take discouragement and despondency out of our lives. Optimism and cheerfulness are products of knowing Him.

The Bible says, "A cheerful heart is good medicine, but a crushed spirit dries up the bones" (Proverbs 17:22, NIV).

If the heart has been attuned to God through faith in Christ, then its overflow will be joyous optimism and good cheer.

Out West an old sheepherder had a violin, but it was out of tune. He had no way of tuning it, so in desperation he wrote to one of the radio stations and asked them at a certain hour on a certain day to strike the tone "A." The officials of the station decided they would accommodate the old fellow, and on that particular day the true tone of "A" was broadcast. His fiddle was thus tuned, and once more his cabin echoed with joyful music.

If we live our lives in tune with the Master, we, too, will find ourselves surrounded by His beautiful music.

BEHIND THE CLOUDS

Thy mercy, O LORD, is in the heavens; and thy faithfulness reacheth unto the clouds. Psalm 36:5

M Y home is on a mountain nearly four thousand feet high. Many times we can see below us the clouds in the valley. Some mornings we wake up to find that we are in lovely sunshine, but the valley below is covered with clouds. At other times thunderstorms come up, and we can see the lightning flash and hear the thunder roar down below, while we are enjoying beautiful sunlight and clear skies above.

Many times I have sat on our rustic front porch and watched the clouds below. I have thought of the clouds of discouragement and suffering that temporarily veil the sunlight of God's love from us. Many people live with a cloud hanging over their lives. Some may be in hospital beds; others are suffering discouragement and bereavement. A heavy cloud hangs over them.

The Bible has a great deal to say about clouds, for they sometimes symbolize the spiritual forces which obscure the face of God. The Bible indicates that clouds are given to us for a purpose and that there is glory in the clouds and that every cloud has a silver lining. It is written in Exodus 16:10, "They looked . . . and, behold, the glory of the LORD appeared in the cloud." Without the clouds there would be no shield from the burning sun. There would be no lavish sunsets, no rain, no light, no beautiful, picturesque landscapes.

Charles Kingsley sensed this truth when he wrote: "No cloud across the sun but passes at the last and gives us back the face of God once more." Longfellow also saw meaning in life's clouds when he said: "Be still, sad heart, and cease repining; Behind the clouds is the sun still shining."

The Bible says that God was in the cloud and that He spoke to His people through a cloud. The Lord said, "Lo, I come unto thee in a thick cloud" (Exodus 19:9). Again, God called to Moses "out of the midst of the cloud" (Exodus 24:16). There are clouds in our lives shadowing, refreshing, and oftentimes draping them in the blackness of night, but there is never a cloud without its bright light.

February 6

THE FOUNTAIN OF LIFE

*For with thee is the fountain of life: in thy light shall we see
light.*   Psalm 36:9

THE more knowledge we acquire, the less wisdom we seem to
have. The more economic security we gain, the more boredom
we generate. The more worldly pleasure we enjoy, the less
satisfied and contented we are with life. We are like a restless
sea, finding a little peace here and a little pleasure there, but
nothing permanent and satisfying. So the search continues!
Men will kill, lie, cheat, steal, and go to war to satisfy their
quest for power, pleasure, and wealth, thinking thereby to
gain for themselves and their particular group peace, security,
contentment, and happiness.

Yet inside us a little voice keeps saying, "We were not
meant to be this way—we were meant for better things." We
have a mysterious feeling that there is a fountain somewhere
that contains the happiness which makes life worthwhile. We
keep saying to ourselves that somewhere, sometime we will
stumble onto the secret. Sometimes we feel that we have
obtained it—only to find it elusive, leaving us disillusioned,
bewildered, and unhappy.

The happiness which brings enduring worth to life is not
the superficial happiness that is dependent on circumstances.
It is the happiness and contentment that fills the soul even in
the midst of the most distressing of circumstances and the
most adverse environment.

Near my home is a spring that never varies its flow at any
season of the year. Floods may rage nearby, but it will not
increase its flow. A long summer's drought may come but it

will not decrease. It is perennially and always the same. Such is the type of happiness for which we yearn—and it can be found in Christ alone!

Have you discovered this spring yet?

February 7

FRETTING . . . OR COMMITTING?

Fret not thyself because of evildoers, neither be thou envious against the workers of iniquity. . . . Commit thy way unto the LORD; trust also in him; and he shall bring it to pass. Psalm 37:1, 5

THERE are no troubles that distress the mind and wear upon the nerves as do borrowed troubles. The psalmist said, "Fret not thyself . . ." The implication is that fretting, complaining, and distress of mind are often self-manufactured and can best be coped with by a change of attitude and transformation of thought.

You cannot allay a baby's anxiety by giving him a rattle when he is hungry. He will keep on crying until his hunger is satisfied by the food his little body demands. Neither can the soul of a mature man be satisfied apart from God. David described the hunger of all men when he said: "As the hart panteth after the water brooks, so panteth my soul after thee, O God" (Psalm 42:1). The Prodigal Son, who had to learn life's lessons by painful experience, said: "How many hired servants of my father's have bread enough and to spare, and I perish with hunger!" (Luke 15:17).

Two conflicting forces cannot exist in one human heart. When doubt reigns, faith cannot abide. Where hatred rules, love is crowded out. Where selfishness rules, there love cannot dwell. When worry is present, trust cannot crowd its way in.

The very best prescription for banishing worry is found in Psalm 37:5: "Commit thy way unto the LORD; trust also in him; and he shall bring it to pass." The word "commit" means to turn over to, to entrust completely.

Some years ago someone gave my little boy a dollar. He brought it to me and said, "Daddy, keep this for me." But in a few minutes he came back and said, "Daddy, I'd better keep my own dollar." He tucked it in his pocket and went out to play. In a few minutes he came back with tears in his eyes, saying, "Daddy, I lost my dollar. Help me find it." How often we commit our burdens to the Lord and then fail to trust Him by taking matters into our own hands. Then, when we have messed things up, we pray, "O Lord, help me, I'm in trouble."

The choice is yours. Do you want to trust your life in God's "pocket" or keep it in your own?

February 8

THE BRIGHT SIDE OF DEATH

Mark the perfect man, and behold the upright: for the end of that man is peace. Psalm 37:37

WE who have made our peace with God should be like the evangelist D. L. Moody. When he was aware that death was at hand, he said, "Earth recedes, heaven opens before me." It appeared as though he was dreaming. Then he said, "No, this is no dream . . . it is beautiful, it is like a trance. If this is death, it is sweet. There is no valley here. God is calling me, and I must go."

After having been given up for dead, Moody revived to indicate that God had permitted him to see beyond that thin veil separating the seen from the unseen world. He had been "within the gates, and beyond the portals," and had caught a glimpse of familiar faces whom he had "loved long since and lost awhile." Then he could remember when he had proclaimed so vociferously earlier in his ministry, "Some day you will read in the papers that D. L. Moody of East Northfield is dead. Don't you believe a word of it. At that moment I shall be more alive than I am now. I shall have gone up higher, that is all—out of this old clay tenement into a house that is immortal; a body that death cannot touch, that sin cannot taint, a body fashioned like unto His glorious body . . . . That which is born of the flesh may die. That which is born of the Spirit will live forever" (*The Life of Dwight L. Moody*, by W. R. Moody). If Moody were to witness to us now, he would surely tell us of the glowing experience that became his as the angelic hosts ushered him into the presence of the Lord.

Can you face death with such confidence? You can if you know and believe God's promises about life after death, promises that caused Moody to rejoice rather than despair.

February 9

HIS STRENGTH, OUR STRENGTH

The salvation of the righteous is of the LORD: he is their strength in the time of trouble. Psalm 37:39

WHATEVER the circumstances, whatever the call, whatever the duty, whatever the price, whatever the sacrifice—His strength will be your strength in your hour of need.

There are physical benefits that come from Christian living. Sin and the sense of inner unworthiness impair physical and mental well-being. The sense of physical impurity and physical immorality, the sense of hatred directed toward our fellow men, the awareness of our own inadequacy and frustration and our inability to achieve the goals to which we aspire—these are the real reasons for physical and mental illness. The sense of guilt and sin that natural man carries within himself renders him unfit for the performance of his duties, renders him sick in both mind and body. It was no accident that Jesus combined healing with His preaching and teaching when He was on earth. There is a very real relationship between the life of the spirit and the health of the body and mind.

Peace with God and the peace of God in a man's heart and the joy of fellowship with Christ have in themselves a beneficial effect upon the body and mind and will lead to the development and preservation of physical and mental power. Thus, Christ promotes the best interest of the body and mind as well as of the spirit, in addition to inward peace, the development of spiritual life, the joy and fellowship with Christ, and the new strength that comes with being born again.

February 10

OBEDIENCE—THE KEY TO EFFECTIVE PRAYER

I waited patiently for the LORD; and he inclined unto me, and heard my cry. Psalm 40:1

EFFECTIVE prayer is offered in faith. The Bible says, "Therefore I say unto you, what things soever ye desire, when ye pray, *believe* that ye receive them, and ye shall have them" (Mark 11:24, italics mine).

Maltbie Babcock said, "Our prayers are to mean something to us if they are to mean anything to God." It goes without saying that if our prayers are aimless, meaningless, and mingled with doubt they will go unanswered. Prayer is more than a wish turned heavenward . . . it is the voice of faith directed God-ward.

This kind of dynamic prayer emanates from an obedient heart.

The Bible says, "And whatsoever we ask, we receive of him, because we keep his commandments, and do those things that are pleasing in his sight" (1 John 3:22).

I know a wealthy father who refused to get his son a bicycle because the boy's report card showed disgracefully low marks, a yard remained unraked, and other assignments had not been carried out. I am sure the father would not have been wise to lavish gifts upon such a disobedient and ungrateful son.

The Bible says, "But if ye will not obey the voice of the Lord, but rebel against the commandment of the Lord, then shall the hand of the Lord be against you . . ." (1 Samuel 12:15).

If you want to get your prayers through to God, surrender your stubborn will to Him, and He will hear your cry. Obedience is the master key to effective prayer.

February 11

TEN COMMANDMENTS FOR THE HOME

Save thy people, and bless thine inheritance. . . . Psalm 28:9

WHAT shall it profit men or women if they gain the whole world but lose their own families?

With a 50 percent divorce rate and more and more two-wage-earner households, the home as we have known it in the past, indeed, as God established it, is truly an endangered species.

Marriage and the family were not quaint ideas cooked up by society. The family was ordained of God before He established any other institution, even before He established the Church.

I want to suggest ten commandments for a solid, happy, God-honoring home:

1. Establish God's chain of command. The Bible teaches that for the Christian, Jesus Christ is to head the home, with the wife under the authority of a

Christlike husband and the children responsible to their parents.

2. Obey the commandment that you love one another.

3. Show acceptance and appreciation for each family member.

4. Family members should respect God's authority over them and the authority God has delegated down the chain of command.

5. It is important to have training and discipline in the home and not just for the family dog!

6. Enjoy one another and take the time to enjoy family life *together*. Quality time is no substitute for quantity time. Quantity time *is* quality time.

7. Do not commit adultery. Adultery destroys a marriage and is a sin against God and against your mate.

8. Everyone in a family should work for the mutual benefit of the family. No child should be without chores or without the knowledge that work brings fulfillment.

9. Pray together and read the Bible together. Nothing strengthens a marriage and family more. Nothing is a better defense against Satan.

10. Every family member should be concerned about whether every other member of the family is truly saved. This extends after the immediate family to grandparents, uncles and aunts, cousins, and in-laws.

No one is truly a success in God's eyes if his family is a mess.

February 12
....

AN EVER-PRESENT HELP

God is our refuge and strength, an ever present help in trouble. Psalm 46:1, NIV

GOD is "an ever present help in trouble," but we sometimes allow bitterness to keep Him at a distance and thus we miss His help.

A young Irish immigrant, Joseph Scriven (1820–1886), was deeply in love with a young woman, and their marriage plans had been made. Not long before their wedding day, however, she was drowned. For months Scriven was bitter, in utter despair. At last he turned to Christ, and through His grace, he found peace and comfort. Out of this experience he wrote the familiar hymn which has brought consolation to millions of aching hearts: "What a friend we have in Jesus, All our sins and griefs to bear!"

Sometimes our way lies in the sunlight. It was so for Joseph Scriven as he approached his wedding day. But like him, we may find that our path also leads through the dark shadows of loss, disappointments, and sorrow. At times like this it is within our power to turn our sufferings into occasions for a firmer grasp of God, and make them channels through which a surer and brighter hope may flow into our souls.

Business losses, pensions that don't pay the bills, loss of work, inflation, the sickness that lays us low, the sorrows that rob our homes of their light, children who rebel—all turned into blessings for those who by them become less attached to the earth and more attached to God.

Trouble will not hurt us unless it does what many of us too often allow it to do—harden us, making us sour, bitter, and skeptical. The trouble we bear trustfully brings to us a fresh vision of God, and, as a result, we discover a new outlook on life.

If we make our sorrow and trouble an occasion for learning more of God's love and of His power to aid and bless, then it will teach us to have a firmer confidence in His providence, and as a result of this, the brightness of His love will fill our lives.

Trust with a childlike dependence on God, and no trouble can destroy you. Even in that last dark hour of death, when your flesh and your heart fail, you will be able to depend in peace upon Him who "is the strength of my heart and my portion forever" (Psalm 73:26, NIV).

February 13

IS GOD YOUR PILOT?

For this God is our God for ever and ever: he will be our guide even unto death. Psalm 48:14

YOU probably have seen the bumper sticker which says, "God is my copilot. "

It sounds nice and very spiritual, until you think about it. God does not want to share the controls over our lives. He wants us to relinquish them and let Him have control of our lives.

The story is told of a little girl whose father is an airline pilot. As they crossed the Atlantic, a storm came up. The flight attendant awakened the little girl and told her to fasten her seat belt because they were in some turbulent weather. The little girl opened her eyes, saw the lightning flashing around the plane, and asked, "Is Daddy at the controls?" The flight attendant replied, "Yes, your father is in the cockpit." The little girl smiled, closed her eyes, and went back to sleep.

God is at the controls of our lives. Or, rather, He wants to be at the controls. But He gives us the freedom to pilot ourselves if we wish. The problem is that we often crack up, much as we could expect to do if we took the controls of an airplane we had not been taught how to fly.

God knows us, how we work, and what is best for us. If we will only relinquish the controls to Him, He will see us safely home.

What about you? Who or what is in control of your life?

Are you still holding on to the controls, or have you allowed God to take control yet? What are you waiting for?

February 14

LOVE AND PEANUT BUTTER

Behold, what manner of love the Father hath bestowed upon us. 1 John 3:1

THE word "love" is used to mean many different things. We say that we "love" the house that we have just bought or that we "love" a particular vacation spot or that we "love" a peanut butter and jelly sandwich. We also "love" a certain television program, and we "love" our husband or wife. It is to be hoped that we don't love our spouse the same way we love a peanut butter and jelly sandwich!

A friend once observed, "Love talked about is easily ignored, but love demonstrated is irresistible." God demonstrated His love toward us "in that, while we were yet sinners, Christ died for us" (Romans 5:8). Now that is *real* love.

If God had only talked about how much He loved us and never proved it by sending Christ to meet our greatest need—the forgiveness of sin and the healing of the breach between God and man when sin entered the world—He would have been a very cruel God. But He did more than talk. He demonstrated His love for us by sending the most precious offering He could make: His only and sinless Son, who became sin on our behalf that we might be delivered from sin and have a home in heaven.

God's love is eternal. It outlasts everything man has ever loved, including a peanut butter and jelly sandwich! It is in experiencing God's love for us that we are able to love others, including those who might be unlovable to us.

WHITER THAN SNOW

. . . Wash me, and I shall be whiter than snow. Psalm 51:7

FOR centuries, the color white has signified purity. Isaiah spoke of purity in terms of the whitest thing he could think of—snow—when he said, "Come now, and let us reason together, saith the LORD: though your sins be as scarlet, they shall be as white as snow . . ." (Isaiah 1:18).

Snow is so white that one can see almost anything that is dropped on it, even up to great distances. We can take the whitest object we can find, like newly washed clothing, but when we place it next to snow it still looks dirty by comparison.

Our lives are like that. At times, we may think of ourselves as morally good and decent, content that "we are not like other men." But compared to God's purity, we are defiled and filthy.

In spite of our sins and uncleanness, God still loves us. He decided to provide for us a purity we could never attain on our own. That is why He gave His Son, Jesus Christ, to die for us on the cross. It is only when our sins have been washed in the blood of Christ that we appear as white as snow in the eyes of God. No human "detergent" of good works or clean thoughts can make us that white, that pure. Only Christ's precious blood can do that, and it is only His blood that can continue to cleanse us from sin after He has saved us.

Reflect on that wonderful truth. Claim it for your own life.

PICKING UP THE PIECES

The sacrifice acceptable to God is a broken spirit; a broken and contrite heart, O God, thou wilt not despise. Psalm 51:17, RSV

CORRIE TEN BOOM tells a story of a little girl who broke one of her mother's demitasse cups. The little girl came to her mother sobbing, "Oh, Mama, I'm so sorry I broke your beautiful cup."

The mother replied, "I know you're sorry and I forgive you. Now don't cry any more." The mother then swept up the pieces of the broken cup and placed them in the trash can. But the little girl enjoyed the guilty feeling. She went to the trash can, picked out pieces of the cup, brought them to her mother and sobbed, "Mother, I'm so sorry that I broke your pretty cup."

This time her mother spoke firmly to her, "Take those pieces and put them back in the trash can. Don't be silly enough to take them out again. I told you I forgave you, so don't cry anymore, and don't pick up the broken pieces anymore."

Guilt is removed with confession and cleansing. "If we confess our sins, he is faithful and just to forgive us our sins, and to cleanse us from all unrighteousness" (1 John 1:9).

However, the story of David's sin (Psalm 51) shows that forgiveness does not preclude the natural consequences of our sin. Murder can be forgiven, but that does not bring the dead to life again.

AN ANSWER FOR ANXIETY

Cast your burden on the LORD, and he will sustain you; he will never permit the righteous to be moved. Psalm 55:22, RSV

"GOD grant me the serenity to accept things I cannot change, the courage to change the things I can, and wisdom to know the difference." I ran across this prayer, and it is one that we should all pray.

Someone once said, "Worry is the interest paid on trouble before it comes due." Let's cast our care on Him, remembering that He is "our salvation also in the time of trouble."

Trust is one answer to anxiety. We find in the first place that we are to cast our care upon the Lord, and this is to be a continuing process. We are not only to take our burdens to the Lord, we are to leave them there. Needless anxiety is contrary to the lessons of nature.

Someone has written a little verse which goes:

> Said the robin to the sparrow,
>   I should really like to know,
> Why these anxious human beings
>   Rush about and worry so.
> Said the sparrow to the robin,
>   Friend, I think that it must be,
> That they have no heavenly Father
>   Such as cares for you and me.

Jesus used the carefree attitude of the birds to underscore the fact that worrying is unnatural. "Behold the fowls of the air: for they sow not, neither do they reap, nor gather into barns; yet your heavenly Father feedeth them" (Matthew 6:26). From this He went on to the lilies of the field. "And why take ye thought for raiment? Consider the lilies of the field, how they grow; they toil not, neither do they spin: And yet I say unto you, that even Solomon in all his glory was not arrayed like one of these" (Matthew 6:28–29).

If He cares for tiny birds and frail flowers, why cannot we count on Him for every aspect of our lives? I know that modern living taxes the faith of the greatest Christians, but none of us should doubt the ability of God to give us grace sufficient for our trials even amid the stresses of this twentieth century. In the middle of our world troubles, the Christian is not to go about wringing his hands, shouting: "What shall we do?" having more nervous tension and worry than anyone else. The Christian is to trust quietly that God is still on the throne. He is a sovereign God, working out things according to His own plan.

February 18

THE REFINER'S FIRE

Praise our God, O peoples, let the sound of his praise be heard; he has preserved our lives and kept our feet from slipping. For you, O God, tested us; you refined us like silver. You brought us into prison and laid burdens on our backs. . . . We went through fire and water, but you brought us to a place of abundance. Psalm 66:8–12, NIV

KIM WICKES, who comes to most of our Crusades, was a little girl, blinded because the retinas of her eyes had been destroyed when she looked at a bomb blast. Her father tried to kill her by throwing her into a river. Desperate and at his wit's end from war and starvation, Kim's father eventually left her at a home for deaf and blind children in Taegu, Korea.

Later she was adopted by some Americans and began the years of study and training which have resulted in a testimony in word and song which has thrilled millions. Her studies have taken her to the finest schools in the world, including study in Vienna. The events in Kim's life could have destroyed many people, but by God's grace she has triumphed over adversity.

Today there are thousands of Christians all over the world who are facing daily pain, persecution, and opposition for their faith. We are now learning of their triumph and survival in many parts of the world. Their faith in Christ is deep and strong. Their willingness to face persecution puts us to shame.

I do not understand how the human body can withstand such persecution as some of our brothers and sisters in Christ are experiencing today—such as in Uganda. I only know that when Jesus Christ is with a person, that one can endure the deepest suffering and somehow emerge a better and stronger Christian because of it. Just as fire refines silver, suffering and persecution purify Christians.

February 19

ANGELIC ACTIVITY

The chariots of God are twenty thousand, even thousands of angels: the LORD is among them, as in Sinai, in the holy place. Psalm 68:17

REPORTS continually flow to my attention from many places around the world telling of visitors of the angelic order appearing, ministering, fellowshiping and disappearing. They warn of God's impending judgment; they spell out the tenderness of His love; they meet a desperate need; then they are gone. Of one thing we can be sure: angels never draw attention to themselves but ascribe glory to God and press His message upon the hearers as a delivering and sustaining word of the highest order.

Demonic activity and Satan worship are on the increase in all parts of the world. The devil is alive and more at work than at any other time. The Bible says that since he realizes his time is short, his activity will increase. Through his demonic influences he does succeed in turning many away from true faith; but we can still say that his evil activities are countered for the people of God by His ministering spirits, the holy ones of the angelic order. They are vigorous in delivering the heirs of salvation from the stratagems of evil men. They cannot fail.

Believers, look up—take courage. The angels are nearer than you think. For after all, God has given "his angels charge of you, to guard you in all your ways. On their hands they will bear you up, lest you dash your foot against a stone" (Psalm 91:11–12, RSV).

February 20

STRENGTH AND WEAKNESS

. . . *The joy of the Lord is your strength.* Nehemiah 8:10, RSV

GOD'S idea of strength and man's idea of strength are opposite one another.

The Lord told Paul, "My strength is made perfect in weakness" (2 Corinthians 12:9). Having learned this lesson, Paul can then say, "When I am weak, then am I strong" (2 Corinthians 12:10).

It is true that God's strength is made perfect in weakness. Otherwise, it would not be God's strength, nor would He get the glory. That is why throughout the Old Testament God ordered the leaders of Israel to reduce the size of their armies or He announced in advance the time and place of conflict and which side was going to win. God wanted the faith of man to be placed in Him and not in human armaments or physical strength. In our own lives, God wants us to be broken in spirit so that He can make us strong at the broken places.

Man likes to place his security in missiles and armies, but the world now has more nuclear weapons and more men under arms than ever before in history. Have all of these weapons, all of these armies brought more security to humanity? On the contrary, they have brought less security because man will still not trust in God.

Isaiah said, "But they that wait upon the Lord shall renew their strength; they shall mount up with wings as eagles; they shall run, and not be weary; and they shall walk, and not faint" (40:31). This is the kind of strength God is prepared to give us if we will only ask Him for it.

Do you have this strength? You can have it. Just ask!

February 21

MORE THAN CONQUERORS

. . . We are more than conquerors through him that loved us. Romans 8:37

so many Christians live defeated lives. Perhaps it is because of some of the language that has crept into our vocabulary. Our intentions are good when we talk about retreats, surrendering, and such, but the Bible speaks of victory, occupation, and becoming overwhelming conquerors. The language is the vocabulary of war. Only victorious armies occupy and conquer. Vanquished armies surrender and retreat.

We sing "Onward, Christian soldiers, marching as to war," but so often when Satan mounts an attack against us we behave as if we are prisoners of war, or worse, conscientious objectors. But as Christians, we don't have to live defeated lives. God wants us to live victorious lives, lives that are constantly conquering sin.

There is only one way to have victory over sin. That is to be so closely walking with Christ that sin no more abounds in your life, that sin becomes the exception with you rather than the rule as it was before.

Discover what it is to walk in the way of Christ. Know what a thrilling experience it is to wake up every morning and sense His presence! Realize what a joyous experience it is at sunset to know the peace of God, and then as you retire, to sleep as only those can sleep who know Christ!

If you determine to walk with Christ and then do it, you will be amazed at the strength He gives you to overcome sin. In that day you, too, will be more than a conqueror through Him who loves you.

February 22

LONGING FOR GOD

My soul longs, yea, faints for the courts of the LORD; my heart and flesh sing for joy to the living God. Psalm 84:2, RSV

WHAT does it mean to "long" for someone? It means that a person is unsatisfied or unfulfilled because there is someone he or she very much wants to be near, to hear that certain voice, to experience that special presence.

Usually, particularly when the object is someone very much loved by the person who is longing for another, there is hardly a waking moment when that person is not on the mind of the one who is "longing for."

Have you ever been underwater for a period of time that is longer than you had expected? You know, as the time ticks away, how desperate you become to reach the surface and breathe the air. The greater the time you are underwater, the more you long for a breath of air until that desire overwhelms you, and you rush to get to the surface as rapidly as possible. You have no other thoughts but quenching your need for air.

That is what it means to "long for God." In another context, it is what it means to "hunger and thirst" after righteousness with the same desires that lead us to quench our physical need for food and water.

How many of us are content to give God only a brief moment of our time, a hasty prayer before a meal, a few coins in the offering plate on Sunday, and forget about Him the rest of the time?

God wants us to long for Him because it is in that longing that we are fulfilled and overwhelmed by God and the reflection of His Son, the Lord Jesus Christ, in our lives.

We are never more fulfilled than when our longing for God is met by His presence in our lives.

February 23

REVIVAL

O Lord . . . revive thy work in the midst of the years. Habakkuk 3:2

HAVE you ever seen someone unconscious? Such a person will usually have vital signs but is not aware of anything that is occurring. There is also a lack of any perception of reality.

There is a difference between revival and resuscitation. Resuscitation is used on a person who is dead and whom the doctors are trying to bring back to life. Revival is for a person who is alive but unconscious. Spiritually, we can be unconscious and completely out of touch with the Spirit of God. We may be unaware of the God who made us and what He wants to do in and through us.

When one comes to Christ in faith and is born again, he or she is brought back from the dead into life. But when revival occurs, a person who is already a Christian is brought back from the brink of apathy, of taking God for granted, of ignoring God and trying to live under one's own power and strength. This can be deadly for others, because the Christian in need of revival is not producing any fruit for God. "I've got mine and that's all that matters" is not an attitude that is pleasing to God.

We have not seen a revival in America since shortly after the turn of the twentieth century. But, as the hymn says, "Lord, send a revival and let it begin with me." If we are to see a revival in our nation, it must begin in the hearts of individual believers. What are you doing in your daily walk with God that will bring revival to your life?

February 24

GOD SPEAKS

I will hear what the Lord will say; for He will speak peace to His people, to His godly ones. . . . Psalm 85:8, NASB

IN every good novel or play there must be conflict. But even Shakespeare could not have created a more powerful plot than the divine dilemma. We know that man is sinful and separated from God. Because God is holy, He couldn't automatically forgive or ignore man's rebellion. Because God is love, He couldn't completely cast man aside. Conflict. How could God be just and the justifier? This is the question Job posed: "But how can a man be in the right before God?" (Job 9:2, NASB).

Radio was just coming of age when I was a boy. We would gather around a crude homemade set and twist the three tuning dials in an effort to establish contact with the transmitter. Often all the sound that came out of the amplifier was the squeak and squawk of static. It wasn't very exciting to listen to all those senseless sounds, but we kept at the controls with anticipation. We knew that somewhere out there was the unseen transmitter, so if contact was established and the dials were in adjustment we could hear a voice loud and clear. After a long time of laborious tuning, the far distant sound of music or a voice would suddenly break through and a smile of triumph would brighten the faces of everyone in the room. At last we were tuned in!

Perhaps you have been puzzled that the prophets said God spoke to them. Does He speak to us? Does He tell us where He is—how we can find Him—how we can be right with Him? God has solved the problem; He does tell us about Himself and His loving concern. The key is a line of communication which is "revelation."

Revelation means "to make known" or "to unveil." Revelation requires a "revealer," who in this case is God. It also requires "hearers"—the chosen prophets and apostles who recorded in the Bible what He told them. Revelation is communication in which God is at one end and man is at the other.

In the revelation that God established between Himself and us we can find a new dimension of living, but we must "tune in." Levels of living we have never attained await us. Peace, satisfaction, and joy we have never experienced are available to us. God is trying to break through. The heavens are calling and God is speaking.

Have you heard God's voice? At the same time you are searching for God, He is speaking to you.

RIGHTEOUSNESS

For the Lord knoweth the way of the righteous: but the way of the ungodly shall perish.   Psalm 1:6

WHAT does it mean to be righteous?

God is pleased with righteousness; indeed He commands us to be righteous (not self-righteous, which means we think more highly of ourselves than we ought to—there is a difference).

Righteousness has nothing to do with doing good works, though good works are a byproduct of being righteous. Jesus spoke of God as the only one who is truly good. The word "good" is a synonym for righteous, so it follows that to be righteous is to be like God. But how can anyone be like God, who is holy and perfect?

There are hundreds of references in Scripture to righteousness and the righteous. Perhaps the greatest insight into this word is found in Genesis 15:6 when Abraham believed the promise of God "and he counted it to him for righteousness."

Righteousness, meaning to be right or just, begins with believing God. It sounds so simple, but how many times do we disbelieve God? God's formulas are so simple that we ignore them because we think there must be more to it than that.

All sin is rooted in unbelief. All righteousness is rooted in belief. Believe God for all His promises and He will count it unto you as righteousness. Believe on the Lord Jesus Christ, God's ultimate standard and incarnation of righteousness, and be saved. Believe in Jesus Christ to deliver you in your day of trouble and learn what the righteousness of Christ can do in and through you.

THE ANSWER TO WORRY

Thou rulest the raging of the sea: when the waves thereof arise, thou stillest them.   Psalm 89:9

"WORRY," says Vance Havner, "is like sitting in a rocking chair. It will give you something to do, but it won't get you anywhere." Worry and anxiety have hounded the human race since the beginning of time, and modern man with all his innovations has not found the cure for the plague of worry.

Physicians tell us that 70 percent of all illnesses are imaginary, the cause being mental distress or worry. In reading hundreds of letters from people with spiritual problems, I am convinced that high on the list is the plague of worry. It has been listed by heart specialists as the number one cause of heart trouble.

Psychiatrists tell us that worry breeds nervous breakdowns and mental disorders. Worry is more adept than Father Time in etching deep lines into the face. It is disastrous to health, robs life of its zest, crowds out constructive, creative thinking, and cripples the soul.

When Sir Walter Raleigh was burdened with a huge debt, his doctor said to him one day: "Sir Walter, if you don't stop worrying, you will die." He looked up sadly, and said: "I can't help worrying as long as that debt is over my head. It may kill me, but you might as well tell my cook to order the water in the kettle not to boil as to command my brain not to worry."

What is the answer? The hymn writer Edward Henry Bickersteth hinted at it when he wrote: "Peace, perfect peace, in this dark world of sin? The blood of Jesus whispers peace within."

The sea was beating against the rocks in huge, dashing waves. The lightning was flashing, the thunder was roaring, the wind was blowing; but the little bird was asleep in the crevice of the rock, its head serenely under its wing, sound asleep. That is peace—to be able to sleep in the storm! In Christ, we are relaxed and at peace in the midst of the confusions, bewilderments, and perplexities of this life. The storm rages, but our hearts are at rest. We have found peace—at last!

February 27

DOES GOD CARE?

I will say of the LORD, He is my refuge and my fortress: my God; in him will I trust.   Psalm 91:2

A REFUGE is a place which is safely out of harm's way. A fortress is a fortified building that is virtually impenetrable by conventional means.

Martin Luther wrote that wonderful hymn which says, "A mighty fortress is our God; a bulwark never failing. Our helper He amidst the flood; of mortal ills prevailing." What a statement about the magnificent power and protection of God!

Does God care for you and me? What greater proof do we need than that God sent His Son, Jesus Christ, to die in our place?

Recently two men were hanged for possession of drugs in a country where capital punishment has been invoked for such crimes. Imagine what these men might have felt had another man rushed in just before the nooses were placed around their necks and offered to take their place, freeing them to go home to their families. What an incredible joy and sense of relief would have come over those condemned men.

God has done precisely that for us. He cared so much for us that even while we were yet sinners and still rebellious, He sent His only Son to die in our place, suffering the penalty that rightly was ours. And God keeps on giving. He meets our daily physical needs. He delivers us from evil when we stay close to Him. And there is never a time when we are separated from His care and concern. How could there be? His Son died for us. Can you think of a better reason why God would care for us?

February 28

ANGEL AT WORK?

For He will give His angels [especial] charge over you, to accompany and defend and preserve you in all your ways [of obedience and service]. Psalm 91:11, AB

THE British express train raced through the night, its powerful headlight piercing the darkness. Queen Victoria was a passenger on the train.

Suddenly the engineer saw a startling sight. Revealed in the beam of the engine's light was a strange figure in a black cloak standing in the middle of the tracks and waving its arms. The engineer grabbed for the brake and brought the train to a grinding halt.

He and his fellow trainmen clambered down to see what had stopped them. But they could find no trace of the strange figure. On a hunch the engineer walked a few yards further up the tracks. Suddenly he stopped and stared into the fog in horror. A bridge had been washed out in the middle and ahead of them it had toppled into a swollen stream. If the engineer had not heeded the ghostly figure, his train would have plummeted down into the stream.

While the bridge and the tracks were being repaired, the crew made a more intensive search for the strange flagman. But not until they got to London did they solve the mystery.

At the base of the engine's head lamp the engineer discovered a huge dead moth. He looked at it a moment, then on impulse wet its wings and pasted it to the glass of the lamp.

Climbing back into his cab, he switched on the light and saw the "flagman" in the beam, seconds before the train was due to reach the washed-out bridge. In the fog, it appeared to be a phantom figure, waving its arms.

When Queen Victoria was told of the strange happening she said, "I'm sure it was no accident. It was God's way of protecting us."

No, the figure the engineer saw in the headlight's beam was not an angel . . . and yet God, quite possibly through the ministry of His unseen angels, had placed the moth on the headlight lens exactly when and where it was needed. Truly "He will command his angels concerning you to guard you in all your ways" (Psalm 91:11, NIV).

February 29

GOD'S SECRET AGENTS

For he will give his angels charge of you to guard you in all your ways. Psalm 91:11, RSV

A SECRET agent is one who works to protect his country, his king, or his president against evil forces that are opposed to the one he serves. These days when we think of secret agents, the fictional character James Bond usually comes to mind. But God has His own secret agents—angels. The American Secret Service is charged with protecting the president of the United States. They usually do an excellent job, but even they will tell you they are not perfect, and someone who is fiercely determined to assassinate the president sooner or later will be successful.

God's angels, however, never fail in their appointed tasks. We will never know how many potentially fatal accidents were avoided because God's angels protected us.

Did you know that the Bible guarantees that every believer will be personally escorted into the presence of Christ by the holy angels? What would you do if you were about to meet the queen of England? You would make preparations so that you would be dressed properly and so that you would say the correct things.

So, too, should you be preparing to meet Christ, because no one knows the day or the hour when life will end and God's angels, who have been protecting you, will then usher you into the presence of Christ.

March

THE FAMILY

All thy children shall be taught of the LORD; and great shall be the peace of thy children. Isaiah 54:13

THE family is the basic unit of society. But from the very beginning, since man sinned against God, the family has been in trouble.

On certain products you will find the label, "For best results follow the instructions of the manufacturer." For best results in marriage and in rearing children and building a stable home, follow the instructions of the One who performed the first wedding in the Garden of Eden. Those instructions are in the Bible. The reason the family is in critical condition today is that we have neglected the rules, the regulations, the formula for a successful home.

You can have the right kind of home. Your home can be united if it is now divided. Perhaps there is so much tension and unhappiness that you wonder whether you can stand it much longer. Perhaps you are seriously contemplating divorce. Don't do it! God can heal any marriage if we allow Him to.

A good friend who has counseled troubled marriages for many years says that whenever he hears someone say, "I don't love her," or "I don't love him anymore," the first question he asks is this: "But are you *willing* to love?"

If we are not willing to love our spouses then God will not be able to restore the love we once had for our mates. Remember, feelings come out of commitment and sacrifice. We love God because He first loved us. We came to feel and understand God's love after He offered it in the person of His Son, Jesus Christ.

Receive God's love and ask Him to restore your love for

your mate. He will.

THE CLOUD OF DISCOURAGEMENT

*May the God of steadfastness and encouragement grant you
to live in such harmony with one another, in accord with
Christ Jesus.* Romans 15:5, RSV

THE root of discouragement is unbelief. Consider what
discourages you. You are not making enough money (you
are not convinced that God can and will supply all of
your needs); you are frustrated in your job (you have
refused to believe that you can be content in whatever
state you are in); you are worried about health problems
(Is not God the great physician? Did He not make your
body and know how every cell functions? Can He not
heal you when and if He wishes?)

Discouragement is a large cloud that, like all clouds,
obscures the warmth and joy of the sun. In the case of
spiritual discouragement the Son of God, the Lord Jesus,
is eclipsed in our lives. Discouragement is Satan's device
to thwart the work of God in our lives. Discouragement
blinds our eyes to the mercy of God and makes us
perceive only the unfavorable circumstances.

There is only one way to dispel discouragement, and it
is not in our own strength or ingenuity. The Bible says,
"Wait on the LORD: be of good courage, and he shall
strengthen thine heart: wait, I say, on the LORD" (Psalm 27:14).

I have never met a person who spent time in daily
prayer and in the study of God's Word and who was
strong in the faith who was ever discouraged for very
long. You cannot be discouraged if you are close
to the One who gives all hope and plenty to be

Unto the Hills   73

encouraged about.

"Be of good cheer," Jesus tells us. "I have overcome the world."

March 3

IN THE BEGINNING

God hath from the beginning chosen you. . . . 2 Thessalonians 2:13

GOD's love did not begin at Calvary. Before the morning stars of the pre-Eden world sang together, before the world was baptized with the first light, before the first blades of tender grass peeped out, God was love.

Turn back to the unwritten pages of countless millennia before God spoke this present earth into existence, when the earth was "without form and void" and the deep, silent darkness of space formed a vast gulf between the brilliance of God's glory and His cherubim and seraphim, who covered their faces with their wings in awe and reverence toward Him who is high and holy.

Yet lofty as the heavens may be, and pure as God's holiness glistens, there comes to our ears the word that the majesty of His love was moved for us, and the Lamb was slain from the foundation of the world.

God thought of you even then, even before He made the world, even before He made you. It is that God who loves you and longs to have the deepest and closest relationship possible with you.

That is what it was like in the beginning. That is what it is still like today, for God never changes, whether it be in His personality or His love for you.

March 4

THE OWL AND THE PELICAN

*I am like a pelican of the wilderness: I am like an owl of
the desert.*   Psalm 102:6

M Y wife has a weakness for books—especially old, choice
religious books which are now out of print. At one time
Foyles in London had a large secondhand religious book
department. One day during the 1954 London Crusade she
was browsing through the books in Foyles when a very
agitated clerk popped out from behind the stacks and asked if
she was Mrs. Graham. When she told him that she was, he
began to tell her a story of confusion, despair, and
frustration. His marriage was on the rocks, his home was
breaking up, and business problems were mounting. He
explained that he had explored every avenue for help and as a
last resort planned to attend the services at Harringay arena
that night. Ruth assured him that she would pray for him,
and she did. That was in 1954.

In 1955 we returned to London. Again my wife went into
Foyles' secondhand book department. This time the same
clerk appeared from behind the stacks, his face wreathed in
smiles. After expressing how happy he was to see her again, he
explained that he had gone to Harringay that night in 1954 as
he had said he would, that he had found the Savior, and that
the problems in his life had sorted themselves out.

Then he asked Ruth if she would be interested in knowing
what verse it was that "spoke to him." She was. Again he
disappeared behind all the books and reappeared with a worn
Bible in his hand. He turned to Psalm 102, which I had read
the night that he had attended the Crusade. He pointed out
verse 6, "I am like a pelican of the wilderness: I am like an
owl of the desert." This had so perfectly described to him his

condition that he realized for the first time how completely God understood and cared. As a result he was soundly converted to the Lord Jesus Christ. And subsequently so was his entire family.

My wife was in London during 1972 at the time of a Harringay reunion. As the ceremonies closed, a gentleman came up to speak to her, but he didn't have to introduce himself. She recognized the clerk from Foyles. He was radiantly happy, introduced his Christian family, and explained how they were all now in the Lord's work—all because God spoke to him when he was "an owl of the desert"!

How graciously God speaks to us in our need . . . often through some obscure passage.

March 5

FOREVER

As for man, his days are as grass; even as a flower of the field, so he flourisheth. Psalm 103:15

THE Bible reminds us that our days are as grass. They are filled with tiny golden minutes with eternity in them. We are exhorted to redeem the time because the days are evil.

Our lives are also immortal. God made man different from the other creatures. He made him in His own image, a living soul. When this body dies and our earthly existence is terminated, the soul lives on forever. One thousand years from this day you will be more alive than you are at this moment. The Bible teaches that life does not end at the cemetery. There is a future life with God for those who put their trust in His Son, Jesus Christ. There is also a future hell of separation from God toward which all are going who have refused, rejected, or neglected to receive His Son, Jesus Christ.

Victor Hugo once said, "I feel in myself the future life." Cyrus the Great is reported to have declared, "I cannot imagine that the soul lives only while it remains in this mortal body."

March 6

WE ARE GOING TO A PLACE

I go to prepare a place for you. . . . John 14:2

THE Lord Jesus could have used any word, any symbol to tell us where we would spend eternity. But He always chose words very carefully, and so in this instance He used the word "place."

I live in a place, high on a mountain in a log cabin in North Carolina. This place has an address. If you send a letter to me, the postman knows where to deliver it.

In saying that He was going to prepare a place for us, Jesus was telling us that when we die, we are going to a precise location. We do not evaporate or disappear. In fact, He said, "In my Father's house are many mansions." We are going to have a place in heaven if we have trusted Christ as our Savior—and not only a place, but a mansion!

When we as Christians die, we go straight into the presence of Christ, straight to that place, straight to that mansion in heaven to spend eternity with God. We are simply changing our address, much as we would if we moved to another place here on earth. If the post office was capable of delivering the mail in heaven, we could fill out a change of address form, because the place we are going to has an address just as the place in which we are now living has an address. It is a real place.

March 7

ANGELS ALL AROUND ME

Bless the LORD, *ye his angels, that excel in strength, that do his commandments hearkening unto the voice of his word.* Psalm 103:20

THERE is much in the news these days about demons and devil worship. Movies like *The Exorcist* attracted wide interest several years ago and packed movie theaters. Today we read of cults that engage in animal and, in some instances, human sacrifice.

Until recently there was far less attention paid to angels, perhaps because so much of the media seems preoccupied with the evil forces in the spirit world and not the good. But if you are a believer in Christ, expect powerful angels to accompany you in your life experiences. You will not always be able to sense their presence. You will not be aware that you did not turn down a certain road, preferring another, because an angel so directed you away from trouble.

The Bible teaches that angels speak and that they appear and reappear. You may have never seen one, but there is much that you have not seen that still exists. You may never have been to the North Pole, either, but it is there.

Often we fail to sense the spiritual forces around us because we operate for the most part on our physical senses, the senses of sight, touch, and taste. Get tuned in to the spiritual realm through God's Word and through regular prayer and sense the angels and the work of God's Holy Spirit in your life. It is like tuning in a radio. The signals are already in the air, but you have to turn the dial to bring them in.

March 8

SATISFYING THE LONGING SOUL

Oh that men would praise the LORD *for his goodness, and for his wonderful works to the children of men! For he satisfieth the longing soul, and filleth the hungry soul with goodness.*   Psalm 107:8—9

WHEN Satan tried to tempt Jesus into the same trap made of "things" that he lures men to in this day, Christ said, "Man shall not live by bread alone, but by every word that proceedeth out of the mouth of God" (Matthew 4:4). Bread is important—but it is not all-important. Pleasure and recreation have their place—but they must not have first place. Money is necessary, but gold is no satisfying substitute for God.

Now, as then, God's Word resounds in our ears: "Hearken diligently unto me, and eat that which is good, and let your soul delight itself in fatness" (Isaiah 55:2). This is the secret of soul-satisfaction: Let your soul delight itself in fatness. Remove the obstructions, tear down the barriers, and let your soul find the fulfillment of its deepest longings in fellowship with God.

I could tell you of many people who have explored every earthly resource for happiness and failed, but eventually came in repentance and faith to Christ, and in Him found satisfaction. The principle reason communism loses ground in the world (when it does) is that it promises material prosperity without spiritual satisfaction. Things, minus God, equal misery. That equation is just as true as two plus two equal four. As Eddie Rickenbacker once said, "Let the moment come when nothing is left but life, and you will find that you do not hesitate over the fate of material possessions."

March 9

SEARCHING

My spirit made diligent search.   Psalm 77:6

WHEN a spacecraft returns from its orbital flight, there is a blackout period of about four minutes when all communications are broken. This is due to the intense heat generated by the spacecraft's reentry into the earth's atmosphere.

The Bible teaches that man is in a period of spiritual blackout. Spiritually, he is *blind*. "We grope for the wall like the blind, and we grope as if we had no eyes: we stumble at noon day as in the night; we are in desolate places as dead men" (Isaiah 59:10). "The god of this world hath blinded the minds of them which believe not" (2 Corinthians 4:4).

Spiritually, man is also *deaf*. "They have ears to hear, and hear not" (Ezekiel 12:2). Jesus went so far as to say, "If they hear not Moses and the prophets, neither will they be persuaded, though one rose from the dead" (Luke 16:31).

Spiritually, man is even *dead*. "Who were dead in trespasses and sins" (Ephesians 2:1).

All of this means that the communication between God and man is broken. There is a wonderful world of joy, light, harmony, peace, and satisfaction to which millions of persons are blind and deaf, and even dead. They search for serenity, they long for happiness, but they never seem to find it.

Many give up the search and surrender to pessimism. Often their despondency leads to a frantic round of cocktail parties where vast amounts of alcohol are imbibed. Sometimes it leads them to narcotics or illicit sex. It is all part of man's desperate search to find an escape from the cold realities of a sin—blighted existence. All the while God is there speaking and beckoning. God is sending forth His message of love, but we must be on the right wavelength. We must be willing to receive His message and then to obey it.

A LAMP AND A LIGHT

Your word is a lamp to guide me and a light for my path.
Psalm 119:105, TEV

WE must become grounded in the Bible. As Christians, we have only one authority, one compass: the Word of God.

In a letter to a friend, Abraham Lincoln said, "I am profitably engaged in reading the Bible. Take all of this Book upon reason that you can and the balance upon faith, and you will live and die a better man."

Coleridge said he believed the Bible to be the Word of God because, as he put it, "It finds me."

"If you want encouragement," John Bunyan wrote, "entertain the promises."

Martin Luther said, "In Scriptures, even the little daisy becomes a meadow."

The Bible is our one sure guide in an unsure world.

Great leaders have made it their chief Book and their reliable guide. Herbert J. Taylor, formerly international president of Rotary, told me that he began each day by reading the Sermon on the Mount aloud. President Ronald Reagan revered the Bible so much that he proclaimed 1984 the "year of the Bible."

We should begin the day with the Book, and as it comes to a close let the Word speak its wisdom to our souls. Let it be the firm foundation upon which our hope is built. Let it be the Staff of Life upon which your spirit is nourished. Let it be the Sword of the Spirit which cuts away the evil of our lives and fashions us in His image and likeness.

....

REVELATION IN SCRIPTURE

For ever, O LORD, thy word is settled in heaven. Psalm 119:89

WHAT does revelation mean? It means that something which has been hidden is to be made known. God, who has existed forever, has revealed Himself to us through Scripture.

God has two textbooks (a textbook is a book which gives the reader facts and instructions). One of God's textbooks is about nature. The other is about revelation.

The laws God has revealed in the textbook of nature have never changed. They tell us of God's mighty power and majesty.

In the textbook of revelation, the Bible, God has spoken verbally; and this spoken word has survived every scratch of human pen. It has survived the assault of skeptics, agnostics, and atheists. It has never been proved wrong by a single archaeological discovery. It remains supreme in its revelation of redemption.

The writers of the Bible repeatedly claim that God spoke. Either God did speak, or these men were the biggest liars in history. But for them to have told two thousand lies on one subject would be incredible.

Jesus quoted frequently from the Old Testament. He never once said He doubted Scripture. The apostle Paul often quoted Scripture. In fact Paul said, "All scripture is given by inspiration of God" (2 Timothy 3:16). Were Jesus and Paul fooled by "liars"?

No, God has spoken truly in history, and He still speaks to us today through that same Word, which stands forever because it is the Word of God.

Get to know the Word of God and you will draw closer to Him.

UNTO THE HILLS

I lift up my eyes unto the hills. From whence does my help come?
My help comes from the LORD, who made heaven and earth.
Psalm 121:1–2, RSV

ISRAEL, the nation in which the Bible was written, is a very "hilly" country. There are mountains and hills everywhere. In fact, the Bible speaks of going "up to Jerusalem," which is "a city set on a hill." Throughout Scripture, there are references to these hills and mountains and encouragement to the Israelites to "look up" to the hills and to look up to heaven.

The disciples looked and saw the resurrected Christ "ascending" to His Father in heaven. We are told that when Jesus returns, He will come in the clouds and we will see Him come just as He left us, from the sky. Looking upward takes the attention of men and women off of their earthly circumstances. It changes their perspective.

If you have ever flown in an airplane, you know that your perspective of what is on the ground is far different from what it was when you were on the ground. Pictures of the earth that have been taken from the moon and from space show an earth that looks much different from our awareness of the planet while we are on it. This is the kind of perspective God wants to give us of ourselves. As we look unto God instead of at ourselves and our circumstances, our perspectives change.

Do not be bogged down in the circumstances of life. Look unto the hills for the guidance of Christ. Keep your eyes upon the eastern sky. "Lift up your heads; for your redemption draweth nigh"(Luke 21 :28)!

March 13

THE WISE BUILDER

Except the LORD build the house, they labor in vain that build it: except the LORD keep the city, the watchman waketh but in vain. Psalm 127:1

Y O U will recall that in the fairy tale *The Three Little Pigs* the pigs built three houses for themselves for protection against the Big Bad Wolf. One little pig built his house of straw. The second little pig built his house of wood. The third little pig built his house of brick. When the Big Bad Wolf came along, he "huffed and he puffed" and blew down the houses that were built of straw and wood, but he could not move the house built of brick.

There is a song still sung in Sunday school classes: "The wise man built his house upon the rock. . . ." The wise man does build his house upon the rock—the Lord Jesus Christ—for nothing built of or on any other substance will stand the test of time.

In big cities I often see wrecking balls destroying old structures to make way for new ones. Some of these "old structures" in America are frequently less than a hundred years old. In Europe, buildings several centuries old are common. But even these buildings can be destroyed, by a natural disaster if not by man.

Only what is built on the solid foundation of Christ will last. As the poem says, "Only one life, 'twill soon be past. Only what's done for Christ shall last."

THE WORK OF THE HOLY SPIRIT

. . . God's love has been poured into our hearts through the
Holy Spirit which has been given to us.   Romans 5:5, RSV

THE Holy Spirit of God plays two important roles.

First, He convicts men of sin: "And when he is come, he will reprove the world of sin, and of righteousness, and of judgment" (John 16:8). This is why before we come to Christ we must acknowledge our sin. We must renounce our sins. The Holy Spirit makes us feel uncomfortable and pricks our consciences. He makes us acknowledge and admit to ourselves and to God that we are sinners, and then He gives us the strength and the power to turn from our sins.

The second role of the Holy Spirit is as a teacher, a guide into all truth. After we have committed our lives to Christ, the Holy Spirit helps us understand the written Word of God. He is our instructor. He is also our comforter in times of trouble and sorrow.

That is why the natural man does not understand the things of the spirit (1 Corinthians 2:14), why the unregenerate man does not have the Holy Spirit, because he has not had his sins forgiven and so has not received his "leader into all truth" and cannot comprehend the Scriptures. It would be like trying to read a book in an unfamiliar language. It would be impossible.

The moment I receive Jesus Christ as Savior, the Holy Spirit takes up residence in my heart. The problem, as A. W. Tozer has noted, is that "though every believer has the Holy Spirit, the Holy Spirit does not have every believer!"

For a student to be taught, he must listen and desire to learn from his teacher. For the Christian to grow in wisdom and knowledge of the Word of God, he must be willing to study God's Word and to be a willing pupil of God's Holy Spirit.

SEARCH AND RESCUE

. . . I have set before you life and death . . . therefore choose life,
that you and your descendants may live. Deuteronomy 30:19, RSV

BEFORE the space shuttle program, American ships and
helicopters used to recover astronauts who had returned to
earth at sea. The tiny spacecraft would be located in the
enormous ocean, and the astronauts would be lifted out of
their capsule into the helicopter, which would then fly them
to the safety of the ship.

I have often thought, as I watched these scenes on
television, how like God this operation is. God hovers over
the entire world, seeking to pluck from sin immortal souls
who are in danger of "drowning" in hell. He tosses out a line
to all those who are in trouble. Some grab on to God's line
and freely receive the gift of His Son, Jesus Christ. They are
pulled to safety, and, eventually, taken to heaven. Others
ignore the line, believing they can make it on their own.

Can you imagine an astronaut or anyone in trouble at sea
refusing to be rescued? Yet vast numbers of people daily
refuse the help of God.

Nations refuse this help as well. Though God has said,
"Righteousness exalts a nation, but sin is a reproach to any
people," nations and national leaders think they can survive
without God's help. We have "In God We Trust" on our
money, but I wonder how often it is really in the money that
we trust?

Our souls send out a distress signal to God. When God
hovers over us dangling a saving lifeline, do we refuse His
help, or do we grasp the line so that we can be saved? The
choice is ours alone. There are eternal benefits that come
from making the right choice. There are also eternal

consequences for making the wrong choice. Which choices have you been making in your life?

REALLY KNOWING GOD

Search me, O God, and know my heart! Try me and know my thoughts!
And see if there be any wicked way in me, and lead me
in the way everlasting. Psalm 139:23–24, RSV

HERE was a wise confession on the part of a great leader. David knew that a people can rise no higher economically, scientifically, and politically than the level of their spiritual resources. Here was a humble admission and an acknowledgment that a nation's sicknesses can be attributed to its spiritual ills.

Weary of assemblies, hearings, conferences, and investigations designed to reveal the root causes of state difficulties, David turned his face to the altar of God. He prayed earnestly for God to begin the revival of his nation by kindling the fires of revival in his own heart.

Not only did he pray that he might know God, but that God might know him. "Search me, O God!"

His heart yearned, as indeed our hearts yearn today, for a personal, vital intimacy with God. In short, he was praying for a new, definite, real experience with his God.

Unless God is revealed to us through personal experience, we can never really know God. Most of us know *about* God, but that is quite different from really *knowing* God.

Is it not logical to believe that the only One who can re-create us is the One who created us in the first place? If your watch were out of order, you wouldn't take it to a blacksmith. If your car needed overhauling, you wouldn't take it to a plumber. If you needed an operation, you wouldn't go to a machine shop.

Our spiritual problems can only be solved by the God who created us originally. He created us in His own image and likeness; today by the grace of His Son, He can re-create us in the likeness of His resurrection. Through faith in Jesus Christ, we are recreated and become partakers of His life.

"Therefore if any man be in Christ, he is a new creature: old things are passed away; behold, all things are become new" (2 Corinthians 5:17).

David's prayer, recorded here in Psalm 139, contained a proper sequence. First he prayed that God might know him; then he prayed that God might cleanse him; and last he prayed that God might direct him. David's transformation, as a result of this prayer, was full and complete. Likewise, his nation, Israel, was brought into harmony with God. We, too, can find peace as we are rightly related to God—and this is the only path to peace.

March 17

WHEN GOD SEEMS SILENT

The LORD is nigh unto all them that call upon him, to all that call upon him in truth. Psalm 145:18

ON THE natural level we tend to neglect the privilege of prayer until we encounter sufferings or difficulty of some kind. We often need to be driven to real prayer by the circumstances that surround us.

Dwight L. Moody was fond of pointing out that there are three kinds of faith in Jesus Christ: *struggling faith*, which is like a man floundering and fearful in deep water; *clinging faith*, which is like a man hanging to the side of a boat; and *resting faith*, which finds a man safe inside the boat—strong and secure enough to reach out his hand to help someone else.

That is the sort of faith you and I have to acquire in order to be effective as Christians—and such faith may be ours through the ministry of suffering in our lives.

Suffering also teaches us patience. These words were found penned on the wall of a prison cell in Europe: "I believe in the sun even when it is not shining. I believe in love even when I don't feel it. I believe in God even when He is silent."

Sometimes God seems so quiet! However, when we see the way He works in lives imprisoned by walls or circumstances, when we hear how faith can shine through uncertainty, we begin to catch a glimpse of the fruit of patience that can grow out of the experience of suffering.

March 18

GOD'S RESTRAINING LOVE

The LORD loveth the righteous. Psalm 146:8

IT is really God's love for man which restrains Him from removing evil from our world by a display of His power. God's plan is to remove evil by a display of His love—the love that He demonstrated at Calvary.

It is in God's love that we find the key to the ultimate solution of the problem of suffering. The answer to the age-old question of suffering rests in an understanding and appreciation of the character of God.

This is what Job discovered. At the height of his suffering and questioning, God revealed Himself in various aspects of His character to Job. Job was given an awesome demonstration of God's wisdom. Through this experience he came to realize that God could be trusted on the basis of His character. Although Job could not understand the ultimate purpose for all of God's actions, he could trust God. Because God knows and understands all things, He can be trusted to do what is best.

There will always be secrets and motives of God which lie beyond the grasp of man. God is infinite; man is finite. Our knowledge and understanding are limited. But based upon what we do know about God's character, demonstrated supremely in the Cross, we can trust that God is doing what is best for our lives.

As Corrie ten Boom once explained, "Picture a piece of embroidery placed between you and God, with the right side up toward God. Man sees the loose, frayed ends; but God sees the pattern."

God is in control. Whatever comes into our lives, no matter how difficult or dangerous it may be, we can confidently say, "We know that in all things God works for the good of those who love him, who have been called according to his purpose" (Romans 8:28).

March 19

THE MAN ON THE MOUNTAIN

Great is our Lord, and of great power: his understanding is infinite. Psalm 147:5

SOME theologians have made attempts to rob God of His warmth, His deep love for mankind, and His sympathy for His creatures. But God's love is unchangeable. He loves us in spite of knowing us as we really are. In fact, He created us because He wanted other creatures in His image in the universe upon whom He could pour out His love, and who, in turn, would voluntarily love Him. He wanted people with the ability to say "yes" or "no" in their relationship to Him. Love is not satisfied with an automaton—one who has no choice but to love and obey. Not mechanized love, but voluntary love satisfies the heart of God.

Were it not for the love of God, none of us would ever have a chance in the future life!

Some years ago a friend of mine was standing on top of a mountain in North Carolina. The roads in those days were filled with curves, and it was difficult to see very far ahead. This man saw two cars heading toward each other. He realized that they couldn't see each other. A third car pulled up and began to pass one of the cars, although there wasn't enough space to see the other car approaching around the bend. My friend shouted a warning, but the drivers couldn't hear, and there was a fatal crash. The man on the mountain saw it all.

This is how God looks upon us in His omniscience. He sees what has happened, what is happening, and what will happen. In the Scriptures He warns us time after time about troubles, problems, sufferings, and judgment that lie ahead. Many times we ignore His warnings.

God sees all and knows all. But we are too limited by the circumstances to see the "big picture."

March 20

THE BEST PLACE TO START

Pride goeth before destruction, and a haughty spirit before a fall. Proverbs 16:18

KING David knew that if the tide of sinful pride continued to rise, his nation would collapse spiritually. He knew that economic depression, moral disintegration, or military defeat inevitably follow spiritual decline.

So he did what all intelligent men should do when they reach the end of their ropes—he turned to God. He stopped asking God to destroy his enemies. It was revealed to him by the Spirit of God that the spiritual tide of his nation could rise no higher than the spiritual level of his own heart. So he fell on his knees in utter humility and prayed this prayer: "Search me, O God, and know my heart: try me, and know my thoughts: and see if there be any wicked way in me, and lead me in the way everlasting" (Psalm 139:23–24).

If we today could only realize that a nation can rise no higher, can be no stronger, and can be no better than the individuals which compose that nation! There is nothing wrong with the world. The trouble lies with the world's people. If the world is bad, it is the people who are bad. If the world is confused, it is the people in the world who are confused. If this is a godless world, it is the people who are godless.

David realized this truth; and in wisdom, he concluded that he should start making things right in himself! Each one of us needs to reach that same conclusion.

March 21

THE PURSUIT OF HAPPINESS

But happy is the man who has the God of Jacob as his helper, whose hope is in the Lord his God. Psalm 146:5, TLB

I ALMOST wish that Thomas Jefferson had not written about "the pursuit of happiness." Jefferson was correct that we should have a "right" to pursue happiness, but the problem today is that so many people are pursuing happiness without knowing exactly what they are looking for or where to find it.

Happiness is a byproduct, not an end in itself. Happiness cannot be pursued any more than one can pursue a cloudless day, grasp it, put it in a bottle, and then bring it out on a rainy day to enjoy again. True happiness is not superficial and fleeting, as a day at an amusement park might be. True happiness begins when one is in a right relationship with God.

In fact, God is the only source of true happiness, because He offers those intangibles that we mistakenly believe can be found on earth: contentment, security, peace, and hope for the future. None of these can be found in a job, a human relationship, money, power, or position. They are God's alone to give.

That is why the Lord Jesus, in His Sermon on the Mount, told where ultimate happiness lies when He said, "Happy are they who hunger and thirst after righteousness, for they shall be filled."

March 22

TRAINING CHILDREN

Train up a child in the way he should go: and when he is old, he will not depart from it. Proverbs 22:6

EVERY child is a free moral agent. But there are certain truths we can teach and certain examples we can set that will make it much more likely a child will accept Jesus Christ as Savior when he is old enough to make such a decision. And for the rebellious child who wanders away from God, working in biblical principles at an early age can greatly enhance the possibility that God will be able to use these truths to bring an errant child back to the fold.

It is important that we follow the commandment, "Do not provoke your children to anger, but bring them up in the discipline and instruction of the Lord" (Ephesians 6:4, RSV). Parents should never give unreasonable and repetitious commands. Nor should they ever give a command that they do not mean to be carried out.

Children want their parents to care enough about them to

be strict. The Bible teaches us to discipline our children. "He that spareth his rod hateth his son: but he that loveth him chasteneth him betimes" (Proverbs 13:24). We are to train our children "precept upon precept, line upon line; here a little, and there a little" (Isaiah 28:10). In other words, when a boy has reached the age of twelve, we cannot suddenly say, "It's very late, but I'm going to try to cram religion into him now." It must start the very moment he has any understanding at all. Precept upon precept, line upon line, it has to be a little here and a little there.

The majority of children acquire the characteristics and habits of their parents. What are they learning from us?

March 23

GIVING

Give, and it shall be given unto you; good measure, pressed down, and shaken together, and running over, shall men give into your bosom. For with the same measure that ye mete withal it shall be measured to you again. Luke 6:38

THE Bible teaches that blessings follow those who give liberally. Proverbs 11:25 says, "The liberal soul shall be made fat: and he that watereth shall be watered also himself."

I have heard countless testimonies from men and women who were afraid to prove God's promise by tithing as commanded by Scripture for fear they would never have enough. Of course, they never did have "enough" because they did not tithe. Then, when at last they decided to obey God and give to Him the first tenth of all their income, they began to prosper and to prove for themselves what has been proved by everyone who has done it, that no one can outgive God.

Two things happen when we give. First, God wants to produce in us the attitude that what we have is not really ours.

Everything we possess belongs to God.

Second, giving is a means by which we meet the needs of others whom God also loves. By giving to others we testify to God's love for them. So giving becomes not only a means by which people's needs are met, it also is a form of evangelism which allows us to tell of God's greatest gift, His Son, the Lord Jesus Christ, who will meet far more than their momentary physical needs.

Giving to God is a guaranteed investment with a certain return. Investment in God is a no-risk, always profitable act that is not subject to the whims of the stock market or of economic uncertainties.

It has been said that our lives should resemble a channel, not a reservoir. A reservoir stores up water. A channel is constantly flowing. God wants us to be a channel of blessing to others. When we are, it is we who receive the greatest blessing of all.

March 24

HOLY, HOLY, HOLY

Holy, holy, holy, is the LORD of hosts: the whole earth is full of his glory. Isaiah 6:3

THE Bible teaches that God is holy, without fault, perfect, and complete. From Genesis to Revelation, God reveals Himself as a holy God. He is so holy that He cannot endure sin, cannot even look upon it.

It was God's holiness that caused Him to turn His back when the Lord Jesus Christ took upon Himself the sin of the entire world at Calvary. It was the only time in the eternal unity of the Trinity that God the Father and God the Son had a rupture in their relationship.

Christ cried out on the cross, "My God, my God, why hast

Thou forsaken me?" What a terribly frightening and horrible moment that was as the blackness of man's sin caused the Father to turn away in disgust. Yet what a glorious moment it was as Christ took upon His holy and sinless self all of the penalty that should be ours because of our sinfulness.

And now, God commands us to be holy as He is. But how can we be holy? When we accept Jesus Christ as our Savior, He comes into our hearts and lives, cleanses us from sin, and makes a home in us. At that moment we begin to grow into the likeness of Christ (theologians call the process "sanctification"), and we continue to grow until that moment when we go to be with Christ and receive our glorified bodies.

How thankful we should be that it was Christ who made all of this possible!

March 25

OUR HOMECOMING PARADE

He will swallow up death in victory; and the Lord GOD will wipe away tears from off all faces.   Isaiah 25:8

ONCE I stood in London to watch Queen Elizabeth return from an overseas trip. I saw the parade of dignitaries, the marching bands, the crack troops, the waving flags. I saw all the splendor that accompanies the homecoming of a queen. However, that was nothing compared to the homecoming of a true believer who has said good-bye here to all of the suffering of this life and been immediately surrounded by angels who carry him upward to the glorious welcome awaiting the redeemed in heaven.

The Christian should never consider death a tragedy. Rather he should see it as the angels do: They realize that joy should mark the journey from time to eternity. The way to life is by the valley of death, but the road is marked with victory all the way. Angels revel in the power of the resurrection of Jesus, which assures us of our resurrection and guarantees us a safe passage to heaven.

Joy should mark our lives not just at the point of transition from this life to the next. The late A. W. Tozer describes the authentic Christian lifestyle this way:

"George Mueller would not preach until his heart was happy in the grace of God; Jan Van Ruysbroeck, the fourteenth century mystic, would not write while his feelings were low, but would retire to a quiet place and wait on God till he felt the spirit of inspiration. It is well-known that the elevated spirits of a group of Moravians convinced John Wesley of the reality of their religion, and helped to bring him a short time later to a state of true conversion."

As that great hymn says, "When we all get to heaven, what a day of rejoicing that will be; when we all see Jesus we'll sing and shout the victory." And why not? Shouldn't the guest of honor receive a homecoming parade?

March 26

REST FROM LABOR

He will swallow up death for ever, and the Lord GOD will wipe away tears from all faces. Isaiah 25:8, RSV

THE Bible speaks of death, for a Christian, as a rest from labor. The Bible says, "Blessed are the dead which die in the Lord . . . that they may rest from their labors" (Revelation 14:13). It is as if the Lord of the harvest says to the weary laborer, "You have been faithful in your task, come and sit in the sheltered porch of my palace and rest from your labors—enter now into the joy of your Lord."

Some of God's saints accomplish more in a few years than others do in a lifetime. The Bible says, "There remaineth therefore a rest to the people of God" (Hebrews 4:9). That rest cannot begin until the angel of death takes them by the hand and leads them into the glorious presence of their Lord.

And Paul said, "We are confident, I say, and willing rather to be absent from the body, and to be present with the Lord" (2 Corinthians 5:8).

Victor Hugo said of death: "When I go down to the grave I can say, like so many others: I have finished my work, but I cannot say I have finished my life. My day's work will begin the next morning. My tomb is not a blind alley. It is a thoroughfare. It closes in the twilight to be open in the dawn."

Confident of the fact that death is not an end but a beginning, we can say with the apostle Paul, "O death, where is thy sting? O grave, where is thy victory?" (1 Corinthians 15:55).

March 27

PERSONAL PEACE

Thou wilt keep him in perfect peace, whose mind is stayed on thee. Isaiah 26:3

I KNOW that modern living taxes the faith of the greatest Christians, but none of us should doubt the ability of God to give us grace sufficient for our trials even amid the stresses of this twentieth century. In the middle of our world troubles, the Christian is not to go about wringing his hands, shouting, "What shall we do?" having more nervous tension and worry than anyone else. The Christian is to trust quietly that God is still on the throne. He is a sovereign God, working out things according to His own plan.

Some section hands on a British railroad found a thrush's nest under a rail, and the hen peacefully sitting on the eggs undisturbed by the roar of the fast trains above and around her. The Bible says, "Thou wilt keep him in perfect peace, whose mind is stayed on thee." Believe me, God's grace is more than adequate for these times. I am learning in my own life, day by day, to keep my mind centered on Christ, and the worries and anxieties and concerns of the world pass away and nothing but "perfect peace" is left in the human heart.

God has taken the responsibility for our care and worry. Who of us has not asked in times of affliction and difficulty—does God care for me? The psalmist voiced the sentiments of many of us when he said, ". . . Refuge failed me; no man cared for my soul" (Psalm 142:4). Martha, over-concerned with her workaday duties, said to Jesus, "Lord, dost Thou not care?" How many faithful, loving mothers, overwhelmed by the burdens of motherhood, have cried anxiously, "Lord, dost Thou not care?" The disciples, tossed by the turbulent sea, cried, "Carest Thou not that we perish?"

That question is forever answered in those reassuring words of Peter: "He careth for you." This is the Word of God, and the world will pass away before it can be altered. You can be positively assured that God does care for you, and if God cares for you and has promised to carry your burdens and cares, then nothing should distress you.

March 28

GOD IS OUR SHEPHERD

He tends his flock like a shepherd: He gathers the lambs in his arms and carries them close to his heart; he gently leads those that have young. Isaiah 40:11, NIV

THE wonderful picture of God as our Shepherd is found in many places in the Old Testament. One of the Psalms begins, "Hear us, O Shepherd of Israel, you who lead Joseph like a flock" (Psalm 80:1, NIV). It's wonderful to know that the everlasting God, the almighty Creator, stoops to be the

Shepherd of His people.

David makes the relationship a personal one in the best known of all psalms. "The LORD is *my* shepherd," he cries exultantly, "I shall lack nothing" (Psalm 23:1, NIV, italics mine). The rest of the psalm tells us what we shall not lack. It speaks of the Shepherd's provision as He leads us to the green pastures, His guidance along the paths of righteousness (that means the right paths), His presence with us in the dark valley. No wonder David testifies, "My cup overflows" (verse 5). Such are God's boundless blessings.

Isaiah adds a further dimension to the picture when he says, "He tends his flock like a shepherd: He gathers the lambs in his arms and carries them close to his heart" (Isaiah 40:11, NIV). The figure here indicates the tender care with which the Lord supports His people on their journey and the strong love with which He enfolds them.

In the New Testament Jesus uses this same figure and applies it to Himself. He says, "I am the good shepherd. The good shepherd lays down his life for the sheep. The hired hand is not the shepherd who owns the sheep and runs away. Then the wolf attacks the flock and scatters it. . . . I am the good shepherd; I know my sheep and my sheep know me" (John 10:11–14, NIV).

Note four things about Jesus the Good Shepherd. He *owns* the sheep: They belong to Him. He *guards* the sheep: He never abandons them when danger is near. He *knows* the sheep; knows them each by name and leads them out (see verse 3). And he *lays down His life* for the sheep; such is the measure of His love.

No wonder, just as a shepherd of real sheep, Jesus is worthy of being followed.

March 29

THE PEACE OF GOD

Fear thou not; for I am with thee: be not dismayed; for I am thy God: I will strengthen thee; yea, I will help thee; yea, I will uphold thee with the right hand of my righteousness. Isaiah 41:10

EVERYONE who knows the Lord Jesus Christ can go through any problem, and face death, and still have the peace of God in his heart. When your spouse dies, or your children get sick, or you lose your job, you can have a peace that you don't understand. You may have tears at a graveside, but you can have an abiding peace, a quietness.

A psychiatrist was quoted in the newspaper as saying that he could not improve upon the apostle Paul's prescription for human worry. Paul said, "Be (anxious) for nothing; but in everything by prayer and supplication with thanksgiving let your requests be made known to God. And the peace of God, which surpasses all comprehension shall guard your hearts and your minds in Christ Jesus" (Philippians 4:6–7, NASB). Be anxious for nothing. How many times do you and I fret and turn, looking for a little peace? God's peace can be in our hearts—right now.

Colossians 3:15 says, "Let the peace of Christ rule in your hearts." Some of you believe that you know Jesus Christ as your Savior, but you haven't really made Him your Lord. You're missing the peace of God in your struggles and turmoils and trials and pressures of life. Is the peace of God in your heart?

We are all familiar with the transformation that took place in Saul on the road to Damascus, when Christ entered his heart and changed him from one of His most destructive enemies to one of His mightiest advocates. Many equally dramatic changes in human personalities are taking place today, and they are being brought about by the selfsame means that transformed Saul into Paul—birth again through Jesus Christ!

There is no human philosophy that can achieve such changes or provide such strength. This mighty strength stands ready to be available at your beck and call at all times.

No man can bring peace to a troubled world because it is not his to give. Christ said, "My peace I give unto you. . . ." It is not the peace of man, but the peace of God. We cannot give what does not belong to us. Ask for God's peace and see what a transformation will take place in your life.

March 30

THROUGH THE TRIALS

See, I have refined you, though not as silver; I have tested you in the furnace of affliction. Isaiah 48:10, NIV

A PRISONER recently released from years at hard labor, without a Bible, drew for his spiritual nourishment on the passages of Scripture which he had memorized since his conversion as a young boy. One he mentioned particularly was Psalm 66. As I read that psalm I was impressed by the fact that the psalmist recognized no secondary causes. Beginning with verse 10 he says, "For *you*, O God, tested us; *you* refined us like silver." Verse 11, "*You* brought us into prison and laid burdens on our backs." Verse 12, "*You* let men ride over our heads; we went through fire and water, but you brought us to a place of abundance" (italics mine).

In the Scriptures we find this also true in the case of Job. Job did not know that Satan had to get permission from God before he could touch Job, much less Job's possessions. Yet when Job had lost everything he did not say, "The LORD gave and the devil has taken away," but "The LORD gave and the LORD has *taken away*; may the name of the LORD be praised" (Job 1:21, NIV, italics mine).

So when we are hurt it is important to remember that God Himself has allowed it for a purpose.

It was a theologian from the nineteenth century, Edward B. Pusey, who said it so well: "God does not take away trials or carry us over them, but strengthens us through them."

March 31

BLESSED BY BURDENS

Shout for joy, O heavens; rejoice, O earth; burst into song, O mountains! For the LORD comforts his people and will have compassion on his afflicted ones. Isaiah 49:13, NIV

COMFORT and prosperity have never enriched the world as adversity has done. Out of pain and problems have come the sweetest songs, the most poignant poems, the most gripping stories. Out of suffering and tears have come the greatest spirits and the most blessed lives.

J. R. Miller wrote, "Many of us find life hard and full of pain. We cannot avoid these things; but we should not allow the harsh experiences to deaden our sensibilities, or make us stoical or sour. The true problem of living is to keep our hearts sweet and gentle in the hardest conditions and experiences."

Our oldest daughter married a Swiss. They have seven children and usually spend their summers in Switzerland and their winters in America. Sometimes when we visit them in Switzerland we take the children and go high up in the Alps on chair lifts. We cross over miles of land, looking down below at some of the most beautiful flowers to be found anywhere in the world. These flowers have survived the heavy snows of winter. The burdens of ice, snow, and winter storms have added to their luster, beauty, and growth. It is hard to believe that just a few weeks earlier these flowers were buried under many feet of snow. Our burdens can have the same effect on our lives.

As Christians face the winds of adversity and the storms of trouble, they rise like the skylark. They are like the trees that survive the storm because their roots are driven deep. They are like the trees that grow on our mountain ridges in North Carolina—trees battered by winds, yet, trees in which we find the strongest wood.

The skylark, the flowers, the trees—all these illustrate Job's words: "When he has tested me, I will come forth as gold" (23:10, NIV). The Christian who understands this aspect of God's nature can find comfort in his suffering and peace in his pain. "Blessed is the man whom God corrects; so do not despise the discipline of the Almighty. For he wounds, but he also binds up; he injures, but his hands also heal" (Job 5:17–18, NIV).

April

April 1

THE FOOL

The fool hath said in his heart, There is no God. Psalm 14:1

APRIL first is April Fool's Day. I'm not sure how this designation was made, but it is usually a time when people will play tricks on you or try to get you to believe in something that is not true. They might say, "Your house is on fire," and when you run to look and find out that it is not, they will shout, "April Fool," causing you to feel foolish that you believed their prank.

God is not like the practical joker. He tells the truth and He never lies. Therefore, while man looks foolish for believing a lie in the form of a practical joke, God calls a person who refuses to believe in Him a fool. In the one case, a person is a fool for believing something that is not true, that was made up. In the other case, a person is described as foolish who refuses to acknowledge God's ample evidence for existing, for His love for us, for His desire that we might come to know Him through Jesus Christ, and for His provision for us throughout our lives.

When one believes the lie of an April Fool's joke, he is momentarily embarrassed, but soon gets over it. When one refuses to believe what God has told him, he will soon enough find out how foolish he has been. Unfortunately, it will be too late, and he will find himself in hell in the company of other fools.

We receive only one life during which we have many chances to come to know God. We are the biggest fools of all if we make the eternal mistake of rejecting the truth that God has communicated to us.

HEADING FOR HEAVEN

For we know that if our earthly house of this tabernacle were dissolved, we have a building of God, a house not made with hands, eternal in the heavens. 2 Corinthians 5:1

WHEN you get ready to go on a trip, there are several things you must do.

First, you must decide where you are going. It does no good to make preparations to travel if you are unsure of your final destination. Next, if you are to travel by plane, bus, train, or boat, you must reserve a ticket and tell the ticket agent your destination. Then you must pay for your ticket, and finally, you must pack what you will need while you are away.

Preparing for heaven is much like going on a journey. First, you must decide that heaven is the place to which you want to go. Next, you must purchase your ticket. But wait! You cannot get to heaven by plane, boat, train, or car.

Jesus said, "I am the way, the truth, and the life. No man comes to the Father but by me" (John 14:6). Jesus is the only way to heaven, and only He can purchase the ticket. We cannot afford it, no matter how much money, power, or influence we have, no matter how many good works we may have done. Only Christ's blood is a sufficient price to purchase this ticket and only by trusting in Christ may we receive it, free of charge. You see, He has already made the purchase and anxiously awaits an opportunity to give it to us, all expenses paid. Now who among us would not love to win an all-expenses-paid trip to the most wonderful place we could ever visit?

After becoming a Christian, all of our life becomes a preparation for our journey. God wants to prepare us through our attitudes, through our service for Him, through our witnessing, tithing, faithful church attendance, and holy living for a place where such attitudes and behavior will be commonplace.

Are you going to heaven? Have you started packing yet?

April 3

THE MESSAGE OF EASTER

"Don't be alarmed," he [the angel] said. "You are looking for Jesus the Nazarene, who was crucified. He has risen! He is not here. See the place where they laid him." Mark 16:6, NIV

ONCE while watching a television news program, I saw a reporter ask people she encountered on the street what Easter meant to them. One person said, "Oh, bunny rabbits, chocolate candy, a fun time for the children." Another observed, "Dyeing eggs, an Easter egg hunt, dinner with relatives." A third person said Easter for her was "some new clothes, maybe a new hat." Only one person of all of those interviewed said Easter meant "the resurrection of Jesus Christ."

Like Christmas, Easter has been popularized and commercialized by merchants and the secular establishment. But the message of Easter is the central focus of Christianity.

The apostle Paul said, "If Christ has not been raised, your faith is futile; you are still in your sins" (1 Corinthians 15:17, NIV). It is as simple as that. If Christ is still dead, then He cannot be our Savior, for He was not the Son of God, and He died like all men.

But, as the Scriptures teach and as hundreds of witnesses testified (none of whom ever recanted that testimony despite threats and death for many of them), if Christ is risen, then we have the ultimate hope of humanity—eternal life with the God who made us and a hope of life beyond the grave.

What does Easter mean to you? It means to me that Christ is risen! Hallelujah!

April 4

THE RESURRECTION IS THE KEY

God hath both raised up the Lord, and will also raise us up by his own power. 1 Corinthians 6:14

THE entire plan for the future has its key in the resurrection. Unless Christ was raised from the dead, there can be no kingdom and no returning King. When the disciples stood at the place where Jesus left this earth, which is called the place of ascension, they were given assurance by angels that the Christ of resurrection would be the Christ of returning glory: "Men of Galilee, why do you stand here looking into the sky? This same Jesus, who has been taken from you into heaven, will come back in the same way you have seen him go into heaven" (Acts 1:11, NIV).

The resurrection is an event which prepares us and confirms for us that future event when He will return again.

Yes, Jesus Christ is alive.

Obviously Christ's physical resurrection is an essential part of God's plan to save us. Have you given yourself to this living Christ?

A woman wrote us this: "Last evening I was alone and watching television. I had no *TV Guide.* Something urged me to turn the dial to the station where the Gospel was being preached. I had been really wrestling with a great problem. I was and am facing death and may or may not be helped through surgery. I had been putting off the operation because I was afraid I had been cut off from God.

"I began to really seek the Lord. The message I heard was God's way of speaking to me and answering my prayers. Now

I feel entirely at peace in my soul."

If you trust the resurrected Christ as your Lord and Savior, He will be with you when you die and will give you life with Him forever. Because of the resurrection, you can be "born again."

April 5

IS MARRIAGE OBSOLETE?

Therefore shall a man leave his father and his mother, and shall cleave unto his wife: and they shall be one flesh. Genesis 2:24

TENS of thousands of couples today are living together outside of marriage. *The New York Times* reports there are nine times as many such couples now as there were ten years ago.

There seems to be a growing rebellion against marriage throughout the world. Living together without marriage is not only accepted, explained away, filmed, and glamorized, but even some church leaders are diluting the scriptural guidelines and rules for marriage in an attempt to soften the problem. There is great pressure in our culture, too, to establish same-sex "marriages" as normal.

But God's truth and God's laws never change. This is not because God is some rigid tyrant, demanding total obedience from subjects weaker than He is. It is because He knows what is best for us and how we best function, physically and spiritually. After all, one who manufactures a product knows far more about it than anyone else. That is why a manual comes with most products that tell us how to assemble the item and how to keep it functioning properly.

God's "manual" is the Bible. God says marriage is holy and sacred and is not to be entered into lightly. God also hates divorce because it is something that man has invented to undermine what God has joined together.

Can there be any question that the social diseases which

now sweep our land as perhaps never before are an indication that man cannot flaunt the laws of God without paying some kind of penalty for his rebellion?

But put Christ first in your life and then first in your marriage and you will have a bond between yourself, your mate, and the Lord that no one can break.

April 6

THE SECOND COMING OF CHRIST

The LORD is coming with fire, and his chariots are like a whirlwind; he will bring down his anger with fury, and his rebuke with flames of fire. Isaiah 66:15, NIV

WHAT would you say about a person who had made a hundred promises to you and kept ninety-nine of them? You probably would think that he was honest enough to fulfill the last promise as well, wouldn't you?

Jesus Christ has fulfilled every promise He ever made, except one. He has not yet returned. Will He?

In both the Old and New Testaments there are references to the return of the Lord. Jeremiah said that at the Lord's coming Jerusalem will be made the throne of His glory and nations shall be gathered in representation. Ezekiel tells of a Jerusalem which is to be restored, a temple which is to be rebuilt, and a land which is to be reclaimed and blessed with prosperity at the Lord's return. Zephaniah gives us the new song that He will teach to Israel and describes the overthrow of the false Christ.

In the New Testament, Matthew likens Christ to a bridegroom coming to receive His bride. Mark sees Him as a householder going on a long journey and entrusting certain tasks to his servants until his return. To Luke, Jesus is a nobleman going to a far country to transact business and leaving his possessions with his servants that they may trade with them until he comes.

John quotes Christ as saying, "I go to prepare a place for you. I will come again and receive you unto myself." The entire book of Revelation tells of the glorious return of Christ. And we can say with the apostle John, who wrote that book, "Amen, even so, come, Lord Jesus."

What would you do differently if you knew He was coming today?

April 7

TWO KINDS OF WISDOM

God hath chosen the foolish things of the world to confound the wise;
and God hath chosen the weak things of the world to confound the things
which are mighty. 1 Corinthians 1:27

TODAY there is more knowledge in the world than ever before. Computers can transmit information in a millisecond to any part of the globe by satellite. More information has been processed, more facts discovered in this century than in all of the other centuries of human history combined.

Yet man has never been further from solving his basic problems, the basis of which is alienation from other men. It is this alienation which produces wars, crime, and all of the other social ills. The United Nations was supposed to be a forum in which men could resolve their differences. Instead, it has been a forum for magnifying them.

Psalm 111:10 says, "The fear of the LORD is the beginning of wisdom." The troubles and problems of the human race have stemmed from the fact that it has followed the wisdom of the world rather than the wisdom of the Lord.

The Bible says there are two kinds of wisdom in the world. First, there is wisdom that is given by God, a wisdom which, after the mind of Christ, views life in terms of eternity. Of this wisdom, the Scripture says, "But the wisdom that is from above is first pure, then peaceable, gentle, and easy to be entreated, full of mercy and good fruits, without partiality, and without hypocrisy" (James 3:17).

The second is the "wisdom of the world" which, God says, "I will destroy . . ." (1 Corinthians 1:19).

Now that you know the choice, which kind of wisdom will you choose?

April 8

MY HOPE IS BUILT ON NOTHING LESS

Blessed is the man that trusteth in the LORD, and whose hope the LORD is. Jeremiah 17:7

ONE of the great hymns of the church, "The Solid Rock," by Edward Mote and William Bradbury, begins, "My hope is built on nothing less, than Jesus' blood and righteousness; I dare not trust the sweetest frame, but wholly lean on Jesus' name. On Christ, the solid Rock, I stand; all other ground is sinking sand."

What is your hope built on? You may hope for a raise in pay at work. You may hope that you pass an exam at school. You may even hope that you win a contest you have entered. Such hopes are based on externals over which we have little control: a favorable view of our work by the boss, the "right" questions being asked by the professor, our name being drawn among thousands of entries.

But the hope we have in Christ is an absolute certainty. It leaves nothing to chance. It is based on the fact of Christ's resurrection and the fact that He has gone ahead of us to get our dwelling place in readiness for our arrival.

In my travels I have stayed at many hotels around the

world. Sometimes when I arrive early, the chambermaids have not had time to clean my room and make the beds, so I must wait. I may hope that the room is ready when I arrive at the hotel, but I have no control over it.

We can be sure that the place Christ is preparing for us will be ready when we arrive because with Him nothing is left to chance. Everything He promised He will deliver, just as He said.

"Happy is he that hath the God of Jacob for his help, whose hope is in the LORD" (Psalm 146:5).

April 9

IT WAS LOVE . . .

"Yea, I have loved thee with an everlasting love: therefore with lovingkindness have I drawn thee. Jeremiah 31:3

IT was love, the love of God, that put words such as these into the mouths and hearts of the prophets: "All we like sheep have gone astray; we have turned every one to his own way; and the LORD hath laid on him the iniquity of us all" (Isaiah 53:6).

It was love, the unerring love of God, that brought these prophecies into precise fulfillment. On a specific day marked on earth's calendar and in a specific place marked on earth's map, the Son of God came to this planet.

It was love that prompted the Son of God to reflect the same affection for the world as did God the Father, and to show a selfless compassion to the sick, the distressed, and the sin-burdened.

It was love that enabled Jesus Christ to become poor that we through His poverty might be rich.

It was love, divine love, that made Him endure the cross,

despising the shame, and made Him endure the contradictions of sinners against Himself.

It was love that restrained Him when He was falsely accused of blasphemy and was led to Golgotha to die with common thieves; He raised not a hand against His enemies.

It was nothing but love that kept Him from calling twelve legions of angels to come to His defense.

It was love that made Him, in a moment of agonizing pain, pause and give life to a repentant sinner who cried, "Lord, remember me when Thou comest into Thy kingdom!"

It was love that, after every known torture devised by degenerate man had been heaped upon Him, caused Jesus to lift His voice and pray, "Father, forgive them; for they know not what they do" (Luke 23:34).

April 10

THE POWER OF THE CROSS

For the preaching of the cross is to them that perish foolishness; but unto us who are saved it is the power of God. 1 Corinthians 1:18

WE can never plumb the depths of sin, or sense how terrible human sin is, until we go to the Cross and see that it was "sin" that caused the Son of God to be crucified. The ravages of war, the tragedy of suicides, the agony of the poverty-stricken, the pain and suffering of the rejected of our society, the blood of the accident victim, the terror of rape and mugging victims of our generation—these all speak as with a single voice of the degradation that besets the human race at this hour. But no sin has been committed in the world today that can compare with the full cup of the universe's sin that brought Jesus to the cross. The question hurled toward heaven throughout the ages has been, "Who is He and why does He die?" The answer comes back, "This is My only begotten

Son, dying not only for your sins but for the sins of the whole world." To you sin may be a small thing; to God it is a great and awful thing. It is the second largest thing in the world; only the love of God is greater.

When we comprehend the great price God was willing to pay for the redemption of man, we only then begin to see that something is horribly wrong with the human race. It must have a Savior, or it is doomed! Sin cost God His very best. Is it any wonder that the angels veiled their faces, that they were silent in their consternation as they witnessed the outworking of God's plan? How inconceivable it must have seemed to them, when they considered the fearful depravity of sin, that Jesus should shoulder it all. But they were soon to unveil their faces and offer their praises again. A light was kindled that day at Calvary. The cross blazed with the glory of God as the most terrible darkness was shattered by the light of salvation. Satan's depraved legions were defeated, and they could no longer keep all men in darkness and defeat.

April 11

OUR GOD FORGETS!

. . . *They shall all know me, from the least of them unto the greatest of them, saith the LORD: for I will forgive their iniquity, and I will remember their sin no more.* Jeremiah 31:34

THE omniscient God has the unique ability that we do not have: He has the ability to forget. The God of grace forgets our sins and wipes them completely from His memory forever! He places us in His sight as though we had never committed one sin.

In theological language, this is called *justification*. The Bible says, "Therefore being justified by faith, we have peace with God through our Lord Jesus Christ" (Romans 5:1).

There is no possibility of true happiness until we have established friendship and fellowship with God. And there is no possibility of establishing this fellowship apart from the Cross of His Son, Jesus Christ. God says, "I will forgive you, but I will forgive only at the foot of the Cross." He says, "I will fellowship with you, but I will fellowship with you only at the Cross." That is the reason it is necessary for us to come to the Cross in repentance of our sin and by faith in His Son to find forgiveness and salvation.

When we come to Christ, God imparts His righteousness to us. It is as if an accounting entry had been made in the books of heaven, declaring us righteous for Christ's sake. The Divine Bookkeeper cancels our debt!

April 12

A NEW HEART NEEDED

I will give them a new heart and a new mind. I will take away their stubborn heart of stone and will give them an obedient heart. Ezekiel 11:19, TEV

THE actinic ray is that property of fire which works chemical change. It turns wood to ashes, tempers steel, and changes the color and form of objects which come in contact with it.

It is this property in the rays of the sun which transforms seeds into plants, buds into flowers, and grass into hay. It is the miracle ray which makes useless things useful through the process of change.

Like the calorific ray, it is also a physical symbol of God's ability to do mightier things in the spiritual realm.

When a man comes in contact with God, he can never be the same again. This "fire" either draws or drives, saves or destroys, helps or hinders. Accepted and utilized, it becomes a boon and a blessing. Rejected, it becomes a bane and a curse. One dying thief was drawn to the warmth of the Savior; he responded and was saved. The other dying thief turned away and rejected God's compassion; he was lost.

God takes the weak and makes them strong. He takes the vile and makes them clean. He takes the worthless and makes them worthwhile. He takes the sinful and makes them sinless.

With this in mind, Ezekiel said, "Thus saith the Lord GOD . . . A new heart also will I give you, and a new spirit will I put within you: and I will take away the stony heart."

April 13

NOW I LAY ME DOWN TO SLEEP

I will both lay me down in peace, and sleep: for thou, LORD, only makest me dwell in safety. Psalm 4:8

MANY people have trouble falling asleep at night. Some take over-the-counter drugs or sleeping pills to help them sleep. Others require prescription drugs in order to get the rest they need.

I am not a doctor and would not presume to prescribe medication, but it is my experience that too many in our culture turn first to drugs and not to God. Often, it is a restless spirit and not a chemical imbalance that keeps us from the rest our bodies need.

The Psalms are, perhaps, the most soothing place in Scripture for one to turn to shut out the stresses and troubles of the day. Some of the Psalms have been set to music, and listening to them on a CD or tape player can help soothe the cares of the world.

God wants us to get our rest. He knows that we need it in order to work effectively while we are awake. So the next time you have difficulty falling asleep at night (and even when you don't), read from some of the Psalms. Pick a quiet time in your house and a quiet place and let God soothe your troubled spirit to a point where you receive His rest and you place your trust and confidence in Him.

April 14

THE VISION IN THE VALLEY

Thus saith the Lord GOD unto these bones: Behold, I will cause breath to enter into you, and ye shall live. Ezekiel 37:5

NICODEMUS was one of the most religious men of his day, and yet Christ told him he must be born again (John 3:3).

This transformation is the theme of Ezekiel's parable of the valley of dry bones. This parable pictures Israel as dried up and nearly lost, with no evidence of life. All that remain are the bones, dry and dead. This is true of hundreds of churches today. The organization is going smoothly, statistics are pouring out, but there is little life. Other churches have either lost their first love or are neither hot nor cold and are being spewed out of the mouth of Christ (Revelation 2:4; 3:15–18).

The thrilling thing about Ezekiel's story, however, is that new life is possible. The miracle of regeneration can occur; the church can be revived on the inside. "Breathe upon these slain, that they may live" (Ezekiel 37:9). Though Ezekiel was talking about Israel, his parable applies equally well to the church of Christ. God's interest is not merely in reaching *outsiders*, important as they are; He is concerned equally with changing the *insiders*.

Some Christians talk of making the world godly by being like it; but on the contrary, history has consistently shown that the church ends in becoming worldly—it loses its spiritual power, its evangelizing spirit, and its purifying influence. The church has compromised with the world and come to terms with it to such a point that it has lost much of its power.

The call of Christ is for rededication to Him—a call to follow Him, to pattern our lives after His. As John Wesley so wisely wrote: "Anything that cools my love for Christ is of the world." That's the way I want to live!

April 15

RENDERING UNTO GOD

I beseech you therefore, brethren, by the mercies of God, that ye present your bodies a living sacrifice, holy, acceptable unto God, which is your reasonable service. Romans 12:1

APRIL 15 in the United States is a day dreaded by most Americans. It is the day when our income taxes are due to be paid to the government. Often there is a frantic rush to complete the forms that should have been done much earlier but were put off. Post offices in big cities stay open until midnight, and thousands of procrastinators hurry down to make sure their returns are postmarked by twelve o'clock so they will not have to pay a penalty.

Jesus told His followers to "render unto Caesar that which is Caesar's and unto God that which is God's" (Matthew 22:21). At such a time of year when we are preoccupied with what we owe the government, we would benefit by thinking about what we owe God. We owe God everything! We have been bought and paid for with a terrible price, the broken body and shed blood of God's Son.

Because we belong to God, if we have trusted in Christ to save us from our sins, God has a right to expect that we would render certain things unto Him. We have an obligation to present our bodies a "living sacrifice, made holy and acceptable to God." We are commanded to present God with our tithes and offerings. And beyond that, God wants to have communion and fellowship with His children, much as those of us who are parents want the same relationship with our own children.

God wants us to speak to Him through prayer and to receive His answers through the reading of His Word and the leadership of His Holy Spirit. God describes all of this as "reasonable," and so it is for One who has done so much for us.

April 16

BE AWARE OF ANGELS

Then Daniel said unto the king, . . . My God hath sent his angel, and hath shut the lions' mouths, that they have not hurt me. . . . Daniel 6:21–22

ANGELS minister to us personally. Many accounts in Scripture confirm that we are the subjects of their individual concern. In his book *Table Talk*, Martin Luther said, "An angel is a spiritual creature created by God without a body, for the service of Christendom and the church."

We may not always be aware of the presence of angels. We can't always predict how they will appear. But angels have been said to be our neighbors. Often they may be our companions without our being aware of their presence. We know little of their constant ministry. The Bible assures us, however, that one day our eyes will be unscaled to see and know the full extent of the attention angels have given us (1 Corinthians 13:11–12).

In the Old Testament, Daniel vividly describes the bitter conflict between the angelic forces of God and the opposing demons of darkness. Before the angel came to him he had spent three weeks mourning (Daniel 10:3). He had no bread, meat, or wine, nor did he anoint himself. As he stood by the Tigris River, a man appeared clothed in linen. His face looked like lightning and his eyes like flaming torches. His voice sounded like the roar of a crowd.

Daniel alone saw the vision. The men who were with him did not. Yet a great dread came upon them, and they ran away to hide. Left alone with the heavenly visitor, Daniel's strength departed from him, so great was the effect of this personage on him.

Many experiences of God's people suggest that angels have been ministering to them. Others may not have known they were being helped, yet the visitation was real. The Bible tells us that God has ordered angels to minister to His people—those who have been redeemed by the power of Christ's blood. We may often be unaware of their presence.

April 17

THE GRAVE IN THE GARDEN

Joseph took the body . . . and placed it in his own new tomb that he had cut out of the rock. He rolled a big stone in front of the entrance to the tomb and went away. . . . There was a violent earthquake, for an angel of the Lord came down from heaven and, going to the tomb, rolled back the stone and sat upon it.
Matthew 27:59–60; 28:2, NIV

THE angel who came to the garden where Jesus' body lay, rolled away the stone and permitted fresh air and morning light to fill His tomb. The sepulcher was no longer an empty vault or dreary dormitory; rather it was a life-affirming place that radiated the glory of the living God. No longer was it a dark prison but a transformed reminder of the celestial light that sweeps aside the shadows of death. Jesus' resurrection changed it.

An unknown poet has said of the tomb, "'Tis now a cell where angels used to come and go with heavenly news." No words of men or angels can adequately describe the height and depth, the length and breadth of the glory to which the world awakened when Jesus came forth to life from the pall of death.

Some anonymous poet has summed up the life and ministry of Christ in these words:

He who is the Bread of Life, began His ministry hungering.
He who is the Water of Life, ended His ministry thirsting.
He who was weary, is our true rest.
He who paid tribute, is the King of kings.
He prayed, yet hears our prayers.
He wept, but dries our tears.
He was sold for thirty pieces of silver, yet redeemed us.
He was led as a lamb to the slaughter, but is the Good Shepherd.
He died and gave His life, and by dying destroyed death for all who believe.

April 18

THE FACT OF THE RESURRECTION

God hath both raised up the Lord, and will also raise up us by his own power. 1 Corinthians 6:14

UPON that great fact hangs the entire plan of the redemptive program of God. Without the resurrection there could be no salvation. Christ predicted His resurrection many times. He said on one occasion, "For as Jonah was three days and three nights in the whale's belly; so shall the Son of man be three days and three nights in the heart of the earth" (Matthew 12:40). As He predicted, He rose!

There are certain laws of evidence which hold in the

establishment of any historic event. There must be documentation of the event in question made by reliable contemporary witnesses. There is more evidence that Jesus rose from the dead than there is that Julius Caesar ever lived or that Alexander the Great died at the age of thirty-three. It is strange that historians will accept thousands of facts for which they can produce only shreds of evidence. But in the face of the overwhelming evidence of the resurrection of Jesus Christ they cast a skeptical eye and hold intellectual doubts. The trouble with these people is that they do not want to believe. Their spiritual vision is so blinded, and they are so completely prejudiced, that they cannot accept the glorious fact of the resurrection of Christ on Bible testimony alone.

The resurrection meant, first, that Christ was undeniably God. He was what He claimed to be. Christ was Deity in the flesh.

Second, it meant that God had accepted His atoning work on the cross, which was necessary for our salvation. "Who was delivered for our offenses, and was raised again for our justification" (Romans 4:25).

Third, it assures mankind of a righteous judgment. "For as by one man's disobedience many were made sinners, so by the obedience of one shall many be made righteous" (Romans 5:19).

Fourth, it guarantees that our bodies also will be raised in the end. "But now is Christ risen from the dead, and become the firstfruits of them that slept" (1 Corinthians 15:20). The Scripture teaches that as Christians our bodies may go to the grave, but they are going to be raised on the great resurrection morning. Then will death be swallowed up in victory. As a result of the resurrection of Christ the sting of death is gone and Christ Himself holds the keys. He says, "I am he that liveth, and was dead; and, behold, I am alive forevermore, Amen; and have the keys of hell and death" (Revelation 1:18). And Christ promises that "Because I live, ye shall live also" (John 14:19).

April 19

THE DEFEAT OF DEATH

And the angel answered and said unto the women, Fear not ye; for I know that ye seek Jesus, which was crucified. He is not here: for he is risen, as he said. Come, see the place where the Lord lay.
Matthew 28:5–6

ON the third day after His death the Bible says, "And behold there was a great earthquake; for the angel of the Lord descended from heaven, and came and rolled back the stone from the door, and sat upon it. His countenance was like lightning, and his raiment white as snow: And for fear of him the keepers did shake, and became as dead men" (Matthew 28:2–4).

Though some Bible students have tried to estimate how much this stone weighed, we need not speculate because Jesus could have come out of that tomb whether the stone was there or not. The Bible mentions it so that generations to come can know something of the tremendous miracle of resurrection that took place.

As Mary looked into the tomb she saw "two angels in white sitting, the one at the head, and the other at the feet, where the body of Jesus had lain" (John 20:11–12). Then one of the angels who was sitting outside the tomb proclaimed the greatest message the world has ever heard: "He is not here: for he is risen." Those few words changed the history of the universe. Darkness and despair died; hope and anticipation were born in the hearts of men.

April 20

SOWING AND REAPING

Sow for yourselves righteousness, reap the fruit of steadfast love; break up your fallow ground, for it is time to seek the LORD, that he may come and rain salvation upon you. Hosea 10:12, RSV

THE Word of God says, "They have sown the wind, and they shall reap the whirlwind" (Hosea 8:7).

The immutable law of "sowing and reaping" has held sway. Our world is now the unhappy residence of a harvest of moral depravity, and we seek in vain for a cure. The tares of indulgence have overgrown the wheat of moral restraint. All humanity is guilty. But each faction of society seeks to place the blame upon others.

The Republicans blame the Democrats; the Democrats blame the Republicans. The Communists accuse the Americans; the Americans accuse the Communists. The East denounces the West; the West denounces the East. Capital finds fault with labor; labor finds fault with capital. An old farmer in Indiana summed it up when he said, "The whole world situation is just a mess!"

But, as a minister of the Gospel, I am an optimist. The world problems are big, but God is bigger! If we will dare to take God into account, confess our sin, and rely unreservedly upon Him for wisdom, guidance, and strength, our world problems can yet be solved. There is yet time for bringing peace, but that time is brief. What we do, we must do quickly.

What have you done recently for God?

April 21

CHRIST CRUCIFIED: AN EXAMPLE OF SUFFERING

Though he were a Son, yet learned he obedience by the things which he suffered; and being made perfect, he became the author of salvation unto all them that obey him. Hebrews 5:8–9

THE New Testament, while insisting that the true purpose for which Jesus suffered was to deal with our sins, also points us to the suffering Savior as a pattern of how we, as His believing people, should endure our sufferings.

Thus the apostle Peter, when addressing Christian slaves, urges them to bear their sufferings submissively, even though they have done no wrong: "To this you were called, because Christ suffered for you, leaving you an example, that you should follow in his steps. 'He committed no sin, and no deceit was found in his mouth.' When they hurled their insults at him, he did not retaliate; when he suffered, he made no threats. Instead, he entrusted himself to him who judges justly" (1 Peter 2:21–23, NIV).

Christ has left us an *example.* The Greek word for *example* is derived from school life and refers to a pattern of writing to be copied by the child learning to write. Christ is our copybook. We look at Him and learn how suffering is to be borne.

In the passage the apostle draws attention to four things about the suffering Savior. First, His holy life: "He committed no sin"; second, His guileless speech: "no deceit was found in his mouth"; third, His patient spirit: "When they hurled their insults at him, he did not retaliate; when he suffered, he made no threats"; and fourth, His implicit faith: "he entrusted himself to him who judges justly."

The author of Hebrews writes, "Consider him who endured such opposition from sinful men, so that you will not grow weary and lose heart" (12:2–3, NIV).

Yes, *consider* Him. In our sufferings and tribulations Jesus Himself must be our chief consideration. We must fix our eyes upon Him. He who suffered for us shows us how we are to bear our sufferings.

April 22
GOD'S RECIPE FOR A NEW HEART

Turn ye even to me with all your heart . . . with weeping, and with mourning. Joel 2:12

THE mourning of repentance is not the weeping of self-pity; it is not regret over material losses nor remorse that our sins have been found out. It is entirely possible to be deeply sorry because of the devastation which sin has wrought in our lives and yet not repent. I have had people pour out their hearts to me with tears, because their sins have been discovered and they are in serious trouble. But true repentance is more than being sorry for our sins and regretting the way we have allowed sin to shatter our lives. True repentance is a turning from sin—a conscious, deliberate decision to leave sin behind—and a conscious turning to God with a commitment to follow His will for our lives. It is a change of direction, an alteration of attitudes, and a yielding of the will. Humanly speaking, it is our small part in the plan of salvation—although even the strength to repent comes from God. But even so, the act of repentance does not win us any merit or make us worthy to be saved—it only conditions our hearts for the grace of God.

The Bible says, "Repent ye therefore, and be converted, that your sins may be blotted out, when the times of refreshing shall come from the presence of the Lord" (Acts 3:19). Our part is repenting. God will do the converting, the transforming, and the forgiving.

It will not be easy to bend our warped, stubborn wills; but once we do, it will be as though a misplaced vertebra has snapped back into place. Instead of the stress and tension of a life out of harmony with God will come the serenity of reconciliation.

April 23

THE EFFECTS OF REVIVAL

And it shall come to pass . . . that I will pour out my spirit upon all flesh; and your sons and your daughters shall prophesy, your old men shall dream dreams, your young men shall see visions. Joel 2:28

WHAT would happen if revival were to break into our lives and our churches today? I am sure of one thing. At the heart of that revival would be a tremendous outpouring of the Holy Spirit.

To begin with, people would have a new vision of the majesty of God. We must understand that the Lord is not only tender and merciful and full of compassion, but He is also the God of justice, holiness, and wrath.

Many Christians have a caricature of God. They do not see God in all of His wholeness. We glibly quote John 3:16, but we forget to quote the following verses, "He who does not believe has been judged already" (verse 18, NAB). Compassion is not complete in itself, but must be accompanied by inflexible justice and wrath against sin and a desire for holiness.

What stirs God most is not physical suffering but sin. All too often we are more afraid of physical pain than of moral wrong. The Cross is the standing evidence of the fact that holiness is a principle for which God would die. God cannot clear the guilty until atonement is made. Mercy is what we need, and that is what we receive at the foot of the Cross.

In her book *The Christian's Secret of a Happy Life*, Hannah Whitall Smith tells us, ". . . What we need is to see that God's presence is a certain fact always, and that every act of our soul is done right before Him, and that a word spoken in prayer is really spoken to Him, as if our eyes could see Him and our hands could touch Him. Then we shall cease to have such vague conceptions of our relations with Him, and shall feel the binding force of every word we say in His presence."

April 24

HE IS OUR HOPE

. . . *The LORD will be the hope of his people, and the strength of the children of Israel.*   Joel 3:16

A LATE British historian, Arnold Toynbee, gave his slogan to the world when he said, "Cling, and hope." In other words, he says the storm is raging; all the ideals that we held a few years ago are crumbling; but he advised the human race to cling and hope.

However, there are thousands of people who day by day find refuge from the storms of life by their living faith in a living God!

To turn to God in an hour such as this in the history of the world is much more than a form of escapism. Multiplied thousands of normal, intelligent people have tried and proved that a vital relationship with Christ is the most satisfying experience in all the world. They have found that faith in Christ is more than adequate for the pressures of this hour.

The governor of an eastern state told eight thousand people at a conference how faith in Christ had given him peace, security, and happiness. What Christ had done for this governor, Christ can do for you, if you surrender your will to Him.

Yet some who read these lines are held in the viselike grip of sin's confusion. The despair of loneliness has settled down upon your soul, and at this very moment you are asking the question, "Is life worth living?"

To scores of people who write every week to our office in Minneapolis, life has ceased to be worth living. For all of them I have good news. God did not create us to be defeated, discouraged, frustrated wandering souls, seeking in vain for peace of heart and peace of mind. He has bigger plans for us. The answer to our problem, however great, is as near as the Bible, as simple as first-grade arithmetic, and as real as one's heartbeat.

The Bible says, "In all these things we are more than conquerors through Him that loved us" (Romans 8:37).

The Bible teaches that "Whatsoever is born of God overcometh the world: and this is the victory that overcometh the world, even our faith" (1 John 5:4).

Upon the authority of God's Word, I declare that Christ is the answer to every baffling perplexity which plagues mankind. In Him is found the cure for care, a balm for bereavement, a healing for our hurts, and a sufficiency for our insufficiency.

April 25

BRIGHT CLOUDS

Ask ye of the LORD rain in the time of the latter rain; so the LORD shall make bright clouds, and give them showers of rain, to every one grass in the field. Zechariah 10:1

I RECEIVED a letter from a nineteen-year-old girl on the West Coast, whose fiancé had just broken off their engagement. Her heart was completely crushed, and life seemed no longer worth living. I wrote telling her that it is not always easy to trace God's designs in our ill-planned hopes and dreams. But rest assured that if we are called according to His purpose, and if we love God, all things do work together for good. Who are we to dictate which way the winds will blow, or how God will maneuver our ship through life's storms? The psalmist said, "He . . . guided them by the skillfulness of his hands" (Psalm 78:72).

Yes, clouds will come. They are part of life. But by God's grace we need not be depressed by their presence. Just as clouds can protect us from the brightness of the sun, life's clouds can reveal the glory of God, and from their lofty height God speaks to us. Like the children of Israel, we are travelers to the Promised Land. As they traveled through the wilderness, the Bible says, "The LORD went before them by day in a pillar of a cloud, to lead them the way" (Exodus 13:21).

If your life is dismal, depressed, and gloomy today, Christ can turn those dark clouds inside out. Many may be discouraged because of sins they can't overcome. Sin can hang over us like a cloud. Sin deforms us. It causes turmoil and fighting down inside. We all need to be free from the failure and sin that binds and chains us. When faced with the clouds of defeat we need to open our hearts and let Him in. Let Him take the clouds of sin out and transform you into a new creature.

April 26

DEATH IS DEAD

So when this corruptible shall have put on incorruption, and this mortal shall have put on immortality, then shall be brought to pass the saying that is written, Death is swallowed up in victory.
1 Corinthians 15:54

DEATH is not natural, for man was created to live and not to die. It is the result of God's judgment because of man's sin and rebellion. Without God's grace through Christ, it is a gruesome spectacle. I have stood at the bedside of people dying without Christ; it was a terrible experience. I have stood at the bedside of those who were dying in Christ; it was a glorious experience. Charles Spurgeon said of the glory that amends the death of the redeemed, "If I may die as I have seen some die, I court the grand occasion. I would not wish to escape death by some by-road if I may sing as they sang. If I may have such hosannas and alleluias beaming in my eyes as I have seen as well as heard from them, it were a blessed thing to die."

Death is robbed of much of its terror for the true believer, but we still need God's protection as we take that last journey. At the moment of death the spirit departs from the body and moves through the atmosphere. But the Scripture teaches us that the devil lurks then. He is "the prince of the power of the air" (Ephesians 2:2). If the eyes of our understanding were opened, we would probably see the air filled with demons, the enemies of Christ. If Satan could hinder the angel of Daniel 10 for three weeks on his mission to earth, we can imagine the opposition a Christian may encounter at death.

But Christ on Calvary cleared a road through Satan's kingdom. When Christ came to earth, He had to pass through the devil's territory and open up a beachhead here. That is one reason He was accompanied by a host of angels when He came (Luke 2:8–14). And this is why holy angels will accompany Him when He comes again (Matthew 16:27). Till then, the moment of death is Satan's final opportunity to attack the true believer; but God has sent His angels to guard us at that time. How thankful we should be for that promise.

WHERE IS YOUR TREASURE?

For where your treasure is, there will your heart be also.
Matthew 6:21

THE rich young ruler who came to Jesus was so filled with his piety, his riches, and his greed that he revolted when Jesus informed him that the price of eternal life was to "sell out" and come and follow Him. He went away sorrowfully, the Bible says, because he could not detach himself from himself. He found it impossible to become "poor in spirit" because he had such a lofty estimate of his own importance.

All around us are arrogance, pride, and selfishness: These are the results of sin. From the heavens comes a voice speaking to a tormented, bankrupt world: "I counsel thee to buy of me gold tried in the fire, that thou mayest be rich; and white raiment, that thou mayest be clothed, and that the shame of thy nakedness do not appear; and anoint thine eyes with eye-salve, that thou mayest see . . . Behold, I stand at the door, and knock: if any man hear my voice, and open the door, I will come in to him, and will sup with him, and he with me" (Revelation 3:18, 20).

Heaven in this life and the life to come is not on a monetary standard. Nor can flesh and blood find the door to the kingdom of heaven with its contentment, peace, joy, and happiness. Only those who are poor in spirit and rich toward God shall be accounted worthy to enter there, because they come not in their own merit but in the righteousness of the Redeemer.

Someone has said, "A man's wealth consists not in the abundance of his possessions, but in the fewness of his wants." "The first link between my soul and Christ," said

C. H. Spurgeon, "is not my goodness but my badness, not my merit but my misery, not my riches but my need."

Where is your treasure? In the bank? In the driveway? In the mirror? Or are you storing up your treasure in heaven?

April 28

MEEKNESS IS NOT WEAKNESS

Blessed are the meek: for they shall inherit the earth. Matthew 5:5

IN our culture, meekness has come to mean weakness. But that is not the biblical view. A wild horse which has been broken is no less strong, but he has been made useful to man.

Jesus was meek, but by no stretch of the imagination was He weak. Jesus was and is God.

What did He mean, then, when He said that the meek will inherit the earth? He was speaking of an attitude, a form of humility that is sorely lacking in our culture. A famous baseball coach once declared that "nice guys finish last." One of the best-selling books a few years ago was *Looking Out for Number One.* The seventies were described by some sociologists as the "me decade."

No person is meek by nature. It is the work of the Spirit of God. Moses was meek, but he was not meek by nature. God worked meekness into him over a forty-year period. Peter was certainly not meek by nature. He was impetuous, saying and doing the first thing that came into his mind. The Holy Spirit of God transformed Peter after the resurrection of Jesus. Before his conversion, Paul was not meek. His job was to persecute Christians! Yet Paul wrote to the church at Galatia, "The fruit of the Spirit is . . . gentleness, goodness . . . meekness."

It is our human nature to be proud, not meek. Only the Spirit of God can transform our lives through the new birth experience and then make us over again into the image of Christ, our example of what pleases God in the way of meekness.

April 29

THE POSSIBILITY OF PURITY

Blessed are the pure in heart: for they shall see God.   Matthew 5:8

PURE hearts will be Christlike. It is God's desire that we be conformed to the image of His Son. If Christ lives within us, and our bodies become the abode of the Holy Spirit, is it any wonder that we should be like Him? And just what do we mean by Christlike?

The Bible says, "Let this mind be in you, which was also in Christ Jesus" (Philippians 2:5). Jesus had a humble heart. If He abides in us, pride will never dominate our lives. Jesus had a loving heart. If He dwells within us, hatred and bitterness will never rule us. Jesus had a forgiving and understanding heart. If He lives within us, mercy will temper our relationships with our fellow men. Jesus had unselfish interests. But even more, Jesus' one desire was to do His Father's will. This is the essence of Christlikeness—eager obedience to the Father's will.

You say, "That's a big order!" I admit that. It would be impossible if we had to measure up to Him in our own strength and with our own natural hearts.

Paul recognized that he could never attain this heart purity by his own striving. He said, "I can do all things through Christ which strengtheneth me" (Philippians 4:13).

Christ provided the possibility of purity by His death on the cross. The righteousness and the purity of God are imputed to men who confess their sins and receive Christ into their hearts.

The greatest happiness that comes to the pure in heart is twofold: not only a proper relationship with others but a sublime relationship with God. "For they shall see God." The gates of Eden swing open once more. God and man walk together once again.

April 30

PEACE IS NOT PASSIVE

Blessed are the peacemakers: for they shall be called the children of God.   Matthew 5:9

TO have peace *with* God and to have the peace *of* God is not enough. This vertical relationship must have a horizontal outworking, or our faith is in vain. Jesus said that we were to love the Lord with all our hearts and our neighbors as ourselves. This dual love for God and others is like the positive and negative poles of a battery—unless both connections are made, we have no power. A personal faith is normally useless unless it has a social application. A notable exception would be the thief on the cross.

I once saw a cartoon of a man rowing a boat toward a golden shore labeled "heaven." All around him were men and women struggling in vain to reach the shore and safety, but he was heedless of their peril. He was singing, "I am bound for heaven, hallelujah!" That is not an adequate picture of the Christian life.

If we have peace *with* God and the peace *of* God, we will become peacemakers. We will not only be at peace with our neighbors, but we will be leading them to discover the source of true peace in Christ. Every person can experience the peace of God through Christ: "For he is our peace" (Ephesians 2:14).

Our lives take on new dimensions when we find peace with God. To explain this in simpler terms, let us visualize a right-angle triangle sitting on its horizontal base. At the apex or highest point in this triangle write the letter "G," representing God. At the point where the perpendicular line meets the base write the letter "Y," representing you. Then, at the opposite end of the horizontal line write the letter "O," which represents others. There, in geometric form, you have a visual diagram of our relationship with God and man. Our lives (which before we found the peace of God were represented by a single dot of self-centeredness) now take in an area in vital contact with two worlds. Peace flows down from God and out to our fellow men. We become merely the conduit through which it flows. But there is peace in being just a "channel."

May

PERSECUTION

*Blessed are they which are persecuted for righteousness' sake: for theirs is
the kingdom of heaven.* Matthew 5:10

WHEN we think of persecution, we rarely think of the kind of
attack for sharing our faith that was commonplace when Jesus
preached the Sermon on the Mount. In those days, persecution
meant beatings, arrest, imprisonment, even death. Yet the Bible
and all of history are full of instances where bold men and
women chose persecution over denial of our Lord.

Today, many of us think we are doing God a favor when
we tell another about Christ, even though we were
commanded to do so. And we think we are suffering real
persecution when someone makes light of our faith.

There are places in the world where Christians can still be
jailed for sharing their faith or face the death penalty for
leading a lost soul to Christ, but they are few and far between.
Most people don't care what others believe in, or if they
believe in anything.

The Christian faith has become a cheap faith because we
too often live as if it has no value. We complain when the
preacher runs over a few minutes on the Sunday sermon and
consider it a great inconvenience to return to services once or
twice more in the same week. No wonder so much of the
world does not consider our faith relevant when we are not
even willing to give of our time, much less our freedom or
lives, for what we say we believe in.

Think about it. Have you ever been persecuted for sharing
your faith in Christ? Has your faith cost you anything? If not,
perhaps you had better re-examine your faith to see if it
measures up to the One who said, "Blessed are ye, when men
shall revile you, and persecute you, and say all manner of evil

against you falsely, for my sake. For so persecuted they the prophets which were before you" (Matthew 5:11).

May 2

FAITH AND WORKS

Faith without works is dead. James 2:17

SINCE biblical times, men and women have argued about the doctrines of faith and works. Which should come first? Which carries the most weight with God?

Jesus Christ did not offer us a choice of faith or works. The Scripture teaches that works without faith have no meaning to God, because we cannot work our way to heaven. Those who seek to testify of what they think is their goodness often talk about paying their taxes on time, never defrauding anyone, being faithful to their spouse, and giving to charity. But God is clear that our righteousness is like a filthy rag. There is nothing we can do to measure up to God's standard.

Once we are saved, however, God expects us—in fact He commands us—to not be hearers of the Word only, but doers as well. Works, when we are in Christ, are an extension of Christ's ministry. In fact, works are not ends in themselves, but they demonstrate God's love toward others so that they will know God loves them and so that they will desire to learn about God's provision for their greatest needs.

The Bible says a man in a ditch is not helped if we pass by him, wish him well, and tell him of God's love. No, God's love is demonstrated by attending to the man's physical needs and helping him out of the ditch. This is how people learn that the Father has sent the Son.

Works must never replace faith and the sharing of the Gospel, but they are a natural extension of faith. Jesus said, "Let your light so shine before men, that they may see your

good works, and glorify your Father which is in heaven"
(Matthew 5:16).

May 3

PRAYING IN PERSECUTION

But I say to you [Jesus said], love your enemies and pray for those who persecute you.   Matthew 5:44, RSV

JESUS, in the Sermon on the Mount, had some commandments for us with regard to our attitude toward persecution. We are to:

1. Rejoice and be exceeding glad (Matthew 5:12)
2. Love our enemies (5:44)
3. Bless them that curse us (5:44)
4. Do good to them that hate us (5:44)
5. Pray for them that despitefully use us and persecute us (5:44)

I have a friend who lost his job, a fortune, his wife, and his home. But he tenaciously held to his faith—the only thing he had left. One day he stopped to watch some men doing stonework on a huge church. One of them was chiseling a triangular piece of stone.

"What are you going to do with that?" asked my friend.

The workman said, "See that little opening away up there near the spire? Well, I'm shaping this down here so it will fit in up there."

Tears filled my friend's eyes as he walked away, for it seemed that God had spoken through the workman to explain the ordeal through which he was passing, "I'm shaping you down here so you'll fit in up there."

After you have "suffered a while, make you perfect . . .

settle you," echo the words from the Bible.

The persecuted for "righteousness' sake" are happy because they are identified with Christ. The enmity of the world is tangible proof that we are on the right side, that we are identified with our blessed Lord. He said that our stand for Him would arouse the wrath of the world. "And ye shall be hated of all men for my name's sake: but he that endureth to the end shall be saved" (Matthew 10:22).

May 4

MAKE ROOM FOR GOD

And she brought forth her firstborn son, and wrapped him in swaddling clothes, and laid him in a manger; because there was no room for them in the inn. Luke 2:7

No room for Jesus? No room for the King of kings? No, but room for others and for other things. There was no room for Jesus in the world that He had made—imagine!

Things have not really changed since that Bethlehem night two thousand years ago. God is still on the fringes of most of our lives. We fit Him in when it is convenient for us, but we become irritated when He makes demands on us. If God would only stay in His little box and come out when we pull the string.

Our lives are so full. There is so much to be done. Are we in danger in all of our busy activities of excluding from our hearts and lives the One who made us? Do we have time enough to begin each day by reading God's Word and praying to the One who made us? Do we have time to make room for God in our prayers? Do we have time to ask God what He wants us to do?

"Oh, come to my heart, Lord Jesus; there is room in my heart for you."

ABUNDANT GIVING EQUALS ABUNDANT LIVING

Take heed that ye do not your alms before men, to be seen of them. . . .
But when thou doest alms, let not thy left hand know what thy right
hand doeth.   Matthew 6:1–3

AGAIN and again in the gospels, Christ mentioned money.
Though His Gospel was spiritual, He had much to say about
the material, because there is always a relationship between
the two, paradoxical though it may seem.

He said, "Render to Caesar the things that are Caesar's,
and to God the things that are God's" (Mark 12:17). And yet
He strongly hinted that God was entitled to some of Caesar's
money, and that Caesar stood in need of the mercy and grace
of God.

So grace and gold are inseparably bound up together; and
as long as God's kingdom is upon earth, the need of earthly
mammon is indicated and is closely tied to our spiritual life.

Our Lord's command was, "Give, and it shall be given unto
you; good measure, pressed down, and shaken together, and
running over . . ." (Luke 6:38). Yet it was more than a
command. It was an invitation to glorious and abundant
living. If a person gets his attitude toward money straight, it
will help straighten out almost every other area of his life.

The chief motive of the selfish, unregenerate person is
"get." The chief motive of the dedicated Christian should be
"give." The Prodigal Son set off a series of negative events
marked for failure when he said to his father, "Give me the
portion of goods that falleth to me" (Luke 15:12) But Jesus
said, "Give, and it shall be given." It is a promise, and we
know that Jesus never breaks His promises.

THE BEST INVESTMENT

Do not lay up for yourselves treasures on earth, where moth and rust consume and where thieves break in and steal, but lay up for yourselves treasures in heaven, where neither moth nor rust consumes and where thieves do not break in and steal. Matthew 6:19–20, RSV

SOME time ago there was a television commercial in which people stopped whatever they were doing when someone began talking about a well-known stockbroker. The message was that when this broker talked, people listened.

What if I were to tell you that, contrary to popular belief, you *can* take it with you, depending, of course, on your definition of "it"? Now, of course, you cannot take your money or your house or your car or investments with you to heaven. You wouldn't need them anyway. But you can send things on ahead so that they will be waiting for you when you arrive.

An old man, a great man of God, lay on his deathbed. He summoned his grandson to come to his side. Calling the boy's name, he said, "I don't know what type of work I will be doing in heaven, but if it's allowed, I am going to ask the Lord Jesus to let me help build your mansion. You be sure you send up plenty of the right materials."

Living a holy life, leading others to Christ as we share our faith, doing good works in Christ's name, all of these things are materials that may be sent on ahead and can never be touched by the fluctuations in the earthly economy, by natural disaster, or by thievery.

What kind of materials are you sending up to heaven? What kind of mansion will you live in when the building process has been completed?

THE INTOLERANT CHRIST

Ye cannot serve God and mammon.   Matthew 6:24

IN loving, compassionate intolerance Jesus says, "Enter ye at the strait gate . . . because strait is the gate, and narrow is the way, which leadeth unto life" (Matthew 7:13–14).

His was the intolerance of a pilot who maneuvers his plane through the storm, realizing that a single error, just one flash of broad-mindedness, might bring disaster to all the passengers on the plane.

Once when we were on a flight from Korea to Japan, we ran through a rough snowstorm; and when we arrived over the airport in Tokyo, visibility was almost zero. The pilot had to make an instrument landing. I sat up in the cockpit with the pilot and watched him sweat it out as he was brought in by ground control. A watchful man in the tower at the airport talked us in.

I did not want these men to be broad-minded. I knew that our lives depended on it. Just so, when we come in for the landing in the great airport of heaven, I don't want any broad-minded advice.

I want to come in on the beam, and even though I may be considered narrow here, I want to be sure of a safe landing there.

Christ was so intolerant of man's lost estate that He left His lofty throne in the heavenlies, took on Himself the form of man, suffered at the hands of evil men, and died a shameful death on a cruel cross to purchase our redemption. So serious was man's plight that the Lord could not look upon it lightly. With the love that was His, He could not be broad-minded about a world held captive by its lusts, its appetites, and its sins.

Having paid such a price, He could not be tolerant about man's indifference toward Him and the redemption He had wrought. He said, "He that is not with me is against me" (Matthew 12:30). He also said, "He that believeth on the Son hath everlasting life: and he that believeth not the Son shall not see life; but the wrath of God abideth on him" (John 3:36).

We have the power to choose whom we will serve, but the alternative to choosing Christ brings certain destruction. Christ said that! The broad, wide, easy, popular way leads to death and destruction. Only the way of the Cross leads home.

May 8

WHERE TO CAST YOUR CARE

Therefore do not be anxious, saying, "What shall we eat?" or "What shall we drink?" or "What shall we wear?"
Matthew 6:31, RSV

HAS God left us alone to cope with the trials, tribulations, and temptations of life? I'm glad He has not! Jesus Christ, our Lord and Savior, has told us in specific terms just what we are to do about worry. The Bible offers a workable formula for care and anxiety.

What are we to do about these past, present, and future worries? The Bible says that we are to cast them upon Him. Our guilty past, our anxious present, and the unknown future are all to be cast upon Christ. All of man's burdens and anxieties are wrapped up in these three words: past, present, and future. For the guilt of the past, God says: "I have redeemed thee" (Isaiah 44:2). "I have loved thee with an everlasting love" (Jeremiah 31:3). "The blood of Jesus Christ his Son cleanseth us from all sin" (1 John 1:7).

For the present Christ says: "I am with you always, even unto the end of the world" (Matthew 28:20). If the burden bearer is with us, then why should we be crushed by our burdens? The French translation of this phrase, "Cast all your care upon Him" is "Unload your distresses upon God." Have you ever seen a dump truck get rid of its load? It would be of no use if it carried its burden forever. The driver simply pushes a button or pulls on a lever and the heavy load is discharged at the prescribed spot.

We were never meant to be crushed under the weight of care. We push the button of faith or pull the lever of trust, and our burden is discharged upon the shoulder of Him who said He would gladly bear it. Cast the anxious present upon Him, for He cares for you—says the Bible. The worries of the future are obliterated by His promises. "Take therefore no thought for the morrow. . . . But seek ye first the kingdom of God, and his righteousness; and all these things shall be added unto you" (Matthew 6:34, 33). This promise, if we obey it, takes all the aimlessness out of life and puts purpose into it. It brings all life into balance, and earth's hours become so joyous that they blend into the glory of eternity. Boredom, fretfulness, and anxiety are lost in the wonder of His wonderful grace.

May 9

GOD AND HISTORY

But seek ye first the kingdom of God, and his righteousness; and all these things shall be added unto you.   Matthew 6:33

I HAVE become confirmed in my belief that the Bible is right in saying that God has fashioned the hearts of men alike. We are not together in today's world linguistically, culturally, or racially. We are divided. We have become a neighborhood without being a brotherhood. Yet there is one area in which I am convinced we are all alike—the spiritual dimension. I believe the hearts of all of us are the same. Our deep needs are identical the world over, for they come from within. Our need is God.

Probably it sounds a bit intolerant and narrow to you for an evangelist to go around the planet preaching the Cross—and you are right; for Jesus said that the gate to the kingdom of heaven is narrow. But we are narrow also in mathematics and in chemistry. If we weren't narrow in chemistry we would be blowing the place up. We have to be narrow. I am glad that pilots are not so broad-minded that they come into an airport any way they want.

Why then should we not be narrow when it comes to moral laws and spiritual dimensions? I believe that Christ is different; that He is unique. I believe that He is the Son of the living God and that He did change my life.

Many intellectuals are asking where history is going; they are speculating on what the end will be. I believe that Christ's prayer, "Thy kingdom come. Thy will be done on earth, as it is in heaven"—the prayer that you and I often pray—is going to be answered. And when the human race stands at the edge of the abyss, ready to blow itself apart, I believe God will intervene in history again. I don't believe any world leader will write the last chapter of history. I believe God will write it. I believe that the future kingdom is to be the kingdom of God, that there is a destiny for the human race far beyond anything we can dream. But it will be God's kingdom and will come in God's way.

A MESSAGE FOR MOTHERS . . . AND OTHERS!

They gave themselves first to the Lord and then to us in keeping with God's will. 2 Corinthians 8:5, NIV

LIVING creatively for Christ in the home is the acid test for any Christian man or woman. It is far easier to live an excellent life among our friends, when we are putting our best foot forward and are conscious of public opinion, than it is to live for Christ in our home. Our own family circle knows whether Christ lives in and through us.

If I am a true Christian, I will not give way at home to bad temper, impatience, faultfinding, sarcasm, unkindness, suspicion, selfishness, or laziness. Instead, I will reveal through my daily life the fruit of the Spirit, which is love, joy, peace, long-suffering, and all the other Christian virtues which round out a Christlike personality.

Only God Himself fully appreciates the influence of a Christian mother in the molding of character in her children. The Bible relates the stories of some women who have had an evil influence on their children. Some of the greatest criminals of history have had bad mothers.

On the other hand, most of the noble characters and fine leaders of history have had good, God-fearing mothers.

We are told that George Washington's mother was pious, and that Sir Walter Scott's mother was a lover of poetry and music. But Nero's mother was a murderess, and the dissolute Lord Byron's mother was a proud and violent woman.

Lord Shaftesbury was correct in his famous utterance, "Give me a generation of Christian mothers, and I will undertake to change the whole face of society in twelve months."

If we had more Christian mothers, we would have less delinquency, less immorality, less ungodliness, and fewer broken homes. Every mother owes it to her children to accept Christ as her personal Savior, that she may be the influence for good in the lives of those whom Christ has graciously given to her.

May 11

HOW TO PRAY

Ask, and it will be given you; seek, and you will find; knock, and it will be opened to you. For every one who asks receives, and he who seeks finds, and to him who knocks it will be opened. Matthew 7:7, RSV

EVEN a child can understand these instructions. Prayer is for God's *children.*

Jesus said, "When ye pray, say, Our Father. . . ."

There were children in our neighborhood for whom I provided all clothing, food, and the necessities of life. They asked freely of me, and their requests were usually granted. They were my children! By virtue of their relationship to me, I had a particular responsibility to them.

God has a particular responsibility to His children; and unless we have been born into the family of God through the new birth, we have no right to ask favors of God. The Bible says, "But as many as received him to them gave he power to become the sons of God, even to them that believe on his name" (John 1:12).

I have had new Christians say to me, "I don't know how to pray. I don't have the right words."

When our children were just learning to talk and had difficulty finding the right words, they still managed to make themselves understood to my wife and me, and the mistakes they made only endeared them to us. In fact, I am sure I treasure their early attempts at conversation more than the words of most adults speaking without hesitation and without error.

Oh, my anxious friend whose prayers have not been answered, God invites you to the intimacy of spiritual sonship. "That ye may be blameless and harmless, the sons of God, without rebuke, in the midst of a crooked and perverse nation, among whom ye shine as lights in the world" (Philippians 2:15).

May 12

CHOOSING CHRIST

No man can serve two masters: for either he will hate the one, and love the other; or else he will hold to the one, and despise the other. Matthew 6:24

WHO is your master? We have to make a choice.

When sin gives an order and we follow it, sin becomes the master of our lives. We become its slave. Jesus said, "You are slaves of sin" (Romans 6:17). When we come to Christ the Scripture says, "Sin shall not have dominion over you" (Romans 6:14). Sin is no longer the master. Christ is.

Right here on this earth there are two worlds: a world dominated by evil and a world dominated by Christ. We have to choose between them. We have to live in this world, but we are not to be part of it. We have to be willing to be different. We have to be willing to be laughed at, sneered at, made fun of. We have to be willing to go to the Cross and take a stand for Christ where we live, where we work, where we study. Everyone must know that we are of Christ.

Those of us who know Christ march to a different drumbeat. You see, most of the world goes in one direction, but the followers of Christ go the other way, marching to the drumbeat of heaven against the flood of evil. That's the reason it's so important for a follower of Jesus Christ to pray daily, to study the Scriptures daily.

God gives people the freedom to choose. If you sense a longing for God, a desire to change and be a new person, that's God speaking to your heart. And when you respond to Him, God will change you.

When you make that choice for Christ, you pay a price. It means that your whole life must change. You must repent, and repentance means to turn around, to change your way of living. That is what's involved in coming to Christ.

God demands an immediate decision from each one of us. He says, "How long will you halt between two opinions?" (1 Kings 18:21). Delay makes the right decision harder. Indecision itself is a choice. If you decide that you are going to wait until some other time, that is a choice away from God. The Bible says, "He, that being often reproved hardeneth his neck, shall suddenly be destroyed, and that without remedy" (Proverbs 29:1). Nowhere in the Bible does it say, "Tomorrow." The Bible says, "Now is the accepted time" (2 Corinthians 6:2). Make a choice for Christ now. Grow to maturity in Him, be His disciple.

May 13

GIVING, NOT GETTING

[Jesus said:] Freely ye have received, freely give. Matthew 10:8

THERE are clearly two philosophies about money. The first is Satan's. He says to every man as he said to Christ, "All these things will I give thee, if thou wilt fall down and worship me" (Matthew 4:9).

The second philosophy is Christ's. "Sell all that thou hast, and [give it to] the poor . . . and come, follow me" (Luke 18:22).

The first is motivated by selfishness; the second, by unselfishness.

The first has greed at the center; the second has God at the heart. The first has an eye for this world; the second has an eye for eternity. The first is slated for failure; the second, for success.

Tell me what you think about money, and I can tell you what you think about God, for these two are closely related. A man's heart is closer to his wallet than almost anything else.

It is a staggering fact that for the past few years we Americans have spent ten times as much for luxuries and nonessentials as we have for charitable and religious purposes. This is more than a cold statistic. It is a commentary on the shallow and superficial religious faith in a nation that is nominally Christian.

The Scripture teaches that we are stewards for a little while of all we earn. If we misuse it, as did the man who buried his talent, it brings upon us the severest judgment of God.

One of the worst sins that we can commit is that of ingratitude. In the midst of sorrow and trouble, this life has many blessings and enjoyments which have come from the hand of God.

Life itself, preservation from the dangers to which life is at every instant exposed, every bit of health that we enjoy, every hour of liberty and free enjoyment, the ability to see, to hear, to speak, to think, and to imagine—all this comes from the hand of God.

Even our capacity for love is a gift from God. We show our gratitude by giving back to Him a part of that which He has given to us. What have you done lately to show your gratitude to God for all that He has done, and is doing, for you?

SAVED TO SERVE

[Jesus said:] The disciple is not above his master, nor the servant above his lord. Matthew 10:24

JESUS invites each of His followers to become His *disciple.* "Jesus said unto them, Come ye after me, and I will make you to become fishers of men" (Mark 1:17). We are saved to serve; we are redeemed to reproduce spiritually; we are "fished out of the miry clay" so that we in turn may become fishers of men.

During our Crusades thousands of young people have surrendered their lives to Christ for full-time vocational Christian service. (All Christians ought to consider themselves in the service of God full time, no matter what their calling.) There is evidence that the new generation of young people is responding to Christ more than any previous generation in American history.

Young people seek adventure and excitement; but youth wants more—it wants something to believe in; it wants a cause to give itself to and a flag to follow. The only cause that is big enough is the cause of Jesus Christ; and its flag is the bloodstained body that was lifted on the cross of Calvary for the redemption of the world.

This invitation to discipleship is the most thrilling ever to come to mankind. Just imagine being a working partner with God in the redemption of the world! Jesus challenged, "If any man serve me, let him follow me; and where I am, there shall also my servant be: if any man serve me, him will my Father honor" (John 12:26).

Christian discipleship gives us the privilege of being associated with Christ intimately. And the faithful discharging of the glorious responsibilities of true discipleship invokes the approval and favor of God Himself.

May 15

The Son of Man came eating and drinking, and they say, "Here is a glutton and a drunkard, a friend of tax collectors and 'sinners.'" But wisdom is proved right by her actions. Matthew 11:19, NIV

THE late Dr. Harry Ironside once said, "Beware lest we mistake our prejudices for our convictions."

To be sure, we must deplore wickedness, evil, and wrongdoing, but our commendable intolerance of sin too often develops into a deplorable intolerance of sinners. Jesus hates sin but loves the sinner.

I was amused and shocked to hear a man of considerable religious background declare on television not long ago that "you didn't catch Jesus associating with questionable people or those whose basic ideas and attitudes were at variance with what Jesus knew to be honorable and right!"

Such a man should have known that Jesus wasn't afraid to associate with anyone! One of the things which the scribes and Pharisees criticized bitterly was His willingness to help and talk to and exchange ideas with anyone, be they publicans, thieves, learned professors, or prostitutes, rich or poor! Even His own followers decried some of the people with whom He was seen in public, but this did not lessen the compassion that Jesus felt for all the members of poor, blinded, struggling humanity.

Jesus had the most open and all-encompassing mind that this world has ever seen. His own inner conviction was so strong, so firm, so unswerving that He could afford to mingle with any group, secure in the knowledge that He would not be contaminated. It is fear that makes us unwilling to listen to another's point of view, fear that our own ideas may be attacked. Jesus had no such fear, no such pettiness of

156 *Unto the Hills*

viewpoint, no need to fence Himself off for His own protection. He knew the difference between graciousness and compromise, and we would do well to learn from Him. He set for us the most magnificent and glowing example of truth combined with mercy of all time, and in departing said, "Go ye and do likewise" (Luke 10:37).

May 16

REST FOR THE WEARY

Come unto me . . . and . . . rest. Matthew 11:28

FEW people know how to rest these days. Even on vacation, many people rush to cram in as much as they can before returning to their jobs, where they spend twice as much energy catching up on the work and mail that has piled up in their absence. Many of us need vacations just to rest from our vacations! Perhaps we have been looking for rest in the wrong places.

Jesus said, "Come unto me and I will give you rest." Like peace, rest can be found only in one place, from one source, and that is the Lord Jesus Christ.

When we rest, truly rest, we place our confidence in something outside of ourselves. We acknowledge that while there may be work to do, it will eventually be done. But there is nothing more important at that moment than resting, than taking our shoes off, stretching out on a couch or in a hammock, and thinking about anything (or nothing) but work.

As we contemplate the all-powerful, always-in-control Lord of our lives and Lord of the world, we can rest in the knowledge that Christ has the whole world in His hands. Despite the headlines in the newspapers and some of the scenes we see on television, we know that all is going according to God's plan and foreknowledge.

Jesus gives us the ultimate rest, the confidence we need, to escape the frustration and chaos of the world around us. Rest in Him and do not worry about what lies ahead. Jesus Christ has already taken care of tomorrow.

May 17

MEEKNESS FROM THE MASTER

Take my yoke upon you, and learn of me; for I am meek and lowly in heart: and ye shall find rest unto your souls. Matthew 11:29

GOD is no respecter of persons. Each of us deserves our just share of happiness. Each of us has the same capacity for God. I should not stand back lamenting my bad luck and my bad breaks in life. I should be joined to the source of power. Take Christ's yoke upon you, "and ye shall find rest unto your soul"!

"But I can't live it! I would surely fail in the attempt to be a Christian!" you protest.

Jesus said, "Take My yoke upon you." It is His yoke, and I may rest assured that He will bear the heavy part of the load.

Before He left His disciples, Christ promised that He would send a Comforter to help them in the trials, cares, and temptations of life. This word *comforter* means "one that helps alongside." He is the Holy Spirit, the powerful Third Person of the Trinity. The moment we are born again He takes up residence in our hearts.

We may not emotionally feel Him there, but here again we must exercise faith. Believe it! Accept it as a fact of faith! He is in our hearts to help us in our Christian walk.

We are told that He sheds the love of God abroad in our hearts. He produces the fruit of the Spirit: "love, joy, peace, long-suffering, gentleness, goodness, faith, meekness, temperance" (Galatians 5:22–23). We cannot possibly manufacture this fruit in our own cannery. It is supernaturally manufactured by the Holy Spirit who lives in our hearts!

I must yield to Him . . . surrender to Him . . . give Him control of my life. Through that surrender I will find happiness!

May 18

THE MIND OF CHRIST

Take my yoke upon you, and learn from me. . . .
Matthew 11:29, AB

THE Bible plainly indicates that our mental powers are to be brought under the control of Christ. "Let this mind be in you which was also in Christ Jesus," says Paul in Philippians 2:5. "Let [don't hinder, allow] this mind be in you" suggests that we can have the mind of Christ, or we can reject it. A popular song describes this attitude with the words "all or nothing at all."

Oliver Barclay observed, "Fundamentally, to love God with all our mind is to let God's revealed truth work through our lives so that our thinking, our attitudes, our worship, and our deeds are consistent. They should all be the result of God's holiness and love and grace toward us. . . . The Bible, when it talks of the mind, is not asking us to develop a philosophy . . . but to allow revealed truth to control us."

The human mind cannot be a vacuum. It will be filled either with good or evil. It will be either carnal or Christlike. We can control the kind of thoughts that enter our minds. Negatively, the mind must be turned away from all evil. We must choose the kind of television programs we see. We must be careful of the kind of things we read; the things we think about; the things that occupy our daydreams. Positively the mind must be set on things that are above. It is not enough to put bad thoughts out of our minds. Godly thoughts must be put in by Bible reading, prayer, and communion with Christ, fellowship with other Christians, Christian fellowship in the church.

Some unknown wise man has suggested, "Give your mind to Christ that you may be guided by His wisdom."

The poet, M. W. Biggs, put it well:

> Be Thou my Object, Lord, this day,
> Controlling all I do or say;
> That thro' this mortal frame of mine,
> Thy blessed traits may ever shine!
>
> Oh! fill me, Lord, with Thy deep love,
> Attract my mind to things above;
> That I a pilgrim here may be,
> And truly serve and follow Thee!

May 19

THE UNIVERSITY OF LIFE

[Jesus said,] "Take my yoke upon you, and learn from me. . . ." Matthew 11:29, RSV

WHAT are the required courses in the university of life? You are going to have to face life; you are going to have to face death; you are going to have to face judgment. You can't really face any of them without Christ. There are three required courses in the university of life. First, life itself. You had no control over the fact that you were born. There is nothing you can do to stop living. "Oh," you say, "I can commit suicide." No, you can't. You were created with a soul or spirit which will live forever. Your body will die and go to the grave, but you, the real you, will live forever. You can kill your body, but you cannot kill you. So "life" is one course you have to take, whether or not you like it. You cannot be unborn.

The second required course is death. The Bible says, "It is appointed unto men once to die" (Hebrews 9:27). Every generation dies. You may die in an automobile accident. You may die of cancer. You may die of heart disease. You may live to old age, but you are going to die. God told Hezekiah, the king, "Thou shalt die, and not live." The Bible says there is "a time to be born, and a time to die" (Ecclesiastes 3:2). Are you ready to die? Adam lived 930 years, but he died. Seth lived 912 years, but he died. Methuselah lived 969 years, but he died.

At the end of every person's life it can be said, "He died." There's a day, an hour, a minute, for your death. A prominent man was quoted in the press as saying, "I've prepared in the course of my life for every eventuality except death. I'm unprepared to die." Are you prepared to die?

The third requirement in this university is to face the judgment of God. "It is appointed unto men once to die, but after this the judgment" (Hebrews 9:27).

If you have received Jesus Christ as your Savior, a wonderful thing has happened. The cross where Jesus died for our sins was a judgment. The Bible says that He was "slain from the foundation of the world" (Revelation 13:8). It was in the plan of God for the redemption of the human race that Jesus Christ should die. That was a judgment. God judged His Son for our sins, instead of us. Jesus became sin for us. And Jesus did it voluntarily, because He loves us.

May 20

A FABULOUS FUTURE?

The kingdom of heaven is like treasure hidden in a field, which a man found and covered up; then in his joy he goes and sells all that he has and buys that field. Matthew 13:44

PRESIDENT Theodore Roosevelt said, "When you educate a man in mind and not in morals, you educate a menace to society."

Science is learning to control everything but man. We have not yet solved the problems of hate, lust, greed, and prejudice, which produce social injustice, racial strife, and ultimately war. Our future is threatened by many dangers, such as the nuclear destruction that hangs over our heads.

However, the greatest danger is from within. Every other civilization before us has disintegrated and collapsed from internal forces rather than military conquest. Ancient Rome is the outstanding example of the fall of a civilization. While its disintegration was hastened by foreign invasions, in the opinion of Arthur Weigall, a world-famous archaeologist, it collapsed "only after bribery and corruption had been rife for generations."

No matter how advanced its progress, any generation that neglects its spiritual and moral life is going to disintegrate. This is the story of man, and this is our modern problem.

The Christian believes in a fabulous future, even though the present structure of modern society should disappear and all its progress should be wiped out by self-destruction as a result of man's failure and folly.

There is a sense in which the kingdom of God is already here in the living presence of Christ in the hearts of all true believers. There is also, however, the ultimate consummation of all things, which is called the kingdom of God. This is the fabulous future! It will be a future in which there will be no war. There will be no poverty. There will be happy and peaceful human relations. There will be full and ample opportunity to exploit all our abilities. There will be a state of complete reconciliation between man and God—between race and race—between nation and nation.

May 21

THE VOICE OF AUTHORITY

And when Jesus had finished these parables, he went away from there, and coming to his own country he taught them in their synagogue, so that they were astonished, and said, "Where did this man get this wisdom and these mighty works? Is not this the carpenter's son? Is not his mother called Mary? And are not his brothers James and Joseph and Simon and Judas? And are not all his sisters with us? Where then did this man get all this?" And they took offense at him. But Jesus said to them, "A prophet is not without honor except in his own country and in his own house." And he did not do many mighty works there, because of their unbelief. Matthew 13:53–58, RSV

JESUS' teaching was unique. He took God out of the theoretical realm and placed Him in the practical. He used no qualifying statements or phrases in declaring His way of life. He didn't use such phrases as "I venture to say" or "Perhaps it's this way" or "It is my considered opinion."

He spoke with authority! He spoke with finality! He spoke as though He knew . . . and He did! When the Sermon on the Mount was completed we read that "the people were astonished at his doctrine: for he taught them as one having authority, and not as the scribes" (Matthew 7:28–29).

His was not the soft, empty conjecture of the philosopher who professes to search for truth but readily admits he has never found it. It was more the confident voice of the mathematician who gives his answers unhesitatingly because the proof of the answer can be found within the problem. Am I listening to Him—or am I a cynic as were so many of His countrymen?

UNUSED POWER

And when he [Jesus] had sent the multitudes away, he went up into a mountain apart to pray: and when the evening was come, he was there alone.   Matthew 14:23

JOHN KNOX prayed, and the results caused Queen Mary to say that she feared the prayers of John Knox more than she feared all the armies of Scotland.

John Wesley prayed, and revival came to England, sparing that nation the horrors of the French Revolution.

Jonathan Edwards prayed, and revival spread throughout the colonies. History has been changed time after time because of prayer. I tell you, history could be altered and changed again if people went to their knees in believing prayer.

What a glorious thing it would be if millions of Americans would avail themselves of the greatest privilege this side of heaven: Jesus Christ died to make communion and communication with the Father possible. He told us of the joy in heaven when one sinner turns from sin to God, and in his heart breathes the simple prayer, "God be merciful to me, a sinner."

Today we have learned to harness the power of the atom, but very few of us have learned how to develop fully the power of prayer. We have not yet learned that a man can be more powerful on his knees than behind the most powerful weapons that can be developed.

We have not learned that a nation is more powerful when it unites in earnest prayer to God than when its resources are channeled into defensive weapons. We have not discovered that the answer to our problems can be through contact with God.

When the disciples came to Jesus and asked, "Lord, teach

us to pray," the Savior answered their request by giving them His model petition, the Lord's Prayer. The Lord's Prayer, however, was only the beginning of His sacred instruction. In scores of passages, Christ offered further guidance, and because He practiced what He preached, His whole life was a series of lessons on prevailing prayer.

Have you learned His lessons yet?

May 23

WORTHY OF OUR WORSHIP

Then they . . . came and worshipped him, saying, of a truth thou art the Son of God. Matthew 14:33

JESUS CHRIST is who He said He is: God in human form. And that is a crucial truth which undergirds the reality of our salvation. Only the divine Savior could die as the perfect and complete sacrifice for our sins. Only the divine Lord could tell us how we should live. Only the risen and ascended Son of God is worthy of our worship and our service. "We confess Jesus Christ as God, our Lord and Savior."

During His time here on earth, He was God in the flesh, true God and true man. He is from eternity to eternity. Jesus Christ, by His death and resurrection, became the Gospel. As His ambassadors we must represent Him in all His fullness totally and truthfully. Anything less disqualifies us from our high and holy calling.

The Nicene Creed that came out of the Council of Nicaea in A.D. 325 affirmed He is "very God of very God, . . . being of one substance with the Father."

By faith Jesus becomes our Lord and Savior. All authority in heaven and on earth has been given to Him (Matthew 28:18). The present evil world system does not yet acknowledge His lordship; it is still under the deceiving power of the prince of this world, Satan (Ephesians 2:2). But those whom Jesus indwells have authority over the evil one and all his demons. The apostle John declares, "Greater is he that is in you, than he that is in the world" (1 John 4:4).

Therefore, in spite of our human limitations and even our failures, the Lord is sovereignly directing His own work of redemption through witnessing for Him. And we are linked to the vast resources of His power so that we don't merely "get by" in our lives and ministries but "in all these things we are more than conquerors through him" (Romans 8:37). And as the context of that inspiring and reassuring verse promises, nothing "shall be able to separate us from the love of God, which is in Christ Jesus our Lord" (Romans 8:39). God can turn the greatest tragedies into that which is for our good and for His glory, for "we know that all things work together for good to them that love God, to them who are the called according to his purpose" (Romans 8:28).

Because Jesus is Savior, He saves us from the penalty of sin. Because He is Lord, He, by His Holy Spirit, gives us power over sin as we daily walk with Him. And some future day He will take us to be with Him, far from the very presence of sin (Hebrews 9:28). Only because Jesus is God and we have confessed Him as Savior and Lord, can He bestow and we receive these benefits, this blessed assurance and hope (Romans 10:9).

May 24

DARE TO BE DISCIPLINED!

Then said Jesus unto his disciples, If any man will come after me, let him deny himself, and take up his cross, and follow me. For whosoever will save his life will lose it; and whosoever will lose his life for my sake shall find it. Matthew 16:24–25

CHRISTIAN living presupposes Christian conviction. But unfortunately, it is possible to have beliefs which do not find expression in conduct. This belief of the head is often confused with real faith. The simple truth is—one really believes only that which one acts upon. When I see a person who claims to be a Christian and believes all the creeds and calls himself an evangelical Christian, but he does not live the Christian life—his life is not characterized by brokenness, tenderness, and love—I remember the words of Jesus when He said, "By their fruits ye shall know them." After being born again we are to demonstrate our faith by our works. As James said, "Faith without works is dead."

The effective Christians of history have been men and women of great personal discipline. The connection between the words "disciple" and "discipline" is obvious. To be a true, effective disciple of Christ we must seek to discipline our lives and endeavor to walk even as He walked. The thing that has hindered the progress of the church is not so much our talk and our creeds; but it has been our walk, our conduct, our daily living. We need a revival of Christian example, and that can only come when professed followers of Christ begin to practice Christian discipline.

Where do we begin? Having found the life which is in Christ, strict disciplinary trails lead to a full-bodied, rich, and complete life.

The great "Prince of Preachers," Charles Haddon Spurgeon, once said, "I bear my willing witness that I owe more to the fire, and the hammer, and the file, than to anything else in my Lord's workshop. I sometimes question whether I have ever learned anything except through the rod. When my schoolroom is darkened, I see most." I echo that sentiment!

GOD'S FORMULA FOR PEACE

Great peace have they who love your law, and nothing can make them stumble.   Psalm 119:165

PSALM 119:165 says that peace is the gift of God. He has a formula for peace. His formula is in the Person of His Son, Jesus Christ, whom He has designated as Prince of Peace. The nations of this world have rejected the peace that God offers. They plan and build for war. Yet there are millions of people around the world who do have peace at this moment because they have found the secret of peace. They have peace in their hearts, as the Bible teaches: "Being justified by faith, we have peace with God through our Lord Jesus Christ."

The real war in which men are engaged is a war of rebellion against God. This rebellion has brought about destruction, suffering, misery, frustration, and a thousand and one ills to the population of the world. God longs to see this rebellion cease. He has sent His Son, Jesus Christ, to the cross as a demonstration of His love and mercy. He asks us to come to that Cross in a repentance of our sins and submission of our will to Him. He promises a peace treaty for all who will come by faith.

Wise old Spurgeon described the peace of God this way:

In the resurrection our nature will be full of peace. Jesus Christ would not have said, "Peace be unto you" (Luke 24:36) if there had not been a deep peace within Himself. He was calm and undisturbed. There was much peace about His whole life; but after the resurrection His peace becomes very conspicuous. There is no striving with scribes and Pharisees, there is no battling with anyone after our Lord is risen.

Do you have Christ's peace in your life?

SELF-DENIAL

Then said Jesus unto his disciples, if any man will come after me, let him deny himself, and take up his cross, and follow me. For whosoever will save his life shall lose it: and whosoever will lose his life for my sake shall find it. Matthew 16:24–25

JESUS CHRIST spoke frankly to His disciples concerning the future. He hid nothing from them. No one could ever accuse Him of deception. No one could ever accuse Him of securing allegiance by making false promises.

In unmistakable language He told them that discipleship meant a life of self-denial, and the bearing of a cross. He asked them to count the cost carefully, lest they should turn back when they met with suffering and privation.

Jesus told His men that the world would hate them. They would be "as sheep in the midst of wolves." They would be arrested, scourged, and brought before governors and kings. Even their loved ones would persecute them. As the world hated and persecuted Him, so it would treat His servants. He warned further, "They will put you out of the synagogues; indeed, the hour is coming when whoever kills you will think he is offering service to God" (John 16:2, RSV).

Many of Christ's followers were disappointed in Him, for in spite of His warnings they expected Him to subdue their enemies and to set up a world political kingdom. When they came face to face with reality, they "drew back and no longer went about with him" (John 6:66, RSV). But the true disciples of Jesus all suffered for their faith.

I think the great pioneer missionary to Africa, David Livingstone, had a handle on what it means to deny self in service to Christ when he said, "People talk of the sacrifice I have made in spending so much of my life in Africa. Can that be called a sacrifice which is simply paid back as a small part of a great debt owed to God, which we can never repay? Is that a sacrifice which brings its own best reward in healthful activity, the consciousness of doing good, peace of mind, and the bright hope of a glorious destiny hereafter? I never made a sacrifice!"

Are you known primarily for self-denial or self-indulgence?

May 27

THEY CANNOT CALL HIM FATHER

For the Son of man shall come in the glory of his Father with his angels, and then shall he reward every man according to his works. Matthew 16:27

GOD is not called "Father" by the holy angels because, not having sinned, they need not be redeemed. And the fallen angels cannot call God "Father" because they cannot be redeemed. The latter case is one of the mysteries of Scripture: God made provision for the salvation of fallen men, but He made no provision for the salvation of fallen angels. Why? Perhaps because, unlike Adam and Eve, who were enticed toward sin by sinners, the angels fell when there were no sinners, so no one could entice them to sin. Thus, their sinful state cannot be altered; their sin cannot be forgiven; their salvation cannot be achieved.

The wicked angels would never want to call God "Father," though they may call Lucifer "father," as many Satan worshipers do. They are in revolt against God and will never voluntarily accept His sovereign lordship, except in that Day of Judgment when every knee will bow and every tongue confess that Jesus Christ is Lord (Philippians 2:9–10). Yet even holy angels who might like to call God "Father" could do so only in the looser sense of that word. As Creator, God is the Father of all created beings; since angels are created beings, they might think of Him this way. But the term is normally reserved in Scripture for lost men who have been redeemed. So in a real sense, even ordinary men cannot call God "Father" except as their Creator God—until they are born again.

Christians are joint heirs with Jesus Christ through redemption (Romans 8:17), which is made theirs by faith in Him based on His death at Calvary. Angels who are not joint heirs must stand aside when the believers are introduced to their boundless, eternal riches. By contrast, Jesus identified Himself with fallen men in the incarnation when He was "made a little lower than the angels for the suffering of death" (Hebrews 2:9). That He chose to taste the death we deserve also shows that the holy angels do not share our sinfulness—nor can they know the joy of our redemption.

May 28

IS THIS THE DAY?

For the Son of man is to come with his angels in the glory of his Father, and then he will repay every man for what he has done.
Matthew 16:27, RSV

THE Greek word *apokulupsis* carries with it the idea of unveiling. It is the unveiling of one who has been hidden. Today the person of Christ is hidden from view though His presence through the Holy Spirit is in our hearts. Today is the day of faith. In that day of His coming it will no longer be faith, but sight.

His first appearing was quiet—the shepherds, the star, and the manger. His second appearing will be with His dazzling warriors from heaven, able to cope with any situation and to defeat the enemies of God until He has subdued the entire earth.

Thus, no Christian has cause to go around wringing his hands, wondering what we are to do in the face of the present world situation. The Scripture says that in the midst of persecution, confusion, wars, and rumors of wars, we are to comfort one another with a knowledge that Jesus Christ is coming back in triumph, glory, and majesty.

Many times when I go to bed at night I think that before I awaken Christ may come. Sometimes when I get up and look at the dawn I think that perhaps this is the day He will come.

The Bible teaches that the coming again of Jesus Christ will be sudden, unexpected, and dramatic. It will come as a surprise and take most people unawares. "For yourselves know perfectly that the day of the Lord so cometh as a thief in the night" (1 Thessalonians 5:2).

May 29

GOD'S KINGDOM

It is easier for a camel to go through the eye of a needle, than for a rich man to enter into the kingdom of God.   Matthew 19:24

GOD's kingdom is not built on the profit motive. The world's favorite verb is "get." The verb of the Christian is "give." Self-interest is basic in modern society. Everyone asks, "What's in it for me?" In a world founded on materialism, this is natural and normal.

But in God's kingdom self-interest is not basic—selflessness is. The Founder, Jesus Christ, was rich, and yet He became poor that we "through his poverty might be rich" (2 Corinthians 8:9). His disciples followed Him, and it was said of them, "Neither said any of them that aught of the things which he possessed was his own" (Acts 4:32). Peter, rich in heavenly goods but poor in worldly goods, said to the lame man on the Temple steps, "Silver and gold have I none; but such as I have give I thee" (Acts 3:6). The apostles realized that there is no permanent value in worldly goods and cherished the abiding values of the Spirit. They lived with eternity in view.

Today we too often hold spiritual things in contempt and lust after the things of this world. Little wonder that the world is in a state of turmoil! Mammon is worshipped, and God is disdained. Pleasure takes precedence over purity, and gain is considered greater than God.

But in God's kingdom he that is greatest among you is the servant of all (see Matthew 23:11). Service to God and mankind are put above self-interest. Jesus said, "Greater love hath no man than this, that a man lay down his life for his friends" (John 15:13). Christ proved His words by doing exactly that for us.

May 30

SIGNS OF HIS COMING

. . . The disciples came to him privately, saying, "Tell us, when will this be, and what will be the sign of your coming and of the close of the age?" Matthew 24:3, RSV

THERE are three Greek words used in the New Testament to describe the coming again of Christ. The first one is *parousia*, which carries with it the idea of the personal presence of Christ. In other words, when Christ returns, He will come *in person*.

The second Greek word is *epiphaneia*, which carries with it the idea of appearing. It is like a star, not seen in the daylight, that suddenly appears in the darkness of night. From it we get our word "epiphany."

The third Greek word is *apokalupsis*, which carries with it the idea of unveiling. It is the unveiling of one who has been hidden.

At Christmas we celebrate the first appearing, which was quiet—the shepherds, the star, and the manger. His Second Coming will be with His dazzling warriors from heaven to cope with any situation and to defeat the enemies of God until He has subdued the entire world.

The Second Coming of Jesus Christ will be a series of events transpiring over a rather long period. There are many debates among theologians as to what some of these passages mean, but one thing almost everyone who loves Jesus Christ agrees on—Jesus Christ is coming back.

When Christ came the first time, He dealt with evil as individual and hereditary. When He comes again, Christ will deal with the practice of evil. He will institute an age of such benevolence that evil cannot reign; and cruelty, oppression, and slavery will no longer exist. All of this will come to pass as a result of the personal reign of Christ, following His return.

For the true believer in Jesus Christ, the future is assured. Tomorrow belongs to you. We wait the distant trumpet announcing the coming of Jesus Christ. The Christian looks to that tomorrow when the kingdom of God shall reign.

HOPE FOR HIS HOUR

Therefore you also must be ready; for the Son of man is coming at an hour you do not expect. Matthew 24:44, RSV

HAVE you ever had something unexpected happen to you? Surprises can be fun or they can be disastrous, depending on where we are and what we are doing. An unexpected check may arrive in the mail just in time to pay a financial obligation. A relative or friend we may love very much might call or visit. Unpleasant surprises might include a traffic accident or word from the bank that our account is overdrawn.

The return of Jesus Christ is going to be a surprise, too. It will be the most glorious and wonderful surprise of all for those who know Him and have committed their lives to Him. For those who are alive, their bodies will be transformed "in the twinkling of an eye" and they will meet Christ in the air! Imagine what a surprise that will be. You are going about your daily routine when, suddenly and without warning, your body is completely transformed into the likeness of Christ's resurrected body, and you "take off" to meet Christ in the air.

For those who do not know Christ, His return will also be a surprise—but a very unpleasant one. For the judgment will soon follow, and those without Christ will spend eternity in hell.

We should use every opportunity we have to tell others of our glorious Savior who wants all of us to meet Him in the air and to live with Him forever.

June

THE SIN OF OMISSION

Then shall he say also unto them on the left hand, Depart from me, ye cursed, into everlasting fire, prepared for the devil and his angels: for I was an hungered, and ye gave me no meat: I was thirsty, and ye gave me no drink: I was a stranger, and ye took me not in: naked, and ye clothed me not: sick, and in prison, and ye visited me not. Then shall they also answer him, saying, LORD, when saw we thee an hungered, or athirst, or a stranger, or naked, or sick, or in prison, and did not minister unto thee? Then shall he answer them, saying, Verily I say unto you, Inasmuch as ye did it not to one of the least of these, ye did it not to me. And these shall go away into everlasting punishment: but the righteous into life eternal. Matthew 25:41–46*

JESUS gave this clear, strong warning against the blighting, murderous sin of omission.

He called those who failed to do good as unto Him, "Cursed." He called those who did good as unto Him, "Righteous."

It is very significant that in every one of Jesus' parables of condemnation the sin condemned is the sin of omission.

For example, the guest at the wedding supper was cast out because he did not wear the wedding garment. The five foolish virgins did not bring oil with their lamps. The man with one talent did not trade with it to his master's profit. The rich man did not minister to the poor man, Lazarus, lying at his gate. The unmerciful servant did not forgive his fellow-servant who owed him a paltry hundred pence.

In the account of the last judgment the people were not asked questions of theology. As important as doctrine is, they were not asked about their doctrinal beliefs. Neither were they asked what sins they had committed. They neglected to do good, and their sin was grave enough to send them into everlasting punishment.

There must be a practical outworking of our faith here in this present world, or it will never endure in the world to come. We need fewer words and more charitable works; less palaver and more pity; less repetition of creed and more compassion.

What are your omissions? And what do you intend to do about them?

June 2

IT'S NOT TOO LATE!

Go ye, therefore, and teach all nations . . . teaching them to observe all things whatsoever I have commanded you: and lo, I am with you always, even unto the end of the world. Matthew 28:20

I SOMETIMES think our world is on the verge of a great gathering which might well be the final one. We may be on the threshold of a mighty world-wide spiritual awakening and harvest. This is a glorious time to be alive.

I have found that people everywhere, all over the world, will respond to the Gospel of Jesus Christ if we present it simply, with Christian compassion. This is true especially in Eastern Europe, as my trips into Russia and Romania have shown.

Yet there are some who are in deep despair. I receive letters daily from people who are discouraged, depressed, and ready to give up. They are yielding to the pessimism of our times, to the mood and spirit of our day. A man in England wrote, "It's too late to do anything about the world."

That isn't true. All is not lost. We still have the Bible, and ". . . the word of God is not bound" (2 Timothy 2:9). We still have the Holy Spirit. We still have the fellowship of believers.

We still have the prayers of God's people. We still have an open door to most of the world for proclaiming the Gospel.

Spurgeon reminds us, "We can learn nothing of the gospel except by feeling its truths. There are some sciences that may be learned by the head, but the science of Christ crucified can only be learned by the heart."

June 3

GOD'S OVERARCHING LOVE

[Jesus said:] I am with you always, to the very end of the age. Matthew 28:20, NIV

THIS is a promise for obedient disciples, and it is marvelously inclusive. Dr. Handley Moule, sometime Anglican Bishop of Durham, England, and a noted Greek scholar, maintained that the *always* could be paraphrased to mean, "I am with you all the days, all day long." That means we can count on Christ's presence not only every day, but every moment of every day. Of the *fact* of His presence there can be no doubt, for His Word cannot fail. What we need is to cultivate the sense of His presence, every day, every hour, every moment.

Some years ago my wife, Ruth, had a terrible fall. She suffered a concussion, was unconscious for nearly a week, broke her foot in five places, and injured her hip. When she regained consciousness she found she had lost a great deal of her memory. What disturbed her most was that she had forgotten so many of the Scriptures she had learned throughout the years. The verses of a whole lifetime were more precious to her than all earthly possessions.

One night when she was praying, because she was so distressed, out of nowhere came the verse, "I have loved thee with an everlasting love. . . ." She has no recollection of ever memorizing this verse, but the Lord brought it back to her.

Gradually, other verses began to come back. But interestingly, while she was still trying to recover her memory, she memorized Romans 8:31–39 and repeated those verses over and over again.

I urge you to memorize this passage. Hide it away in your heart. When persecution, trouble, and adversity arise, these verses will come back to you a thousand times, and remind you of God's overarching love personified in His Son, our Savior.

June 4

THE CRUCIBLE OF SUFFERING

I will not leave you comfortless. . . . John 14:18

NOWHERE has God promised anyone, even His children, immunity from sorrow, suffering, and pain. This world is a "vale of tears," and disappointment and heartache are as inevitable as clouds and shadows. Suffering is often the crucible in which our faith is tested. Those who successfully come through the "furnace of affliction" are the ones who emerge "like gold tried in the fire."

The Bible teaches unmistakably that we can triumph over bereavement. The psalmist said, "Weeping may endure for a night, but joy cometh in the morning" (Psalm 30:5).

Self-pity can bring no enduring comfort. The fact is, it will only add to our misery. And unremitting grief will give us little consolation in itself, for grief begets grief. Ceaseless grieving will only magnify our sorrow. We should not peddle our sorrows and bewail our bad fortune—that will only depress others. Sorrow, or mourning, when it is borne in a Christian way, contains a built-in comfort. "Blessed are they that mourn: for they shall be comforted" (Matthew 5:4).

There is comfort in mourning because we know that Christ is with us. He has said, "Lo, I am with you always, even unto the end of the world" (Matthew 28:20). Suffering is endurable if we do not have to bear it alone; and the more compassionate the Presence, the less acute the pain.

June 5

CHRIST'S EXAMPLE

And when he had sent them away, he departed into a mountain to pray. Mark 6:46

ONE of the most amazing things in all the Scriptures is how much time Jesus spent in prayer. He had only three years of public ministry, yet Jesus was never too hurried to spend hours in prayer. He prayed before every difficult task confronting Him. He prayed with regularity—not a day began or closed on which He did not unfold His soul before His Father.

How quickly and carelessly, by contrast, we pray. Snatches of memorized verses are hastily spoken in the morning; then we say good-bye to God for the rest of the day, until we rush through a few closing petitions at night.

This is not the prayer program that Jesus outlined. Jesus pleaded long and repeatedly. It is recorded that He spent entire nights in fervent appeal.

How little perseverance and persistence and pleading we show. Some time ago the newspapers told of a man in Washington who spent seventeen years securing favorable action on a claim of $81,000 against the government. Yet many people will not pray seventeen minutes for the welfare of their own immortal souls or the salvation of other people.

The Scripture says, "Pray without ceasing." This should be the motto of every true follower of Jesus Christ. Never stop praying, no matter how dark and hopeless your case may seem. Some years ago, a woman wrote me that she had pleaded for ten years for the conversion of her husband, but that he was more hardened than ever. I advised her to continue to plead.

Some time later I heard from her again. She said her husband was gloriously and miraculously converted in the eleventh year of her prayer vigil. That's what it means to "pray without ceasing."

Who have you prayed for lately?

THE CROSS FOR CHRISTIANS

For from within, out of the heart . . . come evil thoughts, fornication, theft, murder, adultery, coveting, wickedness, deceit, licentiousness, envy, slander, pride, foolishness. All these evil things come from within, and they defile a man. Mark 7:21–23, RSV

JESUS indicated that our problem is heart trouble. The greatest need of our great cities at this moment is evangelism. The apostle Paul stood in the heart of pagan, secular, immoral, and violent Corinth and said, "We preach Christ crucified, unto the Jews a stumbling block, and unto the Greeks [Gentiles] foolishness; but unto them which are called, both Jews and Greeks, Christ the power of God, and the wisdom of God" (1 Corinthians 1:23–24).

The proclamation of the Gospel is still the desperate need of men today. We are never going to reverse the moral trends without a spiritual awakening, and we are never going to have a spiritual awakening until the Cross of Jesus Christ is central in all our teaching, preaching, and practice.

David Brainerd, in the journal of his life and work among the American Indians, said, "I never got away from Jesus and Him crucified. And I found that when my people were gripped by this great evangelical doctrine of Christ and Him crucified, I had no need to give them instructions about morality. I found that one followed as the sure and inevitable fruit of the other."

Dorothy Sayers says, "We have been trying for several centuries to uphold a particular standard of ethical values which derives from Christian dogma, while gradually dispensing with the very dogma which is the sole foundation for those values. If we want Christian behavior, then we must realize that Christian behavior is rooted in Christian belief."

As Spurgeon points out, "There are no crown-wearers in heaven who were not cross-bearers here below."

June 7

SURRENDER SELF

[Jesus said,] Whosoever will come after me, let him deny himself, and take up his cross, and follow me. For whosoever will save his life shall lose it; but whosoever shall lose his life for my sake and the gospel's, the same shall save it. Mark 8:34–35

A POLICE sergeant once asked me the secret of victorious Christian living. I told him there is no magic formula. But if any one word could describe it, it would be "surrender."

You may ask, "Billy, how can I surrender my life?" It is surrendered in the same way that salvation comes to the sinner. There needs to be confession of sin and a complete yielding of every area of life, personality, and will to Jesus Christ—plus faith that Christ will accept that commitment. It is not enough for us to have been confirmed or to have made a decision for Christ at an altar. We cannot walk successfully in the glow of that experience for the rest of our lives. Being human, we need to return and renew those vows and covenants with the Lord. We need to take inventory and have spiritual checkups.

Today Christ is calling Christians to cleansing—to

dedication—to consecration—to full surrender. Your response will make the difference between success and failure in your spiritual life. It will make the difference between your needing help and being able to help others.

It will revolutionize your habits, your prayer life, your Bible reading, your giving, your testimony, and your church relationship. This is the Christian's hour of decision!

If you are a Christian and have been suffering defeat, or have been outside the will of God, or do not know the power and thrill and joy that Christ can bring, I beg of you to surrender every area of your life. Give yourself wholly to Christ.

June 8

SENSITIVE TO SUFFERING

For the Son of man also came not to be served but to serve, and to give his life as a ransom for many. Mark 10:45, RSV

OUR son Franklin spent some days on a boat in the South China Sea searching for boat people fleeing the oppressive regime in Vietnam. On board, Ha Jimmy, the first mate, told him that only a week before they had rescued such a boat. It had been boarded by pirates, the passengers robbed, women raped, others wounded. The pirate ship was ramming the smaller boat to destroy all evidence when the rescue ship appeared and they fled.

First the wounded had to be tended to. Then the rescued needed to be fed, bathed, and allowed to rest. Later they were told of Jesus and His love.

One mother on board with several small children saw her baby die. There was nothing to do but put the tiny body overboard and watch it float away. A few days later the next child died. Once more the mother had to watch the little body floating away into the sea.

Ha Jimmy looked at Franklin, his eyes dark with fatigue, and asked, "Franklin, after all she had been through, if I hadn't given her Jesus, what had I really done for her?"

God can use a sensitive Christian to be a rich blessing in the life of one who knows pain and sorrow. Scripture provides guidelines for those who are in a position to help someone suffering.

Someone has said, "To have suffered much is like knowing many languages: It gives the sufferer access to many more people." Lord, help me to use any suffering I might be called upon to endure in that positive fashion.

June 9

ANSWERS TO PRAYER

What things soever ye desire, when ye pray, believe that ye receive them, and ye shall have them.   Mark 11:24

ONE lesson that Jesus would teach us is the victorious assurance that God answers every true petition. Skeptics may question it, humanists may deny it, and intellectuals ridicule it. Yet here is Christ's own promise: "If ye abide in me, and my words abide in you, ye shall ask what ye will, and it shall be done unto you" (John 15:7). Trust that promise with all your soul.

Your Father possesses everything. He "shall supply all your need according to his riches in glory by Christ Jesus" (Philippians 4:19). Let His Holy Spirit help you in your prayer life just as He promised in Romans 8:27, ". . . He maketh intercession for the saints according to the will of God."

With God nothing is impossible. No task is too arduous, no problem is too difficult, no burden is too heavy for His love. The future with its tears and uncertainties is fully revealed to Him.

He understands how much affliction and sorrow you need in order that your soul may be purified and preserved for eternity. Turn to Him, and you can say with Job, "But he knoweth the way that I take: when he hath tried me, I shall come forth as gold" (Job 23:10). No, we are not the masters of our own souls. We must not put our will above God's will. We must not insist on our own way or dictate to God. Rather, we must learn the difficult lesson of praying as the sinless Son of God Himself prayed, "Not my will, but thine, be done."

The Scripture says that the one mediator between God and man is Jesus Christ. We must know Him, and we must pray in His name. Our prayers must be directed according to the will of God, and the Holy Spirit will do that for us.

June 10

THE IMPORTANCE OF PRAYER

But Jesus often withdrew to lonely places and prayed. Luke 5:16, NIV

JESUS considered prayer more important than food, for the Bible says that hours before breakfast, "Very early in the morning, while it was still dark, Jesus got up, left the house and went off to a solitary place, where he prayed" (Mark 1:35, NIV).

To the Son of God, prayer was more important than the assembling and the healing of great throngs. The Bible says, "Crowds of people came to hear him and to be healed of their sicknesses. But Jesus often withdrew to lonely places and prayed" (Luke 5:15–16, NIV).

The precious hours of fellowship with His heavenly Father meant much more to our Savior than sleep, for the Bible says, "Jesus went out into the hills to pray, and spent the night praying to God" (Luke 6:12, NIV).

He prayed at funerals, and the dead were raised. He prayed over the five loaves and two fishes, and fed a multitude with a little boy's lunch. In the contemplation of His imminent suffering on Calvary's cross He prayed, "Not my will, but yours" (Luke 22:42, NIV) and a way was made whereby sinful man might approach a holy God.

Prayer, in the true sense, is not a futile cry of desperation born of fear and frustration. Many people pray only when they are under great stress, or in danger, or facing some crisis. I have been in airplanes when an engine died, then people started praying. I have flown through bad thunderstorms when people who may never have thought to pray before were praying all around me. I have talked to soldiers who told me that they never prayed until they were in the midst of battle. There seems to be an instinct in man to pray in times of danger.

We know "there are few atheists in foxholes," but that kind of Christianity fails to reach into our everyday lives, and it is too shallow to be genuine.

Christian teachers down through the ages have urged the prominence that prayer should have in the lives of believers. Some anonymous wise man has said, "If Christians spent as much time praying as they do grumbling, they would soon have nothing to grumble about."

June 11

DARE TO BE DIFFERENT!

If any man will come after me, let him deny himself, and take up his cross daily, and follow me. Luke 9:23

SOME years ago it was my privilege to speak in the beautiful gothic chapel at West Point. The chapel was filled, and those young people listened earnestly to the Gospel of Jesus Christ.

As I looked out upon those determined, dedicated young faces, who are the cream of American youth, I could not help but think of Jesus' disciples—He made it tough, hard, and rugged to follow Him. He talked about self-denial, cross-bearing, persecution, and even death. He said, "If you are not willing to endure these things, then you are not worthy to be My follower."

While our nation is involved with an increase of crime, immorality, adultery, drunkenness, irreverence, infidelity, and open apostasy, millions of professing Christians have forgotten the Word of Scripture that says, "If any man would follow me, let him take up his cross daily."

Our Lord regarded His followers as a select company who belonged to a different world from other men. Many of the religious people of His day were worldlings, dressed in religious garb that belonged to this world—a world ruled by the prince of darkness, a world dominated by pride, ambition, hate, jealousy, greed, and falsehood. He warned the disciples to be loyal to His teachings and principles. He told them that they were to set their affection on things above.

He also warned them that they would find things exceedingly difficult. Refusing to conform to worldly principles and practices, and living under the lordship of Christ, they would soon become marked men. He told them that the world would hate them.

They could not make their light shine by sinking to the world's low level. It was only by abiding in Christ and living under the ruling power of His Holy Spirit that they could elevate the world. The power and progress of the Christian society would depend on its unlikeness to the world and its likeness to Jesus Christ. It was this very reason that the distinction between the lives of those who lived for this world and those who lived for Christ was so clear that a very deep impression was made on the pagan society of the first century in which the early Christians lived. They influenced thousands to embrace the Christian faith because they out-thought, outlived, and outloved their neighbors. We Christians should dare to be different!

June 12

WORK INSTEAD OF WORRY

Think of the ravens. They do not sow or reap . . . yet God feeds them. And how much more are you worth than the birds! . . . Think of the flowers; they never spin or weave; yet, I assure you not even Solomon . . . was robed like one of these. Now if that is how God clothes the grass in the field . . . how much more will he look after you, you men of little faith! Luke 12:24–28, JB

JESUS did not say that we were not to be industrious, for birds are very industrious. They arise early in the morning and go out to collect the provisions that God has supplied. The flowers flourish and are beautifully clothed, but their roots reach down deep to tap the resources that God has put into the ground for their enrichment.

The birds remind us that food should not be our chief concern and the lilies show us that worrying over appearance does not make us beautiful. Domestic fowls and flowers are protected by human hands, but wild ones such as those described here are cared for by God Himself.

Two conflicting forces cannot exist in one human heart. When doubt reigns, faith cannot abide. Where hatred rules, love is crowded out. Where selfishness rules, there love cannot dwell. When worry is present, trust cannot crowd its way in.

The very best prescription for banishing worry is found in Psalm 37:5: "Commit thy way unto the LORD; trust also in him; and he shall bring it to pass." The word "commit" means to turn over to, to entrust completely.

Think of the things you do not worry about. Perhaps you never worry about whether you will be able to get water out of the faucet in your kitchen, or maybe you do not worry about a tree falling on your house.

Now ask yourself why you do not worry about such things. Is it because, in the case of running water, that it has always been there every time you wanted it, or that a tree has never fallen on your house before? Certainty breeds trust, doesn't it?

We can be just as certain and just as worry-free about God's love, protection, and provision because He has never gone back on a single one of His promises. He never changes. Great is His faithfulness.

June 13

THE HIGHEST CALLING

So likewise, whosoever he be of you that forsaketh not all that he hath, he cannot be my disciple. Luke 14:33

IF I leave my room in the morning without my quiet time, my day is all wrong, my ministry curtailed. I have no close walk, no intimate fellowship with Christ.

We need to have our time of prayer, our time of Bible reading, and above all discipline our minds. The Bible says much about the mind. "Thou wilt keep him in perfect peace whose mind is stayed on Thee." We should make it a habit to center our minds on the Person of Christ.

Let Him take your tongue and nail it to the Cross. The Scripture says that we smite with the tongue. "And the tongue is a fire, a world of iniquity: so is the tongue among our members, that it defileth the whole body, and setteth on fire the course of nature; and it is set on fire of hell" (James 3:6). Take this little muscle of yours in your mouth and nail it to the Cross.

Take those eyes of yours and say with Job, "I've made a covenant with my eyes." Make a list of every area of your life and say, "O Lord, by Thy grace, I reckon myself dead indeed unto sin, I nail these things to the Cross, I identify myself with Thee at the Cross." That is what the Scripture means when it says, "But if by the Spirit you put to death decisively the deeds of the body, ye shall live" (Romans 8:13).

Do you know what Lenin said about a Communist? He said, "A Communist is a dead man on furlough." That's exactly what we ought to be for Jesus Christ—men and women who are living disciplined lives, men and women who are following Christ in a Spirit-filled life. The Spirit-filled life produces the fruit of the Spirit. Having had your heart cleansed by the blood of Christ, having submitted and yielded every area of your life to Him, you can claim by faith to be filled with the Spirit.

When the Standard Oil Company was looking for a representative in the Far East, they approached a missionary and offered him $10,000. He turned down the offer. They raised it to $25,000, and he turned it down again. They raised it to $50,000 and he rejected it once more.

"What's wrong?" they asked.

He replied, "Your price is all right, but your job is too small." God had called him to be a missionary, and that was the highest calling.

DISCIPLESHIP

For which of you, intending to build a tower, sitteth not down first, and counteth the cost . . . ? Luke 14:28

A GENERATION ago, Jim Elliot went from Wheaton College to become a missionary to the Aucas in Ecuador. Before he was killed, he wrote, "He is no fool who gives up what he cannot keep to gain what he cannot lose."

The Christian faith brings its own "blood, sweat, and tears" to those who would follow Jesus Christ. Christ calls us to discipleship. When we come to Him, He takes away one set of burdens—the burden of sin, the burden of guilt, the burden of separation from God, the burden of hopelessness. But He also calls upon us to "Take my yoke upon you and learn from me" (Matthew 11:29). It is not a yoke that is too heavy for us to bear, for Christ bears it with us: "For my yoke is easy and my burden is light" (Matthew 11:30).

Nevertheless, Christ calls us to follow Him, regardless of the cost, and He has never promised that our path will always be smooth. There is no life that is without its own set of burdens. I have chosen Christ, not because He takes away my pain, but because He gives me strength to cope with that pain, and in the long range to realize victory over it. Corrie ten Boom said, "The worst can happen, but the best remains."

The late Dr. Walter L. Wilson once said, "God is more interested in making us what He wants us to be than giving us what we ought to have." Is that the way I'm living my life?

THE ANGELS REJOICE

. . . She calls together her friends and neighbors, saying, "Rejoice with me, for I have found the coin which I had lost." Just so, I tell you, there is joy before the angels of God over one sinner who repents.
Luke 15:9–10, RSV

WHILE angels will play an important role in executing the judgment of God on those who refuse Jesus Christ as Savior and Lord, yet at the same time the Bible tells us that they also rejoice in the salvation of sinners. Jesus tells several striking stories in Luke 15. In the first, a man had a hundred sheep. When one was lost, he left the ninety-nine in the wilderness to seek it. When he found the sheep, he slung it over his own shoulders and brought it back to the fold. At home he summoned all his friends saying, "Rejoice with me: for I have found my sheep which was lost" (verse 6). Jesus said, "I say unto you, that likewise joy shall be in heaven over one sinner that repenteth, more than over ninety and nine just persons, which need no repentance" (verse 7).

His second story is that of a woman who lost a valuable silver coin. She looked everywhere. She swept her house carefully. At last when she recovered the coin she called all her friends and neighbors saying, "Rejoice with me; for I have found the piece which I had lost" (verse 9). "Likewise, I say unto you, there is joy in the presence of the angels of God over one sinner that repenteth" (Luke 15:10).

In these two parables is not Jesus telling us that the angels of heaven have their eyes on every person? They know the spiritual condition of everybody on the face of the earth. Not only does God love you, but the angels love you too. They are anxious for you to repent and turn to Christ for salvation before it is too late. They know the terrible dangers of hell that lie ahead. They want you to turn toward heaven, but they know that this is a decision that you and you alone will have to make. What is your relationship to the Lord?

Isn't it comforting to know that, no matter how alone we may feel, God's angels are watching over us?

June 16

THE NEW PURITANISM

No servant can serve two masters: for either he will hate the one, and love the other; or else he will hold to the one, and despise the other. Ye cannot serve God and mammon. Luke 16:13

BAND-AID remedies are not enough. Only a remedy that goes to the very depths, to touch the sin that has poisoned all facets of life, can meet our needs. Unless we take moral and spiritual action, and do it quickly, we could find ourselves in a totalitarian state with all freedom suppressed in a relatively short time.

The Bible teaches we cannot serve God—the true God—and another god called materialism. But we can serve God with material things if our heart is right toward God. Individually I suggest that we're going to have to adopt lifestyles that are more consistent with the faith that we profess. We must adapt our way of living so as to gain the respect of our children and our children's children, even if it means sacrifice on our part.

Let's admit it. Our generation—yours and mine—we've lived too gaudily and too ostentatiously while millions live on the verge of starvation. And our children are seeing the inconsistency of it all. And they are asking us questions that are hard for you and me to answer. My own children are, at least.

Yes, I'm advocating today what could be called the new

Puritanism, both morally and materially. Our lives must be consistent with the slogan on our coins, "In God We Trust." And I recognize that this can happen only when we have personally committed our lives to God. There's little point in talking about corporate or national dealing with the problem, if we don't come to grips with it individually ourselves.

There is nothing wrong with having things. God often blessed with great wealth those who placed Him first. He knew He could trust them with it and that they would never worship things ahead of Him.

Too often, however, things become our focus of worship, and we desire to serve things rather than God. It is at that point that material goods become our masters, our idols, rather than our servants.

You must choose, even this day, whom you will serve. Will it be God or money?

June 17

CARRIED BY THE ANGELS

And it came to pass that the beggar died, and was carried by the angels into Abraham's bosom. . . . Luke 16:22

IN telling the story in Luke 16 Jesus says that the beggar was "carried by the angels." He was not only escorted; he was *carried.* What an experience that must have been for Lazarus! He had lain begging at the gate of the rich man until his death, but then suddenly he found himself carried by the mighty angels of God!

Another beautiful account of this kind comes from the life of Stephen (Acts 6:8–7:60). In a powerful sermon Stephen declared that even unbelievers "received the law by the disposition of angels, and have not kept it" (Acts 7:53). When he had finished his discourse, Stephen saw the glory of God and Jesus at the Father's right hand. Immediately his enemies stoned him to death, and he was received into heaven. Even as the angels escorted Lazarus when he died, so we can assume that they escorted Stephen; and so they will escort us when by death we are summoned into the presence of Christ. We can well imagine what Stephen's abundant entrance to heaven was like as the anthems of the heavenly host were sung in rejoicing that the first Christian martyr had come home to receive a glorious welcome and to gain the crown of a martyr.

Hundreds of accounts record the heavenly escort of angels at death. When my maternal grandmother died, for instance, the room seemed to fill with a heavenly light. She sat up in bed and almost laughingly said, "I see Jesus. He has His arms outstretched toward me. I see Ben [her husband who had died some years earlier] and I see the angels." She slumped over, absent from the body but present with the Lord. What a glorious experience for the believer!

June 18

MANDATE TO PRAY

Men ought always to pray, and not to faint. Luke 18:1

WE don't have to think that our prayers are bouncing off the ceiling. The living Christ is sitting at the right hand of God the Father. God the Son retains the same humanity He took to save us and is now living in a body that still has nail prints in its hands. He is our great High Priest, interceding for us with God the Father.

The resurrection presence of Christ gives us power to live our lives day by day and to serve Him. "Most assuredly, I say to you, he who believes in Me, the works that I do he will do also; and greater works than these will he do; because I go to

My Father" (John 14:12, NKJV).

The resurrected body of Jesus is the design for our bodies when we are raised from the dead also. No matter what afflictions, pain, or distortions we have in our earthly bodies, we will be given new bodies. What a glorious promise of things to come! "For our citizenship is in heaven, from which we also eagerly wait for the Savior, the Lord Jesus Christ; who will transform our lowly body to be conformed to His glorious body, according to the working by which He is able to subdue all things to Himself" (Philippians 3:20–21, NKJV).

Thousands of people today are excited about Bible prophecy. The revelation of what the Bible says about events past, present, and future has become more prominent in the themes of books, sermons, and conferences. The Second Coming of Christ is a day closer than it was yesterday, and this morning's newspaper describes events that were foretold in God's Word.

June 19

TOO BUSY TO PRAY

Be joyful in hope, patient in affliction, faithful in prayer.
Romans 12:12, NIV

HERE are some thoughts on prayer.

In the morning, prayer is the key that opens to us the treasures of God's mercies and blessings; in the evening, it is the key that shuts us up under His protection and safeguard.

"God's way of answering the Christian's prayer for more patience, experience, hope, and love is often to put him into the furnace of affliction"—Richard Cecil (1748–1810).

"Our prayer and God's mercy are like two buckets in a well; while the one ascends, the other descends"—Mark Hopkins, American educator (1802–1887).

My longtime friend, that great humanitarian missionary and man of prayer, Frank C. Laubuch, said, "Prayer at its highest is a two-way conversation—and for me the most important is listening to God's replies."

"Satan trembles when he sees the weakest saint upon his knees"—William Cowper (1731–1800).

G. Campbell Morgan tells the following story:

A father and his young daughter were great friends and much in each other's company. Then the father noted a change in his daughter. If he went for a walk, she excused herself from going. He grieved about it, but could not understand. When his birthday came, she presented him with a pair of exquisitely worked slippers, saying, "I have made them for you."

Then he understood what had been the matter for the past three months, and he said, "My darling, I like these slippers very much, but next time buy the slippers and let me have you all the days. I would rather have my child than anything she can make for me."

Some of us are so busy for the Lord that He cannot get much of us. To us He would say, "I know your works, your labor, your patience, but I miss the first love" (Revelation 2:2–4).

If there are any tears shed in heaven, they will be over the fact that we prayed so little.

Heaven is full of answers to prayer for which no one ever bothered to ask!

June 20

LATER THAN EVER BEFORE

And then shall they see the Son of man coming in a cloud with power and great glory. Luke 21:27

A LITTLE girl heard a clock strike thirteen times. Breathlessly she ran to her mother and said, "Mother, it's later than it's ever been before." Almost everyone throughout the world will agree. It's later than it's ever been before. The human race is rushing madly toward some sort of climax, and the Bible accurately predicts what the climax is! A new world is coming. Through modern technology and scientific achievement we are catching glimpses of what that new world is. If it were not for depraved human nature, man could achieve it himself. But man's rebellion against God has always been his stumbling block. The penalty for man's rebellion is death. The best leaders and the best brains have many times been stopped by death. The Bible teaches that "it is appointed unto men once to die" (Hebrews 9:27). Today the world longs for a leader such as Abraham Lincoln—but death took him from us.

God will use the angels to merge time into eternity, creating a new kind of life for every creature. Even today's intellectual world speaks of a point when time will be no more. Most scientists agree that the clock of time is running out. Ecologically, medically, scientifically, morally, time seems to be running out. In almost every direction we look, man's time on earth seems to be running out. Self-destruction is overtaking us as a human race.

Will man destroy himself? No! God has another plan!

That plan was inaugurated at the first coming of Jesus Christ. It will be completed at His Second Coming! You and I as Christians can look forward to that climactic event with joyous anticipation!

June 21
....
STUDY THE SIGNS

. . . When these things begin to come to pass, then look up, and lift up your heads; for your redemption draweth nigh. Luke 21:28

THE daily events of our world and the prophecies of the Bible are beginning to coincide. We've been told in Scripture to study the signs and to learn the signs of the times. If only the world had studied the signs of the Old Testament, it would have known that Jesus was coming the first time. But ignorance and blindness concerning the teaching of the Scriptures led men to fail to recognize hundreds of years before Jesus was born that the Old Testament revealed these things.

The Scripture said that He would be born of the tribe of Judah (Genesis 49); He would be born in Bethlehem (Micah 5). He would be born of a virgin (Isaiah 7). He would be called out of Egypt (Hosea 11). He would be a prophet (Deuteronomy 18). His own people would reject Him (Isaiah 53). He would be betrayed and sold for thirty pieces of silver (Zechariah 11). He would be put to death by crucifixion (Psalm 22). The soldiers would cast lots for His clothing (Psalm 22). He would ascend into heaven (Psalm 68). And on and on. Almost every detail which happened to the Lord Jesus Christ was predicted hundreds of years earlier by prophets inspired by the Spirit of God.

Jesus told His disciples that there would be signs for which they could watch when He would come back again. When He warned them on two occasions to beware of setting dates, he said, "Of that day and hour knoweth no man, no, not the angels of heaven, but my Father only" (Matthew 24:36). He also said, "It is not for you to know the times or the seasons, which the Father hath put in his own power." To speculate about a date would be absolutely foolish and unbiblical and against the teachings of our Lord. But we were told to watch for the signs.

Although He warned about speculating on the exact time of His return, Jesus did assure the disciples that there were signs throughout the Scriptures, as well as in His own words, which would make it clear to those who have eyes to see that the time is near. He said, "When these things begin to come to pass, then look up, and lift up your heads; for your redemption draweth nigh" (Luke 21:28). That is the hope that is in the heart of every believer—that our redemption is drawing nigh. Certainly we are two thousand years nearer the coming again of the Lord Jesus Christ than we were when He made those predictions.

Are you excited? I am!

June 22

THE NECESSITY OF THE NEW BIRTH

Jesus answered him, "Truly, truly, I say to you, unless one is born anew, he cannot see the kingdom of God." John 3:3, RSV

WE cannot explain the mystery of our physical birth, but we accept the fact of life. What is it that keeps us from accepting the fact of spiritual life in Christ?

Just as surely as God implants the life cell in the tiny seed that produces the mighty oak, and as surely as He instills the heartbeat in the life of the tiny infant yet unborn, as surely as He puts motion into the planets, stars, and heavenly bodies, He implants His divine life in the hearts of men who earnestly seek Him through Christ.

This is not conjecture; it is a fact. But has it happened to you? Have you been twice born? If you have not been, you are not only unfit for the kingdom of God—you are cheating yourself out of the greatest, the most revolutionary experience known to man.

This new birth is an *eternal* birth. The Bible says, "Being born again, not of corruptible seed, but of incorruptible, by the word of God, which liveth and abideth forever" (1 Peter 1:23). Our physical birth in life is consummated at death; but if we have been born again, death becomes the bright threshold of eternity.

That unknown writer who said, "Better never to have been born at all, than never to have been born again," never uttered a truer statement.

June 23

LOOKING FOR JOY IN ALL THE WRONG PLACES

. . . *For God is love.* 1 John 4:8

SOME years ago there was a popular song which included the lyrics, "I've been looking for love in all the wrong places." What a profound statement that is.

A Christian song puts the despair of looking for love in the wrong place in perspective: "You have searched in vain for something; now you don't want that something you've found. . . ."

How often have you found what you were looking for, only to realize it did not bring the satisfaction you thought it would? It is the ultimate frustration. That frustrating search which never ends if we are looking for fulfillment in the things of this world was never expressed better than on a bumper sticker I saw. It said, "All I want is a little more than I have now."

We look for love, acceptance, and joy in our careers, in money, in power, in all sorts of material things, but if they really brought lasting joy, would we not have testimonies from millions of people around the world to that effect? Wouldn't someone have written a book by now, the title of which might be, "I found joy, love, acceptance, and forgiveness in my new Mercedes Benz"?

The rest of that Christian song I mentioned goes, ". . . Put Jesus first in your life, and turn your life around." Order is

Unto the Hills

very important in most everything we do. By putting Jesus Christ and His will for your life first, everything else will fall into place. When Christ is out of order, or way down on your priority list, your whole life is upside down.

Try putting Christ first and watch how your life is turned around. You will discover where the love, peace, joy, and acceptance you've been searching for is to be found.

June 24

GIVE ME!

The woman said to him, "Sir, give me this water, that I may not thirst, nor come here to draw." John 4:15, RSV

THIS woman who startled a city, who set the people marching out to meet Christ, was a transformed and changed woman. The power of Christ had changed her, and in that very transformation two things were involved:

First, she had repented of her sin. The only thing that may be keeping revival from your life, from your church, from your home, from your community, may be unrepented sin. God can only use cleansed vessels.

The second thing in the preparation of the instrument was prayer. She said, "Give me," and what an intensity of desire must have gone into that prayer! Thus, she repented of her sin, she believed that Christ was the Messiah, and she began to pray. This simple woman was used to transform an entire city.

After the experience of this day, the Scripture says that Jesus went with them. Revival is not more and not less than the presence of Christ in the heart, the home, the community, and the nation. It is the practical application of this fact that we so desperately need to work out in our lifetime.

The cry of the Old Testament prophet was ". . . that the

mountains might flow down at thy presence" (Isaiah 64:1). Nothing less than this will do. The psalmist cried, "Wilt thou not revive us again: that thy people may rejoice in thee?" (Psalm 85:6).

Our greatest need at this moment of confusion and revolution is a moral and spiritual awakening. However, this moral and spiritual awakening is not coming until the people of God repent of their sins, and believe with all their hearts, and begin to pray.

That revival must begin with individuals. In the words of an old hymn, "Lord, send a revival, and let it begin with me."

June 25

MISSION IMPOSSIBLE

Jesus said to her, "You are right in saying, 'I have no husband'; for you have had five husbands, and he whom you now have is not your husband; this you said truly." John 4:17–18, RSV

IN affluent America thousands of us Christians have become too comfortable. We are too much at ease in this world. We have ceased to challenge the world in which we move; and if God wanted to do a great work in our time, we would probably be bypassed.

In John 4:9 we read, ". . . The Jews have no dealings with the Samaritans." The disciples might have thought that the Samaritans were totally outside the kingdom of God. Perhaps they thought these "outsiders" were unreachable and untouchable by the Message.

How many Christians have given up trying to win their neighbors, their business associates, or their school friends to Jesus Christ? They think they are totally uninterested.

Perhaps that friend or neighbor is watching you very carefully to determine whether you back up your belief with your life.

Some of us have already made up our minds that God has no intention of reaching this person and that—they are too hard; they are not interested; they are so materially minded; they are so filled with sin, lust, and pride that they are unreachable.

Thus, when the woman of Sychar who had had six "husbands" was converted to Christ, the disciples were not used.

Many people in history who have been used of God were great sinners and seemed unreachable. John Newton, who wrote the hymn "Amazing Grace," was a slave dealer in Africa and one of the worst sinners who ever lived. Who could ever have believed that he would one day be a clergyman in the Anglican church and become one of the greatest hymn writers of all time!

Even Paul the apostle was Saul the persecutor. Many times God takes the absolutely impossible person and transforms him by His own grace and mercy and providence to become a mighty servant of God. Don't give up on anyone. There is no person beyond the grace of God.

June 26

GOD IS A SPIRIT

God is a Spirit; and they that worship him must worship him in spirit and in truth. John 4:24

THE Bible declares God to be Spirit. In the gospel of John, Jesus is talking to a woman at the well of Sychar. He makes a straightforward statement about God; He says simply, "God is a Spirit." Immediately you imagine a sort of cloudy vapor. But that is not a picture of God.

If I want to know what a spirit is, I can find out from these words of Christ after His resurrection: "Come and touch Me and see, for a spirit has no flesh and bones such as ye see Me have." So I know that spirit is incorporeal—in other words, it is "unbody." Spirit is contrary to body. Spirit is opposite to body. Spirit is something that is not limited by a body. Spirit is not bound in a body. Spirit is not wearable as a body. Spirit is not changeable as a body.

The Bible declares that God is Spirit, that He is not limited to body: He is not limited to shape; He is not limited to force; He is not limited to boundaries or bonds; He is absolutely immeasurable and indiscernible to eyes that are limited to physical things. The Bible declares that because God has no such limitations He can be everywhere at the same time.

I was reared in a small Presbyterian church in Charlotte, North Carolina. Before I was ten years of age my mother made me memorize the "shorter catechism." In that catechism we were asked to define God. The answer we learned was, "God is a Spirit—infinite, eternal, and unchangeable."

Those three words beautifully describe God. He is infinite—not body-bound. Eternal—He has no beginning and no ending. He is the one forever self-existent. The Bible declares that He never changes—that there is no variableness or shadow of turning with Him (James 1:17).

People change, fashions change, conditions and circumstances change, but God never changes. Jesus Christ is the same yesterday, today, and forever.

ARE YOU WILLING TO DO GOD'S WILL?

Jesus saith unto them, My meat is to do the will of him that sent me, and to finish his work.   John 4:34

WE are admonished to seek out the will of the Lord. In Ephesians 5:17 we read, "Wherefore be ye not unwise, but understanding what the will of the Lord is."

To know the will of God is the highest of all wisdom. Jesus said, "If any man will do his will, he shall know of the doctrine, whether it be of God" (John 7:17).

Living in the center of God's will rules out all falseness of religion and puts the stamp of true sincerity upon our service to God. As the Bible says, "Not with eye-service, as men-pleasers but as the servants of Christ, doing the will of God from the heart" (Ephesians 6:6).

You should covet the will of God for your life more than anything in the world.

You can have peace in your heart with little if you are in the will of God; but you can be miserable with much if you are out of His will.

You can have joy in obscurity if you are in the will of God, but you can be wretched with wealth and fame out of His will.

You can be happy in the midst of sufferings if you are in God's will; but you can have agony in good health out of His will.

You can be contented in poverty if you are in the will of God; but you can be wretched in riches out of His will.

You can be calm and at peace in the midst of persecution as long as you are in the will of God; but you can be miserable and defeated in the midst of acclaim if you are out of His will.

All of life swings on this divine hinge: the will of God. So it is all-important that we discover His plan for our lives.

Have you discovered God's plan for your life yet? Have you asked?

ONE WOMAN'S TESTIMONY

Many Samaritans from that city believed in him because of the woman's testimony, "He told me all that I ever did." John 4:39, RSV

THE striking thing about this great revival at Sychar, when an entire city listened to the Gospel, is how God used a former sinner like this woman to be an evangelist. The disciples had gone to the city, and there had been little interest in them.

However, an hour or two later a woman who had been a prostitute threw the entire population into a ferment of excitement; and in a few minutes they were streaming out to meet with Christ. God had not chosen to use the church leaders. He had chosen to use a former prostitute.

As we look at history time and again, we are struck time after time by the fact that God has used the most unlikely and the most unworthy instruments to bring about spiritual awakening.

Time after time the principle is found exemplified that Paul laid down in 1 Corinthians, "God hath chosen the foolish things of the world to confound the wise; and God hath chosen the weak things of the world to confound the . . . mighty; and base things of the world, and things which are despised, hath God chosen, yea, and things which are not, to bring to naught things that are" (1 Corinthians 1:27–28).

Thus, no matter how sinful or unworthy we may feel today God can use us. Throughout history God has chosen ordinary people and unworthy people and the least likely people.

If God could use such a woman two thousand years ago to bring a revival to the city of Sychar, how much more God could use you and me today if we would put ourselves in His hand! He can use us in our community, our town, our city, our country!

June 29

THE LIFE THAT WINS

Truly, truly, I say to you, he who hears My word and believes Him who sent Me, has eternal life and does not come into judgment, but has passed out of death into life. John 5:24, NASB

WHILE it is difficult for us to believe, it is nonetheless true—God will not force the new life upon us against our will. We must be ready to receive Christ as Lord and Savior with all our hearts. Then the miracle of the new birth takes place. It should be as easy for us to believe in the new birth as it is to believe in the atomic bomb.

I know little about nuclear fission, or of uranium and other elements used in making nuclear explosives; yet I believe in the atomic bomb—so do you. But how can we believe that it exists when we possess no scientific knowledge of how it is manufactured and how it works?

The answer is obvious—by reading accounts of its nature and work and by believing and accepting them. The human mind possesses the ability to accept or reject whatever it reads or hears.

I spend much of my time perusing the pages of a Book—the Bible. It has a message for each of us, and that message is, "Ye must be born again."

That message contains both a command and a promise. It implies the possibility that I may have a new, changed, transformed nature. And it also implies more emphatically that I will never see the kingdom of God unless I am born again. Have you accepted the Christ of the Bible into your heart and life? If not, this endless life does not belong to you. If you have opened your heart to Him, it is yours already!

June 30

THE LORD OF LIFE

For as the Father has life in himself, so he has granted the Son also to have life in himself, and has given him authority to execute judgment, because he is the Son of man. John 5:26–27, RSV

WHY is Christianity so different from the religions of the world? It is because Christianity is not a religion. It is a relationship with a living God. Jesus, Son of God the Father and Second Person of the Trinity, is the central figure of our evangelistic message.

Today many voices are making other claims. Atheists say there is no God. Polytheism may allow that Jesus is one of many gods. When I first went to some Far Eastern countries, I had to learn that in giving the invitation to receive Christ I needed to make it clear to my listeners that they were turning from all other gods and turning to the true and the living God as revealed in the Scriptures. We, as "ambassadors for Christ" (2 Corinthians 5:20), boldly echo the ringing conviction of the apostle Peter when he affirmed, "Thou art the Christ, the Son of the living God" (Matthew 16:16). The title "Christ" means "anointed one." It is the term, in the Greek language, for the ancient Hebrew word "Messiah"—the anointed one whom God would send to save His people.

Peter and his fellow Jews, the first believers of the early Christian Church, recognized Jesus Christ as the Messiah promised in the Old Testament. Their period of world history was one of discouragement and despair. The promised Messiah shone as a beacon in the darkness, and His light has never dimmed. "In him was life; and the life was the light of men. . . . That was the true Light, which lighteth every man that cometh into the world" (John 1:4, 9).

July

LET YOUR LIGHT SHINE!

As long as I am in the world, [Jesus said,] I am the light of the world. John 9:5

W E are holding a light. We are to let it shine! Though it may seem but a twinkling candle in a world of blackness, it is our business to let it shine. Light dispels darkness, and it attracts people in darkness to it.

We are blowing a trumpet. In the din and noise of battle the sound of our little trumpet may seem to be lost, but we must keep sounding the alarm to those who are in danger.

We are kindling a fire. In this cold world full of hatred and selfishness our little blaze may seem to be unavailing, but we must keep our fire burning.

We are striking with a hammer. The blows may seem only to jar our hands as we strike, but we are to keep on hammering. Amy Carmichael of India once asked a stonecutter which blow broke the stone. "The first one and the last," he replied, "and every one in between."

We have bread for a hungry world. The people may seem to be so busy feeding on other things that they will not accept the Bread of Life, but we must keep on giving it, offering it to the souls of men.

We have water for famishing people. We must keep standing and crying out, "Ho, every one that thirsteth, come ye to the waters." Sometimes they can't come and we must carry it to them.

We must persevere. We must never give up. Keep using the Word!

Jesus said that much of our seed will find good soil and spring up and bear fruit. We must be faithful witnesses.

The Bible says, "He that winneth souls is wise" (Proverbs 11:30).

"And they that be wise shall shine as the brightness of the firmament; and they that turn many to righteousness as the stars for ever and ever" (Daniel 12:3).

"Ye are the salt of the earth" (Matthew 5:13). Salt makes one thirsty. Does your life make others thirsty for the water of life?

July 2

PRICELESS

I am the door [said Jesus]: by me if any man enter in, he shall be saved. John 10:9

WHEN God said, "Come ye, buy . . . without money and without price" (Isaiah 55:1), He was saying, "Salvation is free!"

God puts no price tag on the Gift of gifts—it is free! Preachers are not salesmen, for they have nothing to sell. They are the bearers of Good News—the good tidings that "Christ died for our sins according to the scriptures" (1 Corinthians 15:3), and that the "grace of God . . . hath appeared to all men" (Titus 2:11). Money can't buy it. Man's righteousness can't earn it. Social prestige can't help us acquire it. Morality can't purchase it. It is as Isaiah quoted: "Without money and without price."

God does not bargain with us. We cannot barter with Him. We must do business with Him on His own terms. He holds in His omnipotent hand the priceless, precious, eternal gift of salvation, and He bids us to take it without money and without price. The best things in life are free, are they not? The air we breathe is not sold by the cubic foot. The water which flows crystal clear from the mountain stream is free for the taking. Love is free, faith is free, hope is free.

We can't reject God's grace on the ground that it is too

cheap, for the most precious things in life come to us without money and without price. Only the cheap, tawdry things have a price tag upon them. Salvation is free—but it is not cheap!

July 3

ABUNDANT LIVING

I am come that they might have life, and that they might have it more abundantly. John 10:10

ONLY those who have been truly converted to Jesus Christ know the meaning of abundant living.

The Bible teaches that worldliness is a force, a spirit, an atmosphere of the cosmos, that is in opposition and in contradiction to all that is godly and Christian. Its goal is selfish pleasure, material success, and the pride of life. It is ambitious, self-centered. God is not necessarily denied; He is just ignored and forgotten.

Three times Christ designated Satan as the prince of this world. He said, "The prince of this world cometh, and hath nothing in me" (John 14:30). In John 16:11, He again said, "Of judgment, because the prince of this world is judged." In John 12:31, He said, "The prince of this world (shall) be cast out."

Thus the Bible is clear that the world's inhabitants are either under the influence of this world with its cunning, deception, and spell; or they are in Christ and under the direction of the Spirit of God. There is no neutral ground. The lines are drawn by the Bible.

Paul wrote to the Ephesians, "Wherein in time past ye walked according to the course of this world, according to the prince of the power of the air, the spirit that now worketh in the children of disobedience. . . . Even when we were dead in sins [God] hath quickened us together with Christ" (2:2, 5).

Now the words "course of this world" carry the meaning of current or flow. There is an undertow, a subtle current, which runs against and in contradiction to the will and the way of God. Its eddies are deep and treacherous. They are stirred and troubled by Satan and intended to trap and ensnare those who would walk godly in Christ Jesus.

Satan employs every device at his command to harass, tempt, thwart, and hurt the people of God. His attack is relentless. Paul wrote, "We wrestle not against flesh and blood, but against principalities, against powers, against the rulers of the darkness of this world, against spiritual wickedness in high places" (Ephesians 6:12).

However, the Christian is not left defenseless in this conflict. God provides the power to give us victory over Satan. Paul said, "We are more than conquerors through him that loved us" (Romans 8:37). And John wrote, "Ye are of God, little children, and have overcome them: because greater is he that is in you, than he that is in the world" (1 John 4:4).

July 4

OUR STATUE OF LIBERTY

If the Son therefore shall make you free, ye shall be free indeed. John 8:36

DURING the national observance of the one hundredth anniversary of the Statue of Liberty in New York Harbor, I was struck by the great emphasis on the number of immigrants who had often left everything behind, coming to America with nothing but the clothes on their backs, risking their very lives for something they valued more highly than everything they had left behind: freedom.

This is a picture of what we must do when we come to Christ. We must forsake allegiance to the things of this world and all that this world has to offer and become immigrants in the kingdom of God. His statue of liberty is in the form of the cross.

The statue in New York Harbor lifts her lamp "beside the golden door."

The statue of liberty on that Golgotha hill lights the way into the eternal life. That light is ours if we will only come to God through the One who said, "I am the light of the world: he that followeth me shall not walk in darkness, but shall have the light of life" (John 8:12).

This light gives freedom to men and women in the darkest of prisons in nations which are intolerant of the preaching of the Gospel. One can have political freedom and still be a prisoner of sin, while one who is in a political prison and knows Christ can be more free than his jailers.

Freedom in Christ is the ultimate freedom to be celebrated not only on special days, but all year around.

July 5

IS HE YOUR LORD—OR JUST YOUR SAVIOR?

He that loveth his life shall lose it; and he that hateth his life in this world shall keep it unto life eternal. John 12:25

MANY Christians can say, "I'm a member of the church. I've been confirmed. I've tried to do my best." But deep in their hearts they haven't really experienced Christ in total commitment. He may be their Savior; but He hasn't yet become their Lord, and Lord and Savior must go together. He is the Lord Jesus Christ.

We are made in the image of God. We are made to glorify God. We are made for God; and without God there is an empty place in our life. That empty place can be filled by a simple surrender to Jesus Christ.

Instant pleasure—we want it. And we want it all now. Paul said, "In the last days . . . men shall be . . . lovers of pleasures more than lovers of God" (2 Timothy 3:1–2, 4). We want pleasure. We are searching for pleasure, and searching for happiness, and searching for kicks, and we get them temporarily; and then comes the morning after. The kick has a kickback. Paul said, "She that liveth in pleasure is dead while she liveth" (1 Timothy 5:6). Physically you're alive, but something is dead inside, and you know it. It's your soul, it's your spirit—dead toward God because you have never really come to the Cross and said, "Lord, I surrender all."

The Scripture says in 1 Corinthians 10:6 that we should not lust. Peter said, "I beseech you as strangers and pilgrims, abstain from fleshly lusts, which war against the soul" (1 Peter 2:11). Lusts fight the soul. They fight the spirit. They fight our relationship with God.

How different it was with William R. Featherstone. He was about sixteen when he wrote, "My Jesus, I love Thee, I know Thou art mine; For Thee all the follies of sin I resign; My gracious Redeemer, my Savior art Thou; If ever I loved Thee, my Jesus, 'tis now." And the psalmist said, "Thou wilt shew me the path of life: in thy presence is fullness of joy; at thy right hand there are pleasures for evermore" (Psalm 16:11) Forevermore. Not the pleasure of a moment. Not the pleasure of an exciting evening that soon is past—but forever. This pleasure is ours on the path of complete surrender.

AN EXAMPLE OF LOVE

By this shall all men know that ye are my disciples, if ye have love one to another. John 13:35

OUR popular music talks constantly about love, and yet divorce rates skyrocket, child abuse is rampant, and our world is shaken by wars, violence, and terrorism. Major news magazines feature cover stories on "The 'Me' Generation." This generation, it seems, would rather see a prizefight than fight for a prize. Not only has the song "Rescue the perishing, care for the dying" disappeared from most of our songbooks, its theme has disappeared from our hearts, except for victims of physical famine, oppressive regimes, and tidal waves. And these are terribly important. It is just that the spiritually perishing need to hear the Gospel.

Several years ago we were visiting India. While we were there a terrible tidal wave hit a fifty-mile section of the coast, killing thousands of people and completely destroying scores of villages and towns. Indian officials graciously provided a helicopter and accompanied us to the area, and we were among the first to view the devastation. I will never forget the terrible destruction and the stench of death—it was as if a thousand atomic bombs had gone off at the same time.

The disaster was virtually ignored by the rest of the world. Why? Because there is so much suffering in the world already that the media cannot cover it all.

Abraham Lincoln once said, "I feel sorry for the man who can't feel the whip when it is laid on the other man's back."

MANY MANSIONS

In my Father's house are many mansions; if it were not so, I would
have told you. I go to prepare a place for you. John 14:2

HEAVEN is a home which is permanent. One of the
unfortunate facts about the houses which men build for
themselves is that they are not permanent. Houses do not last
forever. It is true of the house, the outer shell, and it is true of
the family. How quickly the children grow up and leave home.

As much as our homes mean to us, they are not permanent.
Sometimes I look at my own adult children and can hardly
believe that they are all grown and on their own. The house
that once rang with the laughter of children is now empty.

Those who for Christ's sake had given up houses and lands
and loved ones knew little of home life or home joys. It was
as if Jesus had said to them, "We have no lasting home here
on earth, but my Father's house is a home where we will be
together for all eternity."

The venerable Bishop Ryle is reputed to have said,
"Heaven is a prepared place for a prepared people, and they
that enter shall find that they are neither unknown
or unexpected."

THE RIGHT SIDE OF HEAVEN

There are many rooms in my Father's house; if there were not, I should
have told you. I am going to prepare a place for you, and after I have
gone and prepared you a place, I shall return to take you with me; so
that where I am, you may be too. John 14:2–3, JB

WHEN Jesus said, "In my Father's house are many mansions," we find a very interesting meaning for the word *mansion*. The Greek word used does not mean an imposing house but a resting place. The expression is translated in the margin of the American Standard Version as "abiding places." This comes from the same stem as the English word *remain*.

During Christ's ministry on earth He had no home. He once said, "Foxes have holes and birds of the air have nests, but the Son of Man has no place to lay his head" (Matthew 8:20, NIV). But His home in heaven will last forever.

The early disciples and other Christian pilgrims suffered in many ways, and Jesus knew it—for He suffered more severely than any of His followers. But they were all eagerly anticipating the beauty and permanence of a never-ending home that would last throughout eternity.

A little girl was taking a walk with her father one evening. Looking up at the stars she exclaimed, "Daddy, if the wrong side of heaven is so beautiful, what must the right side be!"

July 9

THE HOLY SPIRIT FOREVER

And I will pray the Father, and he shall give you another Comforter, that he may abide with you for ever; even the Spirit of truth; whom the world cannot receive, because it seeth him not, neither knoweth him; but ye know him; for he dwelleth with you, and shall be in you.
John 14:16–17

DURING His lifetime on earth, Christ's presence could be experienced only by a small group of men at any given time. Now Christ dwells through the Spirit in the hearts of all those who have received Him as Savior. The apostle Paul wrote to the Corinthians: "Know ye not that ye are the temple of God, and that the Spirit of God dwelleth in you?" (1 Corinthians 3:16).

The Holy Spirit is given to every believer—not for a limited time, but forever. Were He to leave us for one moment, we would be in deep trouble.

Walter Knight tells the story about a little boy who had recently received Christ. "Daddy, how can I believe in the Holy Spirit when I have never seen Him?" asked Jim. "I'll show you how," said his father, who was an electrician. Later Jim went with his father to the power plant where he was shown the gyrators. "This is where the power comes from to heat our stove and to give us light. We cannot see the power, but it is in that machine and in the power lines," said the father.

"I believe in electricity," said Jim.

"Of course, you do," said his father, "but you don't believe in it because you see it. You believe in it because you see what it can do. Likewise you can believe in the Holy Spirit because you see what He does in people's lives when they are surrendered to Christ and possess His power."

Thus, by faith you accept the fact that you are indwelt by the Spirit of God. He is there to give you special power to work for Christ. He is there to give you strength in the moment of temptation.

He is there to produce the supernatural fruit of the Spirit, such as "love, joy, peace, long-suffering, gentleness, goodness, faith, meekness, temperance" (Galatians 5:22–23). He is there to guide you over all the difficult terrain you must cross as a Christian.

July 10

COVERED BY CHRIST

[Jesus said,] Abide in me, and I in you. John 15:4

PERSONAL salvation is not merely an occasional rendezvous with Deity; it is an actual dwelling with God. Christianity is not just an avocation; it is a lifelong, eternity-long vocation. David, thrilled with the knowledge that his life was in God, said in Psalm 91:1, "He that dwelleth in the secret place of the Most High shall abide under the shadow of the Almighty."

If you read and reread this beautiful psalm, you will discover that in Him we have a permanent abode and residence, and that all of the comfort, security, and affection which the human heart craves is found in Him.

Modern psychiatrists say that one of the basic needs of man is security. In this psalm we are assured that in God we have the greatest of security: "There shall no evil befall thee, neither shall any plague come nigh thy dwelling. For he shall give his angels charge over thee, to keep thee in all thy ways" (Psalm 91:10–11).

A few years ago in China, two Christian missionaries were undergoing bitter persecution. One night as they were getting ready to retire they heard the sound of voices outside the compound. They lifted the blinds to find their home surrounded with belligerent men who had gathered there to terminate the couple's ministry.

The missionary husband and wife, realizing that God was their only refuge, dropped on their knees and prayed for those who would harm them, and reminded God that He had promised to be with them even unto the end. When they arose from their knees, they noticed that the crowd was dispersing, and the excited murmuring of the departing mob indicated that something unusual had happened. The missionaries thanked God for answered prayer and retired. The next morning as the sun cast its rays upon the compound, a native Christian came to the door and begged an audience with them.

"Do you know why the mob did not kill you last night?"

he asked. "Our God answered prayer," replied the missionary. "Yes," said the native man. "When you were on your knees last night, four creatures like angels dressed in robes of white appeared, and one stood at each corner of your house. The mob trembled and fled, and we Christians who stood helpless in the crowd knew that once more God had intervened."

July 11

THE MEASURE OF REAL LOVE

This is my commandment, That ye love one another, as I have loved you. Greater love hath no man than this, that a man lay down his life for his friends. John 15:12–13

MUCH of the world is callous and indifferent toward mankind's poverty and distress. This is due largely to the fact that for many people there has never been a rebirth. The love of God has never been shed abroad in their hearts.

Many people speak of the social Gospel as though it were separate and apart from the redemptive Gospel. The truth is: There is only one Gospel. Divine love, like a reflected sunbeam, shines down before it radiates out. Unless our hearts are conditioned by the Holy Spirit to receive and reflect the warmth of God's compassion, we cannot love our fellow men as we ought.

Jesus wept tears of compassion at the graveside of a friend. He mourned over Jerusalem because as a city it had lost its appreciation of the things of the spirit. His great heart was sensitive to the needs of others.

To emphasize the importance of people's love for each other, He revised an old commandment to make it read, "Thou shalt love the Lord thy God with all thy heart . . . and thy neighbor as thyself" (Luke 10:27).

St. Francis of Assisi had discovered the secret of happiness when he prayed:

> O Divine Master, grant that I may not so much seek
> To be consoled as to console,
> To be understood as to understand,
> To be loved as to love;
> For it is in giving that we receive;
> It is in pardoning that we are pardoned;
> It is in dying that we are born to eternal life!

Tears shed for self are tears of weakness, but tears of love shed for others are a sign of strength. I am not as sensitive as I ought to be until I am able to "weep o'er the erring one and lift up the fallen." And until I have learned the value of compassionately sharing others' sorrow, distress, and misfortune, I cannot know real happiness.

July 12

MAKE LOVE YOUR MOTIVE!

These things I command you, that ye love one another. John 15:17

WHAT is the great overwhelming evidence that we have passed from death unto life? It is love! Our Lord prayed, "That they all may be one; as thou, Father, art in me, and I in thee, that they also may be one in us: that the world may believe that thou hast sent me" (John 17:21).

Jesus Christ clearly was speaking of visible unity, such as can be seen by the world. His motive for praying was that the world might believe and the world might know. He prayed for unity among believers. There is a kind of unity in diversity, a unity compatible with variety, and it is this pattern which Christ lays down for the Church.

All through the book of Acts there occurs a key phrase:

"with one accord." The apostles were not given to quarreling over secondary points of doctrine. When difficulties did arise, every attempt was made to settle them in a reasonable and charitable spirit under the direction of the Holy Spirit.

God, who wills man's unity in Christ, is a God of variety. So often we want everyone to be the same, to think and speak and believe as we do. Ephesians 2:19–20, Philippians 2:1–4, and many other passages could be called to witness that love is the real key to Christian unity.

In the spirit of true humility, compassion, consideration, and unselfishness—which reflect the mind of the Lord Jesus—we are to approach our problems, our work, and even our differences.

James says that even the demons believe—and shudder. He is protesting against the barrenness of the orthodoxy which is divorced from love and good works. It is possible to be right theologically and yet to be lacking in a spirit of love.

John fills his epistles with the love that we are to have one for another: "We know that we have passed from death unto life, because we love the brethren" (1 John 3:14)—not because we are sound in the Christian faith and believe the Bible from cover to cover. The one great test is love!

July 13

WE ARE IN THE WORLD

If ye were of the world, the world would love his own: but because ye are not of the world, but I have chosen you out of the world, therefore the world hateth you. John 15:19

THE Christian, of course, must live his life in this world. He must infiltrate this world with a purpose—to help win the world. But he does not need to participate in the evils of the world. It is impossible for us to escape from the world, the flesh, and the devil, even in a monastery.

We cannot possibly influence the world unless we live in it and give evidence of the power of the Gospel in our lives. As citizens we must vote and participate in political affairs. We are to participate in civic activities, and most certainly we are to be loyal and faithful to the church.

However, we are not to compromise with the world, the flesh, and the devil. We are not to participate in the sins of the world. There are certain things to which a Christian must say *no*—in politics, in the shop, in the office, even in the neighborhood he must often show that he is a citizen of another world, and many times suffer persecution and misunderstanding because of it.

We should refuse to support anything which does not meet with the approval of our Christian conscience. There are thousands of professing Christians who are betraying their Christian principles because they are more concerned for the world's smile than the condemnation of Jesus Christ.

I have found that the casual Christian has little or no influence upon others. I am finding that it is only the Christian who refuses to compromise in matters of honesty, integrity, and morality who is bearing an effective witness for Christ. The worldly Christian is prepared to do as the world does and will condone practices which are dishonest and unethical because he is afraid of the world's displeasure. Only by a life of obedience to the voice of the Spirit, by a daily dying to self, by a full dedication to Christ and constant fellowship with Him, are we enabled to live a godly life and have a positive influence in this present ungodly world.

NOT OF THE WORLD

[Jesus said,] I have given them thy word; and the world has hated them because they are not of the world, even as I am not of the world.
1 John 17:14, RSV

W E Christians are not to be conformed to the world socially. The world tries to absorb us into its secular society and to conform us to its earthly image, but Christ urges us not to conform. Clearly He says of those who believe in Him, "They are not of the world, even as I am not of the world."

The Gulf Stream is in the oceans, and yet it is not a part of it. Believers are in the world, and yet they must not be absorbed by it. The Gulf Stream maintains its warm temperatures even in the icy water of the North Atlantic. If Christians are to fulfill their purposes in the world, they must not be chilled by the indifferent, godless society in which they live.

Much of our talk as Christians is worldly, not spiritual. It is easy to fall into the conversational conformity of the world and spend an evening discussing politics, the new model cars, and the latest entertainment. We often forget that we are to edify one another with holy conversation and that our conversation should be on heavenly, and not exclusively on earthly, things.

It is true that Jesus dined with publicans and sinners, but He did not allow the social group to overwhelm Him and conform Him to its ways. He seized every opportunity to present a spiritual truth and to lead a soul from death to life. Our social contacts should not only be pleasant, they should be made opportunities to share our faith with those who do not yet know Christ.

THE WORLD'S WORTHLESS PENNY

[Jesus said,] I pray for them . . . for they are thine. And all mine are thine, and thine are mine; and I am glorified in them.   John 17:9–10

I BELIEVE unselfconsciousness is characteristic of the fruit of the Holy Spirit. The person who says, "I am Spirit-filled" sets himself up for some pretty uncomfortable scrutiny. Did any apostle or disciple say of himself, "I am filled with the Holy Spirit"? But others would say of them, "They were filled with the Holy Spirit." The person who is self-consciously loving, self-consciously joyful, self-consciously peaceful, has about him the odor of self. And as one Christian sagely observed: "Self is spiritual B.O."

A little child playing one day with a very valuable vase put his hand into it and could not withdraw it. His father, too, tried his best to get the little boy's hand out, but all in vain. They were thinking of breaking the vase when the father said, "Now, my son, make one more try. Open your hand and hold your fingers out straight as you see me doing and then pull."

To their astonishment the little fellow said, "Oh no, Father. I couldn't put my fingers out like that because if I did I would drop my penny."

Smile if you will—but thousands of us are like that little boy, so busy holding on to the world's worthless penny that we cannot accept liberation. I beg you to drop that trifle in your heart. Surrender! Let go and let God have His way in your life.

Now after you have given yourself completely to Christ in surrender to Him, remember that God has accepted what you have presented. "Him that cometh to me I will in no wise cast out" (John 6:37).

You have come to Him; now He has received you. And He will in no wise cast you out!

July 16

REDUCED TO ROBOTS

These are recorded so that you may believe that Jesus is the Christ, the son of God, and that believing this you may have life through his name. John 20:31, JB

IN Christ we can become new people. "If anyone is in Christ, he is a new creation; the old has gone, the new has come!" (2 Corinthians 5:17, NIV). God can produce great good out of any life dedicated to Him.

If God were to remove all evil from our world (but somehow leave man on the planet), it would mean that the essence of "humanness" would be destroyed. Man would become a robot.

Let me explain what I mean by this. If God eliminated evil by programming man to perform only good acts, man would lose his distinguishing mark—the ability to make choices. He would no longer be a free moral agent. He would be reduced to the status of a robot.

Let's take this a step further. Robots do not love. God created man with the capacity to love. Love is based upon one's right to choose to love. We cannot force others to love us. We can make them serve us or obey us. But true love is founded upon one's freedom to choose to respond. Man could be programmed to do good, but the element of love would be lost. If man were forced to do good, suffering would be eliminated—and so would love. What would it be like to live in a world without love?

Thus we can see that God's use of His power to eliminate evil would not prove to be a positive solution to the problem of suffering. The results of such action would create greater dilemmas. Either man would be reduced to the status of a robot in a loveless world or he would be annihilated. Given the choice, I would choose to be responsible for my actions rather than to be a robot without responsibility!

July 17

LIFE AND LIGHT

. . . These are written, that ye might believe that Jesus is the Christ, the Son of God; and that believing ye might have life through his name. John 20:31

C. T. STUDD, the famous Cambridge cricketer and missionary pioneer, wrote the following couplet while still a student at Cambridge:

> Only one life, 'twill soon be past;
> Only what's done for Christ will last.

Life is a glorious *opportunity* if it is used to condition us for eternity. If we fail in this, though we succeed in everything else, our life will have been a failure. There is no escape for the man who squanders his opportunity to prepare to meet God.

D. L. Moody said, "Let God have your life; He can do more with it than you can!" D. L. Moody also said, "A holy life will produce the deepest impression. Lighthouses blow no horns; they only shine."

Our lives are also *immortal*. God made man different from the other creatures. He made him in His own image, a living soul. When this body dies and our earthly existence is terminated, the soul or spirit lives on forever. One hundred years from this day you will be more alive than you are at this moment. The Bible teaches that life does not end at the cemetery. There is a future life with God for those who put their trust in His Son, Jesus Christ. There is also a future hell of separation from God toward which all are going who have refused, rejected, or neglected to receive His Son, Jesus Christ.

Victor Hugo once said, "I feel in myself the future life." Cyrus the Great is reported to have declared, "I cannot imagine that the soul lives only while it remains in this mortal body." Nothing but our hope in Christ will take the sting out of death and throw a rainbow of hope around the clouds of the future life. Our anchor is in Jesus Christ, who abolished death and brought life and immortality to light through the Gospel.

July 18

THE CHURCH THAT SHOOK THE WORLD

They were all filled with the Holy Spirit. . . . Acts 2:4, RSV

WE read in the book of Acts that the early Church was filled with the Holy Spirit. They had no church buildings, no Bibles, no automobiles, no planes, no trains, no television, no radio. Yet they turned their world "upside down" for Christ. They instituted a spiritual revolution that shook the very foundations of the Roman Empire. They were young, vigorous, virile, powerful. They lived their lives daily for Christ. They suffered persecution and even death gladly for their faith in Christ. What was the secret of their success—even in the face of opposition and death? One reason beyond doubt is that they hungered and thirsted after righteousness. And those with whom they came in contact could not help but be impressed by the quality and purity of their lives and their love.

The reason certain false philosophies and religions are

making such inroads in the world today is that somewhere along the line the people who were supposed to live Christian lives failed. We have failed to meet the standards and requirements that Jesus set forth. If we would live for Christ, we must be willing to count all else as "nothing but refuse." We must be as dedicated, as committed, and as willing to sacrifice all as some followers of false religions are.

The great masses of the unbelieving world are confused as they gaze upon the strife within and among religious bodies. Instead of a dynamic, growing, powerful, Christ-centered Church, we see division, strife, pettiness, greed, jealousy, and spiritual laziness—while the world is standing on the brink of disaster.

The great need in Christendom today is for Christians to learn the secret of daily, wholehearted recommitment to Christ.

July 19

TRANSFORMING FIRE

This Jesus God raised up, and of that we are all witnesses.
Acts 2: 32, RSV

WITNESS the transformation in Simon Peter. He was so weak before Pentecost that, in spite of his bragging to the contrary, he swore and denied Christ. He was cowed by the crowd, shamed by a little maid, and took his place with the enemies of Christ.

But see him after he had been baptized with fire! He stands boldly before the same rabble that had crucified Jesus, and looking into their faces, unafraid, says, "Therefore let all the house of Israel know assuredly, that God hath made that same Jesus, whom ye have crucified, both Lord and Christ" (Acts 2:36).

Peter, the weak, was transformed to Peter, the rock. Saul, the slaughterer, was transformed to Paul, the missionary. All of the disciples were changed from ordinary individuals into virtual firebrands for God. Their faith and zeal started a conflagration which spread throughout Asia Minor, Europe, and the entire world. The world today still feels the powerful impact and influence of this little band of dedicated men who dared to expose themselves to the "Divine Flame."

A bar of raw steel may be purchased for a few dollars. But when that bar of steel has been thrust into the fires and processed, when it has been tempered and forged and made into tiny watch springs for expensive watches, it is worth thousands of dollars. Fire and the skilled hands of master artisans made the difference, enhancing the value.

Just as the sun by its heat and light performs a thousand miracles a day in the plant kingdom, God through the refining fire of His Spirit performs a thousand miracles a day in the spiritual realm. His regenerating power is ever at work in the world, taking the ashes of burned-out lives and changing them to dynamic channels, dedicated to winning the salvation of others!

July 20

AND THE ANGELS REJOICE!

Neither is there salvation in any other: for there is none other name under heaven given among men, whereby we must be saved. Acts 4:12

THE one and only way you can be converted is to believe on the Lord Jesus Christ as your own personal Lord and Savior. You don't have to straighten out your life first. You don't have to try to give up some habit that is keeping you from God. You have tried all that and failed many times. You can come "just as you are." The blind man came just as he was. The leper came just as he was. The thief on the cross came just as he was. You can come to Christ right now wherever you are and just as you are and the angels of heaven will rejoice!

Some of the greatest and most precious words recorded in all of Scripture were spoken by Satan himself (not that he intended it to be so). In his discussion with God about Job, he said, "Hast not thou made a hedge about him, and about his house, and about all that he hath on every side? Thou hast blessed the work of his hands and his substance is increased in the land" (Job 1:10).

As I look back over my life I remember the moment I came to Jesus Christ as Savior and Lord. The angels rejoiced! Since then I have been in thousands of battles with Satan and his demons. As I yielded my will and committed myself totally to Christ—as I prayed and believed—I am convinced that God "put a hedge about me," a hedge of angels to protect me.

The Scripture says there is a time to be born and a time to die. And when my time to die comes an angel will be there to comfort me. He will give me peace and joy even at that most critical hour, and usher me into the presence of God, and I will dwell with the Lord forever. Thank God for the ministry of His blessed angels!

July 21

THE FRUIT OF THE SPIRIT

And when they had prayed, the place was shaken where they were assembled together; and they were all filled with the Holy Ghost, and they spake the word of God with boldness. Acts 4:31

WHAT does it mean to be filled with the Spirit? It is not necessarily an emotional experience, nor will it necessarily bring us some type of spiritual experience that is obvious or open. *To be filled with the Spirit is to be controlled by the Spirit.* It is to be so yielded to Christ that our supreme desire is to do His will. When we come to Christ the Spirit comes to dwell within us—whether we are aware of His presence or not. But as we grow in Christ, our goal is to be controlled by the Spirit.

We should seek to produce the fruit of the Spirit in our lives.

You say, "I am powerless to produce such fruit. It would be utterly impossible for me to do so!"

With that I agree! That is, we can't produce this fruit in our own strength. Remember, the Bible says, "The fruit of the Spirit is love, joy, peace, long-suffering, gentleness, goodness, faith, meekness, temperance" (Galatians 5:22–23). When the Spirit of God dwells in us He will produce the fruit. It is ours only to cultivate the soil of our hearts through sincere devotion and yieldedness that He might find favorable ground to produce that which He will.

I might have a fruit tree in my yard; but if the soil isn't enriched and the bugs carefully destroyed, it will not yield a full crop.

As Christians, we have the Spirit of God in us. But ours is the responsibility to keep sin out of our lives so that the Spirit can produce His fruit in us.

July 22

THE PRIVILEGE OF PRAYER

[The disciples said,] . . . We will devote ourselves to prayer, and to the ministry of the word. Acts 6:4, RSV

WE must desire the will of God. Even our Lord, contrary to His own disposition at the moment, said, "O my Father, if this cup may not pass away from me, except I drink it, thy will be done" (Matthew 26:42).

Prayer couples us with God's true purposes for us and the world. It not only brings the blessings of God's will to our own personal life, but it brings us the added blessing of being in step with God's plan.

Remember, too, that our prayer must be for God's glory. The model prayer which Jesus has given us concludes with, "Thine is the kingdom, and the power, and the glory." If we are to have our prayers answered, we must give God the glory. Our Lord said to His disciples, "And whatsoever ye shall ask in my name, that will I do, that the Father may be glorified in the Son" (John 14:13).

What a privilege is ours: the privilege of prayer! Christian, examine your heart, reconsecrate your life, yield yourself to God unreservedly, for only those who pray through a clear heart will be heard of Him. The Bible says, "The effectual fervent prayer of a righteous man availeth much" (James 5:16).

We are to pray in times of adversity, lest we become faithless and unbelieving. We are to pray in times of prosperity, lest we become boastful and proud. We are to pray in times of danger, lest we become fearful and doubting. We need to pray in times of security, lest we become self-sufficient. Sinners, pray to a merciful God for forgiveness! Christians, pray for an outpouring of God's Spirit upon a willful, evil, unrepentant world. Parents, pray that God may crown your home with grace and mercy! Children, pray for the salvation of your parents!

Christian, saint of God, pray that the dew of heaven may fall on earth's dry, thirsty ground, and that righteousness may cover the earth as the waters cover the sea. Pray, believing, with this promise of our Savior in mind, "What things soever ye desire, when ye pray, believe that ye receive them, and ye shall have them" (Mark 11:24).

"Satan trembles when he sees the weakest saint upon his knees"—so pray, Christian, pray!

A DRAMATIC DELIVERY

And Peter came to himself, and said, "Now I am sure that the Lord has sent his angel and rescued me from the hand of Herod." Acts 12:11, RSV

THE SCRIPTURES are full of dramatic evidences of the protective care of angels in their earthly service to the people of God. Paul admonished Christians to put on all the armor of God that they may stand firmly in the face of evil (Ephesians 6:10–12). Our struggle is not against flesh and blood (physical powers alone), but against the spiritual (superhuman) forces of wickedness in heavenly spheres. Satan, the prince of the power of the air, promotes a "religion" but not true faith; he promotes false prophets. So the powers of light and darkness are locked in intense conflict. Thank God for the angelic forces that fight off the works of darkness. Angels never minister selfishly; they serve so that all glory may be given to God as believers are strengthened. A classic example of the protective agency of angels is found in Acts 12:5–11.

As the scene opened, Peter lay bound in prison awaiting execution. James, the brother of John, had already been killed, and there was little reason to suppose that Peter would escape the executioner's ax either. The magistrates intended to put him to death as a favor to those who opposed the Gospel and the works of God. Surely the believers had prayed for James, but God had chosen to deliver him through death. Now the church was praying for Peter.

As Peter lay sleeping an angel appeared, not deterred by such things as doors or iron bars. The angel came into the prison cell, shook Peter awake, and told him to prepare to escape. As a light shone in the prison, Peter's chains fell off, and having dressed, he followed the angel out. Doors supernaturally opened because Peter could not pass through locked doors as the angel had. What a mighty deliverance God achieved through His angel!

July 24

THE IMPACT OF CHRISTLIKE LIVING

The disciples were filled with joy, and with the Holy Ghost.
Acts 13:52

AT times people have said to me, "Christians are all hypocrites—I don't want anything to do with Christ!" But that is an excuse to keep from having to face the truth that is in Christ. Instead, understand His teaching and examine His life. And if you know Christ and have committed your life to Him, learn from Him and live a consistent life for Him. Do others see something of Christ—His love, His joy, His peace—in your life?

True Christians are supposed to be happy! Our generation has become well versed in Christian terminology, but is remiss in the actual practice of Christ's principles and teachings. Therefore, our greatest need today is not more Christianity but more true Christians.

The world may argue against Christianity as an institution, but there is no convincing argument against a person who through the Spirit of God has been made Christlike. Such a one is a living rebuke to the selfishness, rationalism, and materialism of the day. Too often we have debated with the world on the letter of the law when we should have been living oracles of God, seen and read of all people.

It is time that we retrace our steps to the source and realize afresh the transforming power of Jesus Christ.

Jesus said to the woman at Jacob's well, "Whosoever drinketh of the water that I shall give him shall never thirst"

(John 4:14). This sinsick, disillusioned woman was the symbol of the whole race. Her longings were our longings! Her heart-cry was our heart-cry! Her disillusionment was our disillusionment! Her sin was our sin! But her Savior can be our Savior! Her forgiveness can be our forgiveness! Her joy can be our joy!

July 25

JOY IN TRIBULATION

. . . Strengthening the souls of the disciples, exhorting them to continue in the faith, and saying that through many tribulations we must enter the kingdom of God. Acts 14:22, RSV

NOWHERE does the Bible teach that Christians are to be exempt from the tribulations and natural disasters that come upon the world. It does teach that the Christian can face tribulation, crisis, calamity, and personal suffering with a supernatural power not available to the person outside of Christ.

Thousands of Christians have learned the secret of contentment and joy in trial. Some of the happiest Christians I have met have drunk the full cup of trial and misfortune. Some have been lifelong sufferers. They have had every reason to sigh and complain, being denied so many privileges and pleasures that they see others enjoy, yet they have found greater cause for gratitude and joy than many who are prosperous, vigorous, and strong.

They have learned to give thanks "always and for everything . . . in the name of our Lord Jesus Christ to God the Father" (Ephesians 5:20, RSV).

Christians can rejoice in tribulation because they have eternity's values in view. When the pressures are on, they look beyond their present predicament to the glories of heaven. The thoughts of the future life with its prerogatives and joys help to make the trials of the present seem light and transient.

The early Christians were able to experience joy in their hearts in the midst of trials, troubles, and depression. They counted suffering for Christ not as a burden or misfortune but as a great honor, as evidence that Christ counted them worthy to witness for Him through suffering. They never forgot what Christ Himself had gone through for their salvation, and to suffer for His name's sake was regarded as a gift rather than a cross.

July 26

BELIEVING IS AN EXPERIENCE

Believe on the Lord Jesus Christ, and thou shalt be saved. . . .
Acts 16:31

BELIEVING is an experience as real as any experience, yet multitudes are looking for something more—some electric sensation that will bring a thrill to their physical bodies, or some other spectacular manifestation. Many have been told to look for such spiritual thrills, but the Bible says that "a man is justified by faith," and not by feeling. A man is saved by trusting in the finished work of Christ on the cross and not by bodily sensations and religious ecstasy.

But you will say to me, "What about feeling? Is there no place in saving faith for any feeling?" Certainly there is room for feeling in saving faith, but we are not saved by it. Whatever feelings there may be are the result of saving faith, but feeling never saved a single soul.

When I understand something of Christ's love for me as a sinner, I respond with a love for Christ, and love has feeling. But love for Christ is a love that is above the sensual accompaniments of human love. It is a love that is free from all self. The Bible says, "Perfect love casteth out fear" (1 John 4:18). And those who love Christ have a confidence in Him that raises them above all fear.

When I understand that Christ in His death gained a decisive victory over death and over sin, then I lose the fear of death. The Bible says, "Forasmuch then as the children are partakers of flesh and blood he also himself likewise took part of the same; that through death he might destroy him that had the power of death, that is, the devil" (Hebrews 2:14). Surely this is a feeling. Fear is a kind of feeling, and to overcome fear with boldness and confidence in the very face of death is feeling and experience. But again I say, it is not the feeling of boldness and confidence that saves us, but it is Christ who saves us, and boldness and confidence result from our having trusted in Him.

July 27

THE CHRISTIAN AND CONSCIENCE

And herein do I exercise myself, to have always a conscience void of offense toward God, and toward men.   Acts 24:16

ONE of the ways God has revealed Himself to us is in the conscience. Conscience has been described as the light of the soul. Even when it is dulled or darkened by sin, it can still bear witness to the reality of good and evil, and to the holiness of God. What causes this warning light to go on inside me when I do wrong?

Conscience can be our gentlest counselor and teacher, our most faithful friend, and sometimes our worst enemy when we sin. There are no punishments or rewards on this earth comparable to those of the conscience. The Scripture says, "Man's conscience is the lamp of the eternal" (Proverbs 20:27, MOFFATT). In other words, conscience is God's lamp within man's breast. In his *Critique of Pure Reason,* Immanuel Kant said there were just two things that filled him with awe—the starry heavens and conscience in the breast of man.

The conscience in its varying degrees of sensitivity bears a witness to God. Its very existence within us is a reflection of God in the soul of man. Without conscience we would be like rudderless ships at sea and like guided missiles without a guidance system.

George Bernard Shaw, the great Irish novelist, said, "Better keep yourself clean and bright; you are the window through which you must see the world." And Benjamin Franklin rhymed, "Keep conscience clear, then never fear." If conscience is so vital a concept to these worldly writers, how much more concerned should I as a Christian be that my conscience is "void of offense toward God, and . . . men"? And our consciences can be purified as we allow God's Word, the Bible, to clean and enlighten them.

July 28

THE FALSE AND THE TRUE

For they exchanged the truth . . . for a lie, and worshipped and served the creature rather than the Creator who is blessed forever. Amen. Romans 1:25, NASB

M Y major in college was anthropology, which the dictionary explains as a science dealing with the races, customs, and beliefs of mankind. I have also had the privilege of traveling extensively on every continent. I have found from personal experience that what I learned from anthropology is true: Man has naturally and universally a capacity for religion—and not only a capacity, for the vast majority of the human race practices or professes some form of religion.

Religion can be defined as having two magnetic poles, the

biblical and the naturalistic. The biblical pole is described in the teachings of the Bible. The naturalistic pole is explained in all the man-made religions. In humanistic systems there are always certain elements of truth. Many of these faiths have borrowed from Judeo-Christianity; many use portions and incorporate their own fables. Other religions or faiths have in fragments what Christianity has as a whole.

The apostle Paul described the naturalistic pole when he said that men "exchanged the glory of the incorruptible God for an image in the form of corruptible man and of birds and four-footed animals and crawling creatures" (Romans 1:23, NASB).

A false, naturalistic religion is like the imitation of high fashion. I've read that after an exclusive showing of original designs in one of the fashion centers of the world like Paris, copies will soon appear in the mass merchandising stores under different labels. The very presence of counterfeits proves the existence of the real. There would be no imitations without a genuine product. God's original design has always had imitators and counterfeits!

July 29

PEACE IS OUR PORTION

Therefore being justified by faith, we have peace with God through our Lord Jesus Christ. Romans 5:1

THERE is only one way of salvation, and that is God's way. God has outlined the road to heaven. He has made the rules simple and plain. He has given us the equation and the compass.

The way outlined in His immutable Book is to receive the Lord Jesus Christ as Savior. Jesus said he that climbs up some other way is a thief and a robber. It is the way of the Cross that leads home. It is the grace of God and only the grace of God that brings salvation.

Grace implies that we cannot work for salvation. We cannot make our own way to heaven. We can only come God's way and that is by receiving His unmerited favor in Christ Jesus.

On that memorable night two thousand years ago in Bethlehem, the angels hovered over the Judean hills and sang in unison, "Glory to God in the highest, and on earth peace, good will toward men" (Luke 2:14).

The centuries have rolled by, and still the world longs for and looks for the peace that the angels sang about on that first Christmas morning. "Where is His peace?" you ask.

I'll tell you where it is. It abides in the hearts of all who have trusted His grace. And in the same proportion that the world has trusted in Christ, it also has peace. I could say to the leaders of all governments today that there can be no peace until Christ has come to the hearts of men and brought His peace.

There is no discord, there is no strife in heaven, for Christ reigns supreme there. There is no conflict in the heart where Christ abides, for His words, "Peace I leave with you" (John 14:27), have been proven in the test tubes of human experience over and over again, in the lives of those who have trusted His grace.

July 30

THE HIGHEST JOY

By whom also we have access by faith into this grace wherein we stand, and rejoice in hope of the glory of God. Romans 5:2

WE are not surprised that the early Christians rejoiced in suffering, since they looked at it in the light of eternity. The nearer death, the nearer a life of eternal fellowship with Christ. When Ignatius was about to die for his faith in 110 A.D. he cried out, "Nearer the sword, then nearer to God. In company with wild beasts, in company with God."

The Christians of the early Church believed that "the sufferings of this present time are not worth comparing with the glory that is to be revealed to us" (Romans 8:18, RSV). Thus they could regard present difficulties as of little consequence and could endure them with patience and cheerfulness.

In all ages Christians have found it possible to maintain the spirit of joy in the hour of trial. In circumstances that would have felled most men, they have so completely risen above them that they actually have used the circumstances to serve and glorify Christ. Paul could write from prison at Rome, "I want you to know, brethren, that what has happened to me has really served to advance the gospel" (Philippians 1:12, RSV).

Charles Haddon Spurgeon shares this unique perspective on joy:

Confident hope breeds inward joy. The man who knows that his hope of glory will never fail him because of the great love of God, of which he has tasted, that man will hear music at midnight; the mountains and the hills will break forth before him into singing wherever he goes. Especially in times of tribulation he will be found "rejoicing in hope of the glory of God." His profoundest comfort will often be enjoyed in his deepest affliction, because then the love of God will specially be revealed in his heart by the Holy Ghost, whose name is "the Comforter." Then he will perceive that the rod is dipped in mercy, that his losses are sent in fatherly love, and that his aches and pains are all measured out with gracious design. In our affliction God is doing nothing to us which we should not wish for ourselves if we were as wise and loving as God is. O friends! you do not want gold to make you glad, you do not even need health to make you glad; only get to know and feel divine love, and the fountains of delight are unsealed to you— you are introduced to the highest joy!

July 31

POWER IN PRAYER

By whom [Christ] also we have access by faith into this grace wherein we stand. . . . Romans 5:2

For through him we both [Jew and Gentile] have access by one Spirit unto the Father. . . . Ephesians 2:18

THE Bible tells us to pray in Christ's name.

Jesus said, "And whatsoever ye shall ask in my name, that will I do, that the Father may be glorified in the Son" (John 14:13).

We are not worthy to approach the holy throne of God except through our Advocate, Jesus Christ.

The Bible says, "Seeing then that we have a great high priest, that is passed into the heavens, Jesus the Son of God . . . let us therefore come boldly unto the throne of grace" (Hebrews 4:14, 16).

God, for Christ's sake, forgives our sins. God, for Christ's sake, supplies our needs. God, for Christ's sake, receives our prayers. The person who comes with confidence to the throne of grace has seen that his approach to God has been made possible because of Jesus Christ.

The late Dr. Donald Grey Barnhouse reminds us:

I am not so sure that I believe in "the power of prayer," but I do believe in the power of the Lord who answers prayer. When the rules are met, then God pours out all blessings on those who come to Him in prayer. There is real power. There is comfort in time of need; strength in time of weakness; forgiveness when we have sinned; consolation in time of bereavement; joy in time of sorrow.

When one has accepted God's terms of approach through the redemption that is provided by Christ, there is immediate access to Him, and all the promises of God become certified to us.

Am I praying as if this were true?

August

August 1

GOD'S GYROSCOPE

The love of God is shed abroad in our hearts by the Holy Ghost which is given unto us.   Romans 5:5

YEARS ago when I traveled to Europe to preach I liked to travel by sea, to enjoy the five days on the ship. On one of my voyages Captain Anderson of the United States took me down to see the ship's gyroscope. He said, "When the sea is rough, the gyroscope helps to keep the ship on an even keel. Though the waves may reach tremendous proportions, the gyroscope helps to stabilize the vessel and maintain a high degree of equilibrium." As I listened, I thought how like the gyroscope is the Holy Spirit. Let the storms of life break over our heads. Let the enemy Satan come in like a flood. Let the waves of sorrow, suffering, temptation, and testing be unleashed upon us. Our souls will be kept on an even keel and in perfect peace when the Holy Spirit dwells in our hearts.

Talking about the secret of Spirit-filled living, the great evangelist D. L. Moody said, "I believe firmly that the moment our hearts are emptied of pride and selfishness and ambition and everything that is contrary to God's law, the Holy Spirit will fill every corner of our hearts. But if we are full of pride and conceit and ambition and the world, there is no room for the Spirit of God."

Is your life on course or off? If it is off course, perhaps you need the equilibrium of God's gyroscope—His Holy Spirit. Seek Him and His will for you today.

GOD IS NOT BLIND

God commendeth his love toward us, in that, while we were yet sinners,
Christ died for us.   Romans 5:8

OURS is the God of law who, loving the earth's people, and realizing that we had offended in every point, sent His only Son to redeem us to Himself and to instill the law of the Spirit of life within us. His eyes of compassion have been following man as he has stumbled through history under the burden of his own wretchedness.

Yet Calvary should prove even to the most skeptical that God is not blind to man's plight, but that He was willing to suffer with him. The word *compassion* comes from two Latin words meaning "to suffer with." God's all-consuming love for mankind was best demonstrated at the cross, where His compassion was embodied in Jesus Christ. "God was in Christ, reconciling the world unto himself" (2 Corinthians 5:19).

Never question God's great love. Jeremiah the prophet wrote, "The LORD hath appeared of old unto me, saying, Yea, I have loved thee with an everlasting love: therefore with loving-kindness have I drawn thee" (Jeremiah 31:3).

Paul speaks of God as one "who is rich in mercy, for his great love wherewith he loved us" (Ephesians 2:4). It was the love of God that sent Jesus Christ to the cross.

Young people talk about love. Most of their songs are about love. "The supreme happiness of life," Victor Hugo said long ago, "is the conviction that we are loved." "Love is the first requirement for mental health," declared Sigmund Freud. The Bible teaches that "God is love" and that God loves you. To realize that is of paramount importance.

Nothing else matters so much. And loving you, God has wonderful plans for your life. Who else could plan and guide your life so well?

August 3

THE WAY BACK TO GOD

Greater love hath no man than this, that a man lay down his life for his friends. John 15:13

GOD is love. Many people have misunderstood that part of God's nature. The fact that God is love does not mean that everything is sweet, beautiful, and happy and that God's love could not possibly allow punishment for sin.

God's holiness demands that all sin be punished, but God's love provided a plan of redemption and salvation for sinful man. God's love provided the Cross of Jesus Christ by which man can have forgiveness and cleansing. It was the love of God that sent Jesus Christ to the cross.

Who can describe or measure the love of God? Our Bible is a revelation of the fact that God is love. When we preach justice, it is justice tempered with love. When we preach righteousness, it is righteousness founded on love. When we preach atonement, it is atonement necessitated because of love, provided by love, finished by love.

When we preach the resurrection of Christ, we are preaching the miracle of love. When we preach the return of Christ, we are preaching the fulfillment of love.

No matter what sin we have committed, no matter how black, dirty, shameful, or terrible it may be, God loves us. We may be at the very gate of hell itself, but God loves us with an everlasting love.

Were it not for the love of God, none of us would ever have a chance in the future life. But thanks be unto God, He is love! Because He is a holy God, our sins have separated us from Him, but because of His love there is a way of salvation, a way back to God through Jesus Christ, His Son.

August 4

GOD'S SAFETY ZONE

Since we have now been justified by his blood, how much more shall we be saved from God's wrath through him! Romans 5:9, NIV

AN old preacher in England, who had lived on the American prairies in his youth, was involved in street corner evangelism in the small towns and villages. He attracted an audience with his wild-West stories describing how the Indians had saved their wigwams from prairie fires by setting fire to the dry grass adjoining their settlement. "The fire cannot come," he explained, "where the fire has already been. That is why I call you to the Cross of Christ."

He continued his graphic analogy by explaining, "Judgment has already fallen and can never come again!" The one who takes his stand at the Cross is saved forevermore. He can never come into condemnation, for he is standing where the fire has been. The saved person is in God's safety zone, cleansed by the blood of Christ.

August 5

THE SACRED SUMMIT

Knowing this, that our old man is crucified with him, that the body of sin might be destroyed, that henceforth we should not serve sin. Romans 6:6

CALVARY is the summit of love. "The law was given by Moses, but grace and truth came by Jesus Christ" (John 1:17).

"God commendeth his love toward us, in that, while we were yet sinners, Christ died for us" (Romans 5:8). The Scripture says that we are sinners. We have broken those Ten Commandments. We are under the sentence of death and deserve judgment. We deserve hell. The Cross, where Christ died in our place and where we can find forgiveness, is the only place to find forgiveness and have eternal life.

Jesus Christ was crucified between two thieves on a rugged cross on Calvary. Jesus gave His head to the crown of thorns for us. He gave His face to the human spittle for us. He gave His cheeks and His beard to be plucked off for us. He gave His back to the lash for us. He gave His side to the spear for us. He gave His hands and feet to the spikes for us. He gave His blood for us. Jesus Christ, dying in our place, taking our sins on that cross, is love.

But that's not the end of the story. He rose again, and He is the living Christ. Christ is alive. If Christ be not alive, there is no hope for any of us. But He is alive! And the Scripture says, "If thou shalt confess with thy mouth the Lord Jesus, and shalt believe in thine heart that God hath raised him from the dead, thou shalt be saved" (Romans 10:9).

So what does this mean to me? It means that because Christ lives, I live also if I am in Him and He is in me. And the life that I now live in the flesh I live by faith in the Son of God who loved me and gave Himself for me (see Galatians 2:20).

August 6

DEATH DEFEATED

Knowing that Christ being raised from the dead dieth no more; death hath no more dominion over him. Romans 6:9

WHEN my wife and I were students in college, we used to

take long walks into the country. Nearby was an old graveyard where we would go to read the epitaphs on the tombstones. Ever since then, I have liked to go to old cemeteries in various parts of the world. When we wander through a graveyard and look at the tombstones or go into a church and examine the old monuments, we see one heading on most of them: "Here lies." Then follows the name, with the date of death and perhaps some praise of the good qualities of the deceased. But how different is the epitaph on the tomb of Jesus! It is neither written in gold nor cut in stone. It is spoken by the mouth of an angel and is the exact reverse of what is put on all other tombs: "He is not here: for he is risen, as he said" (Matthew 28:6).

At the end of his great book *Fathers and Sons*, Ivan Turgenev describes a village graveyard in one of the remote corners of Russia. Among the many neglected graves was one untouched by man, untrampled by beast. Only the birds rested upon it and sang at daybreak. Often from the nearby village two feeble old people, husband and wife, moving with heavy steps and supporting one another, came to visit this grave. Kneeling down at the railing and gazing intently at the stone under which their son was lying, they yearned and wept. After a brief word they wiped the dust away from the stone, set straight a branch of a fir tree, and then began to pray. In this spot they seemed to be nearer their son and their memories of him. And then Turgenev asks, "Can it be that their prayers, their tears, are fruitless? Can it be that love, sacred, devoted love, is not all powerful? Oh no, however passionate, sinning, and rebellious the heart hidden in the tomb, the flowers growing over it peep serenely at us with their innocent eyes. They tell us not of eternal peace alone, of that great peace of indifferent nature; they tell us, too, of eternal reconciliation and of life without end."

Turgenev was offering hope of an eternal reconciliation.

But upon what is that hope based? It is based upon the resurrection of Jesus Christ.

DEATH HAS NO POWER

Death has no power over him any more. Romans 6:9, JB

CHRIST died for our sins, and by His death He destroyed death. In Christ, we no longer regard death as the king of terrors. Paul wrote, "I desire to depart and be with Christ, which is better by far" (Philippians 1:23, NIV). Why? Was it because he worked so hard for Christ and had suffered so much? No! He was ready because half a lifetime earlier he had met Christ on the Damascus road. In 1 John 3:14 we read that we have already "passed from death to life." You can have eternal life now. The conquest of death is the ultimate goal of Christianity. Physical death is a mere transition from life on earth with Christ to eternal life in heaven with Christ. For Christians there is such a thing as the shadow of death. Death casts a shadow over those who are left behind.

Dr. Donald Grey Barnhouse was a prince among American Presbyterian clergymen. I knew him well. He died a few years ago. His first wife had died from cancer while still in her thirties. At the time, all three of his children were under twelve. He had such victory that he decided to preach the funeral sermon himself.

En route to the funeral they were overtaken by a large truck which, as it passed them, cast a large shadow over their car. He asked one of his children, "Would you rather be run over by that truck or its shadow?"

"By the shadow, of course!" replied the twelve-year-old daughter. "A shadow can't hurt you."

With that answer, Dr. Barnhouse said to his three

256 *Unto the Hills*

motherless little children, "Your mother has been overrun not by death, but by the shadow of death." At the funeral he spoke on Psalm 23: "Though I walk through the valley of the shadow of death, I will fear no evil, for You are with me" (verse 4, NKJV).

Nothing can harm us, including death, when we have trusted Christ as Savior because Christ has conquered death—so shall we.

August 8

DIVINE DISCIPLINE

Neither yield ye your members as instruments of unrighteousness unto sin: but yield yourselves unto God, as those that are alive from the dead, and your members as instruments of righteousness unto God. Romans 6:13

PAUL, who was a splendid example of a disciplined Christian, said, "I beseech you therefore, brethren, by the mercies of God, that ye present your bodies a living sacrifice, holy, acceptable unto God, which is your reasonable service" (Romans 12:1). Since our bodies are to be the temples of the Holy Spirit, they must be worthy of Him who indwells us. This exhortation calls for us to discipline our bodies as well as our minds. We must pray as Jeremy Taylor once prayed, "Let my body be a servant of my spirit, and both body and spirit servants of Jesus."

When you serve sin, your body is dedicated to the service of sin. Your appetites, whetted by Satan, rage unthrottled. Your God-given creative impulses are sacrificed to Satan on the altar of lust. A sinner, in a sense, is a dedicated person, yielded to his appetites and selfish desires. But when Christ comes into the human heart we are to yield our bodies to Him. Our human frame is often a rebellious and unruly servant. Only through rigid discipline are we able to master it into complete subjection to Christ. We must guard against appetites which blight the conscience, wither the soul, and weaken our witness for Christ.

Perhaps many things are lawful, but are they expedient? They may bring pleasure to us, but do they bring glory to Christ? Paul was so desirous of making every thought and act glorify Christ that He said, "If an indulgence offend my brother, I will not indulge anymore." He had given his body as a living sacrifice to Christ. We need that kind of self-discipline today.

Alexander MacLaren, the forceful Baptist preacher and writer who died in 1910, put this whole matter of self-sacrifice in clear perspective when he wrote, "All along the Christian course, there must be set up altars to God on which you sacrifice yourself, or you will never advance a step."

August 9
....

THE SECRET IS SURRENDER

Know ye not, that to whom ye yield yourselves servants to obey, his servants ye are to whom ye obey; whether of sin unto death, or of obedience unto righteousness? Romans 6:16

OF Eric Liddell, the missionary and great runner whose story is told in the film *Chariots of Fire*, someone has said, he was ". . . ridiculously humble in victory, utterly generous in defeat." That's a good definition of what it means to be meek. Meekness involves being yielded.

The word "yield" has two meanings. The first is negative, and the second is positive. It means "to relinquish, to abandon"; and also "to give." This is in line with Jesus' words: "He that loseth [or abandoneth] his life . . . shall find it" (Matthew 10:39). What a description of Eric Liddell!

We have heard the modern expression, "Don't fight it—it's bigger than both of us." Those who submit to the will of God do not fight back at life. They learn the secret of surrender, of yielding to God. He then fights for us!

The Bible says, "For as ye have yielded your members servants to uncleanness and to iniquity . . . even so now yield your members servants to righteousness unto holiness" (Romans 6:19).

Instead of filling your mind with resentments, abusing your body by sinful diversion, and damaging your soul by willfulness, humbly give all over to God. Your conflicts will diminish, and your inner tensions will often vanish.

Then your life will begin to count for something. It will begin to yield, to produce, to bear fruit. You will have the feeling of belonging to life. Boredom will melt away, and you will become vibrant with hope and expectation. Because you are meekly yielded, you will begin to "inherit the earth" of good things which God holds in store for those who trust Him with their all.

August 10

THE SICKNESS OF SIN

For the wages of sin is death; but the gift of God is eternal life through Jesus Christ our Lord. Romans 6:23

THE changing of men is a primary mission of the church. The only way to change men is to get them converted to Jesus Christ. Then they will have the capacity to live up to the Christian command to "love thy neighbor" (Matthew 22:39).

There is no doubt that today we see social injustice everywhere. However, looking on our American scene Jesus would see something even deeper.

If only we would begin at the root of our problems, which

is the disease of human nature that the Bible calls sin! This is why Christ came and died on the cross, this is why He shed His blood—to do something about this disease that mankind is suffering from.

We in the church today are in danger of becoming blundering social physicians, giving medicine here and putting ointment there on the sores of the world. But the sores break out again somewhere else. The great need is for the church to call in the Great Physician, who alone can properly diagnose the case. He will look beneath the mere skin eruptions and pronounce the cause of it all: "Sin!"

If we in the church want a cause to fight, let's fight sin. Let's reveal its hideousness. Let's show that Jeremiah was correct when he said, "The heart is deceitful above all things, and desperately wicked" (Jeremiah 17:9). Then when the center of man's trouble is dealt with, we can say with D. L. Moody, "Looking at the wound of sin will never save anyone. What you must do is look at the remedy."

August 11

THE SECRET OF SUBMISSION

I do not understand my own actions. For I do not do what I want, but I do the very thing I hate. Romans 7:15, RSV

PAUL himself spoke of his struggle. He spoke of desiring to please God, but in himself he found no strength to do so. The things he did not want to do he sometimes did; and the things he wanted to do he did not do.

Many of us ask these questions: "Why do I, as a Christian, do some of the things I do? Why do I, as a Christian, leave undone the things I ought to have done?"

Many name the name of Christ but do not dwell in Him. They have unclean hands, unclean lips, unclean tongues, unclean feet, unclean thoughts, unclean hearts—and yet claim to be Christians. They claim Christ, attend church, try to pray—and yet they know there are things in their souls that are not right. There is no joy in their hearts, no love for others. In fact, there is little evidence of the fruit of the Spirit in their lives. The fire in their souls has been quenched.

Yet as we look around, we do know some people who are living different lives. They bear the fruit of the Spirit. But some get only snatches of victory. Once in a while they will have a day that seems to be a victorious day over temptation, but then they slide right back into the same old rut of living, and hunger and long for the righteousness of daily growth.

Self-analysis can lead to depression. We need to keep our attention focused on Christ.

August 12

OF FEAR AND FAITH

For you did not receive a spirit that makes you a slave again to fear, but you received the Spirit of sonship. And by him we cry, "Abba, Father."
Romans 8:15, NIV

WHEN I understand something of Christ's love for me as a sinner, I respond with a love for Christ—and love has feeling. But love for Christ is a love that is above human love, though there is a similarity. There is also feeling. But feelings come and go. Commitment stays. We who have committed ourselves to Christ have feelings that come and go—joy, love, gratitude, and so on. But the commitment remains unchanged. Feelings are important, but not essential. The Bible says, "Perfect love casteth out fear" (1 John 4:18). And those who love Christ have that confidence in Him that raises them above fear. Psychologists tell us there is destructive fear and healthy fear. Healthy fear is *instructive*, causing us to care for our bodies and our loved ones—Jesus told us to fear Satan.

When I understand that Christ in His death gained a decisive victory over death and over sin, then I lose the fear of death. The Bible says that "He also himself likewise took part of the same; that through death he might destroy him that had the power of death, that is, the devil; And deliver them who through fear of death were all their lifetime subject to bondage" (Hebrews 2:14–15). It is not the feeling of boldness and confidence that saves us, but it is our faith that saves us, and boldness and confidence result from our having trusted in Christ. The Bible says that we are to fear the Lord. This is reverential fear. It is this kind of fear of the Lord that puts all other fears in proper perspective.

Old John Witherspoon, the only cleric to sign the Declaration of Independence, had this to say on the subject: "It is only the fear of God that can deliver us from the fear of man."

August 13

CHILDREN OF GOD

The Spirit itself beareth witness with our spirit, that we are the children of God. Romans 8:16

W E have three great enemies: sin, Satan, and death. Because Christ rose from the dead, we know that sin and death and Satan have been decisively defeated. And because Christ rose from the dead, we know there is life after death, and that if we belong to Him we need not fear death or hell. Jesus said, "I am the resurrection and the life. He who believes in me will live, even though he dies; and whoever lives and believes in me will never die" (John 11:25–26, NIV). He also promised, "In my Father's house are many rooms; if it were not so, I would have told you. I am going there to prepare a place for you. And if I go and prepare a place for you, I will come back and take you to be with me that you also may be where I am" (John 14:2–3, NIV). We know these words are true, because Jesus died on the cross and rose again from the dead. What a glorious hope we have because of Jesus' resurrection!

> No eye has seen,
>   no ear has heard,
> no mind has conceived
>   what God has prepared for those
>   who love him.
>
> 1 Corinthians 2:9, NIV

Our confidence in the future is based firmly on the fact of what God has done for us in Christ. No matter what our situation may be, we need never despair because Christ is alive. "Now if we died with Christ, we believe that we will also live with him. . . . For the wages of sin is death, but the gift of God is eternal life in Christ Jesus our Lord" (Romans 6:8, 23, NIV).

August 14

TEACHING BY TRIALS

I consider that our present sufferings are not worth comparing with the glory that will be revealed in us. Romans 8:18, NIV

AFFLICTION can be a means of refining and of purification. Many a life has come forth from the furnace of affliction more beautiful and more useful. We might never have had the songs of Fanny Crosby had she not been afflicted with blindness. George Matheson would never have given the world his immortal song, "O Love That Will Not Let Me Go," had it not been for his passing through the furnace of affliction. The "Hallelujah Chorus" was written by Handel when he was poverty-stricken and suffering from a paralyzed right side and right arm.

Job, who was called upon to suffer as few men have suffered, said, "But he knoweth the way that I take: when he hath tried me, I shall come forth as gold" (Job 23:10).

Affliction may also be for our strengthening and Christian development.

The other day a doctor told me that the man who had fought disease all of his life would be better able to resist it than the man who had never been sick a day in his life. "It's the fellows who have never been sick who die in a hurry," he said.

David said, "Before I was afflicted I went astray: but now have I kept thy word" (Psalm 119:67). We learn through the trials we are called upon to bear.

August 15

EARNEST PRAYER

For we know not what we should pray for as we ought: but the Spirit itself maketh intercession for us with groanings which cannot be uttered. Romans 8:26

THIS kind of prayer can span oceans, cross burning deserts, leap over mountains, and penetrate jungles to carry the healing, helping power of the Gospel to the objects of our prayer.

This kind of mourning, this quality of concern, is produced by the presence of God's Spirit in our lives. That "the Spirit itself maketh intercession" indicates that it is actually God pleading, praying, and mourning through us.

Thus we become co-laborers with God, actual partners with Him: our lives are lifted from the low plane of selfishness to the high plane of creativeness with God.

John Knox spent much time in prayer, and the Church in Scotland expanded into new life. John Wesley prayed long and often, and the Methodist movement was born. Martin Luther prayed earnestly, and the Reformation was under way.

God desires that we Christians be concerned and burdened for a lost world. If we pray this kind of prayer, an era of peace may come to the world and hordes of wickedness may be turned back. "As soon as Zion travailed, she brought forth her children" (Isaiah 66:8).

How much do you pray? If someone were to examine your prayer life, would he find that you are more excited about watching football or visiting a friend than talking to God?

August 16

THE JOYOUS CHRISTIAN'S SECRET

We know that in everything God works for good with those who love him, who are called according to his purpose. Romans 8:28, RSV

THE sick room can become a "spiritual gymnasium" where one's soul is exercised and developed. Sickness is one of the "all things" which work together for good to those who love God. Don't resent it. Don't be embittered by it. You who are lying on hospital beds realize today that it is the love-stroke of a loving heavenly Father who loves you so much He will not pamper you but will bring all things for your ultimate good.

Christ is the answer to sadness and discouragement.

This is a world of thwarted hopes, broken dreams, and frustrated desires. G. K. Chesterton said, "Everywhere there is speed, noise, and confusion, but nowhere deep happiness and quiet hearts."

But Christ can take the discouragement and despondency out of our lives. He can put a spring in one's step and give one a thrill in his heart and a purpose in his mind. Optimism and cheerfulness are products of knowing Christ.

The Bible says, "A merry heart doeth good like a medicine; but a broken spirit drieth the bones" (Proverbs 17:22).

If my heart has been attuned to my God through faith in Christ, then its overflow will be joyous optimism and good cheer.

The joy of the Lord is my strength! Do you feel God's joy? It only comes when we spend time with Him.

August 17

SEE BEYOND THE MYSTERIES

O the depth of the riches both of the wisdom and knowledge of God! How unsearchable are his judgments, and his ways past finding out! Romans 11:33

AS we look at the world in which we live, there are many confusions, bewilderments, and mysteries that seemingly have no solution. Man, however, has always been bewildered and confused by things which are beyond his understanding.

Primitive man, like modern man, probed the universe for its secrets and looked up at the night sky in awe and wonder at the mystery of the black space with its myriads of inexplicable lights.

It was the mystery of gravitation which challenged Sir Isaac Newton in 1685 to explore the reasons why objects heavier than air were attracted to the center of the earth.

It was the mystery of lightning that prompted Benjamin Franklin to attach a key to the tail of a kite during a thunderstorm, to prove the identity of lightning and electricity.

It was the mystery of the latent power of the atom which challenged Einstein, Fermi, and others to probe into the dormant energy in matter. Atomic energy is now a household word.

Some of the mysteries of the past have been fathomed by science. Others still puzzle mankind. This fact remains: All of the garnered wisdom of the ages is only a scratch on the surface of man's search for the knowledge of the universe.

For the most part, God retains His secrets, and man, standing on his intellectual tiptoes, can comprehend only a small fraction of the Lord's doings.

This inability fully to comprehend the mysteries of God does not in any way curtail the Christian faith. On the contrary, it enhances our belief. We do not understand the intricate pattern of the stars in their courses, but we know that He who created them does, and that just as surely as He guides them, He is charting a safe course for us.

August 18

A LIVING SACRIFICE

. . . Present your bodies a living sacrifice . . . your reasonable service. And be not conformed to this world. Romans 12:1–2

WE Christians are not to be conformed to the world physically. These bodies of ours are intended to be temples of the Spirit of God. We are not to prostrate them before the temples of Baal. We are to present them wholly to God as a "living sacrifice." Our dress, our posture, our actions, should all be for the honor and glory of Christ. We are to be "holy" in the deepest sense of the word.

God's purpose for us is that we ought to be conformed to the image of His Son. The world may exert its pressure to deform us, but we are told, "Be ye transformed . . . that ye may prove what is that good, and acceptable, and perfect will of God" (Romans 12:2).

On the cover of your Bible and mine appear the words, "Holy Bible." Do you know why the Bible is called holy? Why should it be called holy when so much lust and hate and greed and war are found in it? I can tell you why. It is because the Bible tells the truth. It tells the truth about God, about man, and about the devil. The Bible teaches that we exchange the truth of God for the devil's lie about sex, for example, and drugs, and alcohol, and religious hypocrisy.

Jesus Christ is the ultimate truth. Furthermore, He told the truth. Jesus said that He was the truth, and the truth would make us free. It is in this freedom that we are to ". . . present our bodies a living sacrifice. . . ."

August 19

BECOMING A DISCIPLE

So no one can become my disciple unless he first sits down and counts his blessings—and then renounces them all for me. Luke 14:33, TLB

DO you know what it means to be a disciple? A disciple is, literally, a scholar, a learner, especially one who believes in the doctrine of his teacher and follows him. A disciple acknowledges there is one who knows more than he does. A disciple is a person who realizes he needs to learn more than he knows now—and the more he learns the more he realizes he needs to learn.

A disciple must spend time with his teacher in order to gain wisdom, knowledge, and understanding. He knows he cannot get it by osmosis or any other way. It would be like trying to graduate from college without ever attending classes. It is impossible to do. One must interact with one's professors, asking questions, receiving answers, and studying the assigned material.

All of us who belong to Christ are (or ought to be) His disciples. Unlike the original disciples, we cannot physically spend time with Jesus. But we can hear Him speak and learn from Him just the same by reading what He said when He was here, by speaking to Him through prayer, and by determining to be obedient to His teachings. This is the ultimate proof that one is a disciple: if he follows the commands of his teacher.

Jesus said that he who keeps God's commandments is the one who truly loves God. Are you a disciple of the Lord Jesus?

August 20

THE FAMILY OF FAITH

Clothe yourself with the Lord Jesus Christ, and do not think about how to gratify the desires of the sinful nature. Romans 13:14, NIV

CHRIST must be vitally real to us if we are to remain faithful to Him in the hour of crisis. And who knows how near that hour may be? The wheels of God's judgment can be heard by discerning people in the assembly of the United Nations, in the conferences of political leaders, in the offices of the editors of great newspapers or television networks around the world—and among the people throughout the nations. Things are happening fast! The need for a turning to God has never been more urgent.

The words of Isaiah, whom God used to confound an ancient godless aggressor, are appropriate for us today: "Seek the LORD while he may be found; call on him while he is near. Let the wicked forsake his way and the evil man his thoughts. Let him turn to the LORD, and he will have mercy on him, and to our God, for he will freely pardon" (55:6–7, NIV).

In his encounter with Goliath, David proved that outward armor is not nearly so important as the man within the armor. Unless men of purpose, integrity, and faith stand together in unswerving loyalty to Jesus Christ, the future of the world is dark indeed.

To prepare ourselves for the suffering and persecution which seems so inevitable, we need also to foster and strengthen the small group movement, the concept of "Christian cells." One obvious area where this process should take place is in the family. In the United States today, as well as in other parts of the world, we are witnessing the breakdown and erosion of the family unit. Divorce is rampant, and "living together" without the formality of a wedding ceremony is increasingly common. It is only the strong Christian family unit that can survive the coming world holocaust. And only as Jesus Christ is vitally real to us as family members can we build strong families!

August 21

IS IT WRONG TO ASK WHY?

For none of us liveth to himself, and no man dieth to himself. For whether we live, we live unto the Lord; and whether we die, we die unto the Lord: whether we live therefore, or die, we are the Lord's. Romans 14:7–8

MOST of us know what it means to be stunned by the sudden passing of a dedicated friend, a godly pastor, a devout missionary, or a saintly mother. We have stood at the open grave with hot tears running down our cheeks and have asked in utter bewilderment, "Why, O God, why?"

The death of the righteous is no accident. Do you think that the God whose watchful vigil notes the sparrow's fall and who knows the number of hairs on our heads would turn His back on one of His children in the hour of peril? With Him there are no accidents, no tragedies, and no catastrophes as far as His children are concerned.

Paul, who lived most of his Christian life on the brink of death, expressed triumphant certainty about life. He testified, "To me, to live is Christ and to die is gain" (Philippians 1:21, NIV). His strong, unshakable faith took trouble, persecution, pain, thwarted plans, and broken dreams in stride.

He never bristled in questioning cynicism and asked, "Why, Lord?" He knew beyond the shadow of a doubt that his life was being fashioned into the image and likeness of his Savior; and despite the discomfort, he never flinched in the process.

It was Sir Walter Scott who asked, "Is death the last sleep? No, it is the final awakening."

August 22

A BEACON OF HOPE

That we through patience and comfort of the scriptures might have hope . . . the God of hope fill you with all joy and peace in believing, that ye may abound in hope, through the power of the Holy Ghost.
Romans 15:4, 13

WHEN I referred to the future that God is planning, a student at the University of Hawaii asked me, "Isn't this a form of escapism?" I said, "In a sense, yes; and before the devil gets through with this world, we are all going to be looking for the exit signs."

C. S. Lewis, in his remarkable little book *Christian Behavior,* said, "Hope is one of the theological virtues. This means that a continual looking forward to the eternal world is not, as some modern people think, a form of escapism or wishful thinking, but one of the things a Christian is meant to do. It does not mean that we are to leave the present world as it is. If you read history, you will find that the Christians who did most for the present world were just those who thought most of the next. It is since Christians have largely ceased to think of the other world that they have become so ineffective in this. Aim at heaven and you will get earth thrown in. Aim at earth and you will get neither."

In the midst of the pessimism, gloom, and frustration of this present hour, there is one bright beacon light of hope, and that is the promise of Jesus Christ: "If I go and prepare a place for you, I will come again" (John 14:3).

During the years of the Second World War, the words of General Douglas MacArthur echoed in the ears of the people of the Philippine Islands while they were under enemy occupation. He had promised, "I shall return," and he kept the promise. Jesus Christ has also promised, "I shall return," and He will keep that promise.

August 23

JOY IN BELIEVING

May God, the source of hope, fill you with all joy and peace by means of your faith in him, so that your hope will continue to grow by the power of the Holy Spirit. Romans 15:13, TEV

JESUS said, "Let not your heart be troubled . . . believe . . . in me" (John 14:1). When faith is strong, troubles become trifles.

There can be comfort in sorrow because *in the midst of mourning God gives a song.* God says in Job 30:9, "I am their song." In Job 35:10 Elihu asks, "Where is God my maker, who giveth songs in the night?" His presence in our lives changes our mourning into song, and that song is a song of comfort. Sometimes it must be night to have that song!

This kind of comfort is the kind which enabled a devout Englishman during World War II to look at a deep, dark hole in the ground where his home stood before the bombing and say, "I always did want a basement, I did. Now I can jolly well build another house like I always wanted."

This kind of comfort is the kind which enabled a young minister's wife in a church near us to teach her Sunday school class of girls on the very day of her husband's funeral. Her mourning was not the kind which had no hope—it was a mourning of faith in the goodness and wisdom of God; it believed that our heavenly Father makes no mistakes.

I often think of the two shortest verses in the Bible in this connection. "Jesus wept" is the shorter of the two. But in the original Greek I understand this "shortest" verse has three words whereas the verse from 1 Thessalonians 5:16 ("Rejoice evermore") has only two. However, it is easy to see the lovely connection between the two verses. The Christian's joy flows from the sympathy and grace of his Savior. Jesus wept—we rejoice evermore.

August 24

A GOAL FOR GOODNESS

I myself am convinced, my brothers, that you yourselves are full of goodness, complete in knowledge and competent to instruct one another. Romans 15:14, NIV

THOREAU wrote, "If a man does not keep pace with his companions, perhaps it is because he hears a different drummer. Let him step to the music which he hears, however measured or far away." As Christians we have no alternative but to march to the drumbeat of the Holy Spirit, following the measured steps of goodness, which pleases God.

We can do good deeds, and by practicing principles of goodness can witness to those around us that we have something "different" in our lives—perhaps something they themselves would like to possess. We may even be able to show others how to practice the principles of goodness in their own lives. But the Bible says, "Your goodness is as a morning cloud, and as the early dew it goeth away" (Hosea 6:4). True goodness is a "fruit of the Spirit," and our efforts to achieve it in our own strength alone can never succeed.

We should be careful that any goodness the world may see in us is the genuine fruit of the Spirit and not a counterfeit substitute, lest we unwittingly lead someone astray.

The immortal John Wesley gave us a goal for goodness that puts all this in perspective for me:

> Do all the good you can,
> By all the means you can,
> In all the ways you can,
> In all the places you can,
> At all the times you can,
> To all the people you can,
> As long as ever you can.

August 25

DIFFERENT IS NOT ENOUGH

Moreover it is required in stewards, that a man be found faithful.
1 Corinthians 4:2

WE Christians should stand out like a sparkling diamond against a rough and dark background. We should be more wholesome than anyone else. We should be poised, cultured, courteous, gracious, but firm in the things we do or do not do. We should laugh and be radiant; but we should refuse to allow the world to pull us down to its level.

The greatest need today in Christendom is a revival within the church of dedicated, separated, disciplined living. The people in our country's military academies are living separated, dedicated, and disciplined lives in order to be officers in the armed forces. They are being trained for future leadership and service. Certainly we Christians can do no less in order to serve in the army of Jesus Christ.

The Bible says, "I beseech you therefore, brethren, by the mercies of God, that ye present your bodies a living sacrifice, holy, acceptable unto God, which is your reasonable service. And be not conformed to this world: but be ye transformed by the renewing of your mind, that ye may prove what is that good, and acceptable, and perfect, will of God" (Romans 12:1–2).

Christ meant that His followers are to be different. But merely being different is not enough. We are to be the cleanest, the most holy, the kindest, the most unselfish, the friendliest, the most courteous, the most industrious, the most thoughtful, the truest, and the most loving people on earth. Dr. Albert Schweitzer, the great missionary doctor and statesman, told Christians why we're here: "To be glad instruments of God's love in this imperfect world is the service to which man is called." We're called to serve.

In your life is there a time and place for serving God?

August 26

PAUL KNEW FOR SURE

For we know in part and we prophesy in part, but when perfection comes, the imperfect disappears. 1 Corinthians 13:9–10, NIV

THINGS didn't always work out according to his own plans and ideas, but Paul did not murmur or question. His assurance was this: "We know that in all things God works for the good of those who love him, who have been called according to his purpose" (Romans 8:28, NIV).

When his tired, bruised body began to weaken under the

load, he said in triumph, "We know that if the earthly tent [our bodies] we live in is destroyed, we have a building from God, an eternal house in heaven, not built by human hands" (2 Corinthians 5:1, NIV).

The world called him foolish for his belief that men could become partakers of eternal life through faith. But he realized exultantly, "I know whom I have believed, and am convinced that he is able to guard what I have entrusted to him for that day" (2 Timothy 1:12, NIV).

Every one of these triumphant affirmations rings with the note of hope and the assurance of life immortal. Though the Christian has no immunity from death and no claim to perpetual life on this planet, death is to him a friend rather than a foe, the beginning rather than the end, another step on the pathway to heaven rather than a leap into a dark unknown.

For many people, the corrosive acids of materialistic science have eroded away their faith in everlasting life. But let's face it—Einstein's equation $E = MC^2$ is no satisfactory substitute for Faith + Commitment = Hope.

Paul believed in Christ and committed his all to Christ. The result was that he knew Christ was able to keep him forever. Strong faith and living hope are the result of unconditional commitment to Jesus Christ.

August 27

THE LAST ENEMY

The last enemy that shall be destroyed is death. 1 Corinthians 15:26

THE Bible speaks of death as a departure. When Paul approached the valley of the shadow of death he did not shudder with fear; rather he announced with a note of triumph, "The time of my departure is at hand" (2 Timothy 4:6).

The word "departure" literally means to pull up anchor and to set sail. Everything which happens prior to death is a preparation for the journey. Death marks the beginning, not the end. It is a solemn, dramatic step in our journey to God.

Many times I have said farewell to my wife and children as I have departed for a distant destination. Separation always brings a tinge of sadness, but there is the high hope that we shall meet again. In the meantime the flame of love burns brightly in her heart and in mine.

So is the hope of the believing Christian as he stands at the grave of a loved one who is with the Lord. He knows, as did Paul, that "He is able to keep that which [he has] committed unto him against that day" (2 Timothy 1:12). He says "Goodbye," but only until the day breaks and the shadows flee away.

August 28

DEATH: NOT JUST A MYSTERY

Lo! I tell you a mystery. We shall not all sleep, but we shall all be changed. 1 Corinthians 15:51, RSV

PAUL did not describe death as a mystery. He was quite open about death and the fact that Christ had defeated it, so that we would have nothing to fear. What Paul described as a mystery was the transformation of these mortal bodies we now inhabit into immortal bodies that will be precisely like Jesus Christ's resurrected body. This transformation is a mystery because it transcends human thoughts, scientific inquiry, and even human understanding.

How can a miraculous process be reduced to mere language? It cannot and that is why Paul referred to it as a "mystery."

Yes, the dead in Christ shall rise first (talk about a mystery!) and then those of us who remain (after witnessing this incredible event) will be changed in a moment, "in the twinkling of an eye." We will be caught up in the air to meet the Lord, and so we shall be with the Lord forever. Talk about flying first class!

God wanted Christ to be first in everything and so He preceded us in death and into a resurrected life to show us what it would be like. As we trust Him to save us from the penalty of sin, which is death and eternal separation from God in a literal hell, we can also follow Him in newness of life, through the grave, without fear, comforted in the knowledge that He waits on the other side of a very short journey to take our hand and welcome us into His (and our) dwelling place where the mansion He has prepared for us stands in readiness.

Mystery? Yes, but God has given us enough facts so that we might trust Him for the rest.

August 29

COME HOME!

For the perishable must clothe itself with the imperishable, and the mortal with immortality. When the perishable has been clothed with the imperishable, and the mortal with immortality, then the saying that is written will come true: "Death has been swallowed up in victory."
1 Corinthians 15:53–54, NIV

WHAT this means is that once we have reached heaven, we will no longer be troubled or inhibited by physical or bodily limitations. Can you imagine that? The crippled, diseased, wasted bodies will be strong and beautiful and vigorous.

Once there was a widow and her son who lived in a miserable attic. Years before, she had married against her parents' wishes and had gone with her husband to live in a foreign land.

He had proved irresponsible and unfaithful, and after a few years he died without having made any provision for her and the child. It was with the utmost difficulty that she managed to scrape together the bare necessities of life.

The happiest times in the child's life were those when the mother took him in her arms and told him about her father's house in the old country. She told him of the grassy lawn, the noble trees, the wild flowers, the lovely pictures, and the delicious meals.

The child had never seen his grandfather's home, but to him it was the most beautiful place in all the world. He longed for the time when he would go there to live.

One day the postman knocked at the attic door. The mother recognized the handwriting on the letter he brought and with trembling fingers broke the seal. There was a check and a slip of paper with just two words: "Come home."

Someday a similar experience will be ours—an experience shared by all who know Christ. We do not know when the call will come. It may be when we are in the midst of our work. It may be after weeks or months of illness. But someday a loving hand will be laid upon our shoulder and this brief message will be given: "Come home."

All of us who know Christ personally need not be afraid to die. Death to the Christian is "going home."

August 30

VICTORY IN JESUS

Thanks be to God, who gives us the victory through our Lord Jesus Christ. 1 Corinthians 15:57, RSV

THE victory is yours. Claim it! It is your birthright. Browning said, "The best is yet to be." This doesn't mean the Christian can never suffer defeat or experience low periods in life. But it does mean that the Savior goes with you no matter the problem. The peace comes in the midst of problems and in spite of them.

From the old *Gospel Herald* comes this appropriate story:

> Haydn, the great musician, was once asked why his church music was so cheerful, and he replied, "When I think upon God, my heart is so full of joy that the notes dance and leap, as it were, from my pen, and since God has given me a cheerful heart, it will be pardoned me that I serve Him with a cheerful spirit."

The strength for our conquering and our victory is drawn continually from Christ. The Bible does not teach that sin is completely eradicated from the Christian in this life, but it does teach that sin shall no longer reign over you. The strength and power of sin have been broken. The Christian now has resources available to live above and beyond this world. The Bible teaches that whosoever is born of God does not practice sin. It is like the little girl who said that when the devil came knocking with a temptation, she just sent Jesus to the door.

August 31

COMFORTED BY CHRIST

Blessed be the God and Father of our Lord Jesus Christ, the Father of mercies and God of all comfort, who comforts us in all our affliction, so that we may be able to comfort those who are in any affliction, with the comfort with which we ourselves are comforted by God.
2 Corinthians 1:3–4, RSV

A DEAR friend and trusted counselor once told me that sometimes the greatest test comes to us when we ask God the question, "Why?"

As Charles Hembree has pointed out, "In the full face of afflictions it is hard to see any sense to things that befall us, and we want to question the fairness of a faithful God. However, these moments can be the most meaningful of our lives."

One of God's great servants, Paul Little, was killed in an automobile accident in 1975. I immediately asked God, "Why?" Paul was one of God's outstanding young strategists and Bible teachers. He was a theological professor, a leader of InterVarsity Christian Fellowship, and a former member of our team. I am sure his wife, Marie, must have asked in the agony of her heart, "Why?" And yet, a few months later when she came to our team retreat, she manifested a marvelous spirit as she shared her victory with the wives of our team members. Instead of our comforting her, she was comforting us.

Alexander Nowell once said, "God does not comfort us that we may be comforted but that we may be comforters." We are to pass along the comfort with which God has comforted us.

Look around you. There are countless opportunities to comfort others, not only in the loss of a loved one, but also in the daily distress that so often creeps into our lives.

When we are a comfort and encouragement to others, we are sometimes surprised at how it comes back to us many times over.

September

THE GOD OF ALL COMFORT

*Blessed be God, even the Father of our Lord Jesus Christ, the Father of
mercies, and the God of all comfort; who comforteth us in all our
tribulation, that we may be able to comfort them which are in any
trouble, by the comfort wherewith we ourselves are comforted of
God.* 2 Corinthians 1:3–4

HOW often as a child did you stub your toe, bruise a leg, or
cut a hand, and, running to the arms of your mother, you
sobbed out your pain? Lovingly caressing you and tenderly
kissing the hurt, she gave to you her special "healing magic,"
and you went your way half healed and wholly comforted.
Love and compassion contain a stronger medicine than all the
salves and ointments made by man.

Yes, when a loved one dies it is natural for us to feel a sense
of loss and even a deep loneliness. That will not necessarily
vanish overnight. But even when we feel the pain of
bereavement most intensely, we can also know the gracious
and loving presence of Christ most closely. Christ—who
suffered alone on the cross, and endured death and hell alone
for our salvation—knows what it is to suffer and be lonely.
And because He knows, He is able to comfort us by His
presence. "Blessed be God, even the Father of our Lord
Jesus Christ, the Father of mercies, and the God of all
comfort; who comforteth us in all our tribulation, that we
may be able to comfort them which are in any trouble, by the
comfort wherewith we ourselves are comforted of God"
(2 Corinthians 1:3–4).

So there can be a blessedness in the midst of mourning.
From suffering and bereavement God can work into us new
measures of His strength and love.

NO DEPOSIT, NO RETURN

Now it is God who makes both us and you stand firm in Christ. He anointed us, set his seal of ownership on us, put his Spirit in our hearts as a deposit, guaranteeing what is to come.
2 Corinthians 1:21–22, NIV

WHEN we purchase something of great value—a house, for example—we are usually required to put down a deposit to indicate our sincerity and to promise that our intentions are serious and that we intend to go through with the deal. It is a form of insurance, a guarantee that adds substance to our word.

In recent years we have seen the production of large quantities of "no deposit, no return" cans and bottles. The stores selling these items do not expect to get them back, and so we are not required to pay a deposit on them when we make our purchase. We simply discard them when the contents have been consumed.

God has made some incredible promises to us. He has promised that we might have a relationship with Him through His Son. He has promised never to leave us or forsake us and to be with us always. The Bible is full of promises from God to man.

Someone might ask, "What insurance do we have that God is serious? Let us see what kind of deposit He is prepared to put down." God's deposit is the most precious investment anyone could make: His wonderful Son. Not only is Jesus Christ a sufficient "down payment" on God's promises, He is, in fact, payment in full! There are no more payments to be made. "Jesus paid it all, all to Him I owe. Sin had left a crimson stain; He washed it white as snow."

Because of God's deposit on our lives, He is obligated to meet His promises. And so He has. And so He will.

"Having therefore these promises, dearly beloved, let us cleanse ourselves from all filthiness of the flesh and spirit, perfecting holiness in the fear of God" (2 Corinthians 7:1).

September 3

THE POSITIVE SIDE OF AFFLICTION

We are afflicted in every way, but not crushed; perplexed, but not driven to despair; persecuted, but not forsaken; struck down, but not destroyed; always carrying in the body the death of Jesus, so that the life of Jesus may also be manifested in our bodies. 2 Corinthians 4:8–10, RSV

THE apostle Paul could write, "With all our affliction, I am overjoyed" (2 Corinthians 7:4, RSV).

In all his sufferings and sorrows Paul experienced a deep, abiding joy. He writes of being "sorrowful, yet always rejoicing" (2 Corinthians 6:10, RSV). With sincerity he declared that for Christ's sake he was "content with weaknesses, insults, hardships, persecutions, and calamities" (2 Corinthians 12:10, RSV).

I have found in my travels that those who keep heaven in view remain serene and cheerful in the darkest day. If the glories of heaven were more real to us, if we lived less for material things and more for things eternal and spiritual, we would be less easily disturbed by this present life.

In these days of darkness and upheaval and uncertainty, the trusting and forward-looking Christian remains optimistic and joyful, knowing that Christ someday must rule, and "if we endure, we shall also reign with him" (2 Timothy 2: 12, RSV). As someone has said, "Patience [*hupomone*] is that quality of endurance that can reach the breaking point and not break."

At the same time I am equally certain that Christians who have spent years at hard labor or in exile, have passed through periods of discouragement—even despair. Those who have seen loved ones die have felt deep loss and intense suffering. Victory for them has not come easily or quickly. But eventually the peace of God does come, and with it His joy.

September 4

A LOVE TAP FROM OUR HEAVENLY FATHER

For our light affliction, which is but for a moment, worketh for us a far more exceeding and eternal weight of glory. 2 Corinthians 4:17

CHRIST is the answer to suffering.

Sickness, sorrow, and sin all are the result of the fall of man in the Garden. Sickness is a by-product of transgression; but that does not mean that Christians are never afflicted. The Bible says, "Many are the afflictions of the righteous: but the LORD delivereth him out of them all" (Psalm 34:19).

Job was afflicted; Paul had an infirmity; Lazarus was sick; and good people throughout history have been promised no immunity from disease and infirmity. Scores of people write every month and ask me, "Why do Christians suffer?" Rest assured that there is a reason for Christian people being afflicted. One reason why God's people suffer, according to the Bible, is that it is a disciplinary, chastening, and molding process.

The Bible says, "Thou shalt also consider in thine heart, that, as a man chasteneth his son, so the LORD thy God chasteneth thee" (Deuteronomy 8:5).

Again the Scripture says, "Blessed is the man whom thou chastenest, O LORD, and teachest him out of thy law" (Psalm 94:12).

Again the Bible says, "For whom the LORD loveth he correcteth; even as a father the son in whom he delighteth" (Proverbs 3:12).

From these Scriptures we learn that the chastening of affliction is a step in the process of our full and complete development. It can sometimes be a love tap from our heavenly Father to show us that we have wandered from the pathway of duty.

In the last essay he wrote before he died, great Christian apologist C. S. Lewis said, "We have no right to happiness; only an obligation to do our duty." Of course it is in our duty that happiness comes. Try it.

September 5

THE NEW PERSON

What shall we say then? Shall we continue in sin that grace may abound? God forbid. How shall we, that are dead to sin, live any longer therein? Romans 6:1–2

THE prophet Ezekiel said, "A new heart also will I give you, and a new spirit will I put within you" (Ezekiel 36:26). In the book of Acts, Peter called it repenting and being converted. Paul speaks of it in Romans as being "alive from the dead" (Romans 6: 13). In Colossians Paul calls it "[a putting off of] the old man with his deeds; and [putting] on the new man which is renewed in knowledge after the image of him that created him" (3:9–10). In Titus he calls it "the washing of regeneration and renewing of the Holy Ghost" (3:5). Peter said it was being "partakers of the divine nature" (2 Peter 1:4). John termed it passing "from death unto life" (John 5:24). In the Church of England catechism it is called "a death unto sin and a new birth unto righteousness."

Thus the Bible teaches that man can undergo a radical spiritual and moral change that is brought about by God Himself. The word that Jesus used, and which is translated "again," actually means "from above." The context of the third chapter of John teaches that the new birth is something that God does for man when man is willing to yield to God. Man does not have within himself the seed of the new life; this must come from God Himself.

One day a caterpillar climbs up into a tree where nature throws a fiber robe about him. He goes to sleep, and in a few weeks he emerges a beautiful butterfly. So man—distressed, discouraged, unhappy, hounded by conscience, driven by passion, ruled by selfishness, belligerent, quarrelsome, confused, depressed, miserable, taking alcohol and barbiturates, looking for escapisms—can come to Christ by faith and emerge a new man. This sounds incredible, even impossible, and yet it is precisely what the Bible teaches.

Do you feel you are in a cocoon? Turn to Christ and ask Him to give you your beautiful wings so that you might soar above your problems and be victorious over them.

September 6

THE OLD AND THE NEW

Therefore, if any one is in Christ, he is a new creation; the old has passed away, behold, the new has come.
2 Corinthians 5:17, RSV

I ONCE heard a carpenter say that it is always better and usually more economical to construct a new house than to patch up an old one. This is even more true in the spiritual realm. There is nothing in our old nature worth salvaging. Our thoughts are full of deceit. Our mouths are filled with cursing and bitterness. The way of peace we have not known. The Bible says, "There is none that doeth good, no, not one" (Psalm 14:3; compare Romans 3:12).

The old nature with its deceitfulness, its depravity, and its wickedness must give way to a new nature. And this is exactly what God stands ready to do. God says, "A new heart also will I give you, and a new spirit will I put within you" (Ezekiel 36:26).

What a challenge! It is much more difficult to change our dispositions than it is our apparel. As a matter of fact, it is utterly impossible for me to change my disposition in my own strength. Thus, the new birth is something that must be done for me by another; and God has promised to do that which I cannot do for myself. And He will do it for you, too!

September 7

AMBASSADORS FOR CHRIST

Now then we are ambassadors for Christ, as though God did beseech you by us: we pray you in Christ's stead, be ye reconciled to God.
2 Corinthians 5:20

WHAT is an ambassador? An ambassador is a person, a friend of authority. He is a servant of the government in a foreign land. He is not free to set his own policies or develop his own message. In the same way we are called to live under the authority of Jesus Christ and the authority of the Scriptures. We are servants. We must live under the authority of the Word of God. We are called not to do our will, but Christ's.

What does it mean to live under the authority of the Word of God? *First* of all, it means that we live under the authority of God in our personal lives. "Be ye holy as I am holy" (Leviticus 20:7), say the Scriptures. We are to be holy people of God; we are to live what we preach in our personal lives: a disciplined devotional life. The world today is looking for holy men and women to live under the authority of the Word of God. They're not going to listen to what we say unless we back it up with the way we live in our personal relationships.

Second, we are under the authority of the Word of God in our social relationships as well. As Christians we're not isolated persons; we are part of society with all of its difficulties and problems and hopes. The Bible has much to say about social justice and social actions. This is a difficult area. The Christian knows this. Human society is affected by sin, and we know that any effort we make to improve society will always be incomplete and imperfect. We are not going to build a Utopia on earth. Why? Because of human nature. Sin keeps us from building a paradise on earth.

But we are to work for social justice—that is our command in Scripture—we're to do all we can so that we can live a peaceable and a free life, and a life of human dignity. Only Christ can change hearts, but that does not mean that we neglect social and political responsibilities. Christ is concerned about the whole man, including the society in which he lives. Many of the great social reforms of the nineteenth century in Great Britain and America were inspired by evangelical Christians. But the time came when many forgot that the Gospel was both vertical and horizontal. This is rapidly changing now. Evangelicals are once again proclaiming a balanced Gospel of personal salvation on the one hand and social responsibility on the other.

Third, we are under authority in our service. It is God who has called us to serve. We are not free to choose the place or the manner in which we will serve Him. I am always amazed at the variety of gifts that God has given to the Church. Every person has been given a gift from God. You may be a farmer, or a laborer, or a doctor, or a professor, but you have been given a gift of the Holy Spirit. Paul says, "Stir up the gift that is within you" (2 Timothy 1:6). What is your gift? Each of us is to put his gift into action for God.

JESUS TOOK OUR JUDGMENT

For he hath made him to be sin for us, who knew no sin; that we might be made the righteousness of God in him. 2 Corinthians 5:21

There is therefore now no condemnation to them which are in Christ Jesus. Romans 8:1

THE Bible says the judgment for sin that I deserved is already passed. Christ took my judgment on the cross. Every demand of the law has been met. The law was completely satisfied in the offering that Christ made of Himself for sins. "The LORD hath laid on him the iniquity of us all" (Isaiah 53:6). "Who his own self bare our sins in his own body on the tree" (1 Peter 2:24). "But this man, after he had offered one sacrifice for sins for ever, sat down on the right hand of God" (Hebrews 10:12).

The law had said, "The wages of sin is death" (Romans 6:23), and "The soul that sinneth, it shall die" (Ezekiel 18:4). I deserved judgment and hell, but Christ took that judgment and hell for me. Christ Himself said, "Verily, verily, I say unto you, he that heareth my word, and believeth on him that sent me, hath everlasting life, and shall not come into condemnation; but is passed from death unto life" (John 5:24). No statement could be any plainer that the true believer in Jesus Christ shall not come into judgment. That judgment is past. "For thou hast cast all my sins behind thy back" (Isaiah 38:17). God said through Jeremiah the prophet, "I will remember their sin no more" (31:34).

We shall never understand the extent of God's love in Christ at the Cross until we understand that we shall never have to stand before the judgment of God for our sins. Christ took our sins. He finished the work of redemption. I am not saved through any works or merit of my own. I have preached to thousands of people on every continent, but I shall not go to heaven because I am a preacher. I am going to heaven entirely on the merit of the work of Christ. I shall never stand at God's judgment bar. That is all past.

Once while crossing the North Atlantic, I looked out my porthole when I got up in the morning and saw one of the blackest clouds I had ever seen. I was certain that we were in for a terrible storm. I ordered my breakfast sent to my room and spoke to the steward about the storm. He said, "Oh, we've already come through that storm. It's behind us."

If we are believers in Jesus Christ, we have already come through the storm of judgment. It happened at the Cross.

September 9

THE CHRISTLIKE CHRISTIAN

Sorrowful, yet always rejoicing; poor, yet making many rich; having nothing, and yet possessing everything. 2 Corinthians 6:10, NIV

THESE words from the apostle Paul remind me of Amy Carmichael. Though bedridden as a result of an accident some twenty years before her death, and in almost constant pain, she continued to minister through her devotional writings and poetry. Her keen insight and her refreshingly spiritual writings revealed the depth of her walk with Christ. She remains a striking example of a Christian whose physical suffering enabled her to reflect the character of Christ. She lived a life of rejoicing in the midst of tribulation. Her face radiated the love of Christ, and her life epitomized the saintly stature the surrendered Christian can reach if he reacts to suffering by rejoicing in it.

During those years of physical pain, Amy Carmichael

wrote the many books that have blessed untold thousands around the world. Without the "blessing" of being confined to her bed, she might have been too busy to write.

There is a story about Martin Luther going through a period of depression and discouragement. For days his long face graced the family table and dampened the family's home life. One day his wife came to the breakfast table all dressed in black, as if she were going to a funeral service. When Martin asked her who had died, she replied, "Martin, the way you've been behaving lately, I thought God had died, so I came prepared to attend His funeral."

Her gentle but effective rebuke drove straight to Luther's heart, and as a result of that lesson the great Reformer resolved never again to allow worldly care, resentment, depression, discouragement, or frustration to defeat him. By God's grace, he vowed, he would submit his life to the Savior and reflect His grace in a spirit of rejoicing, whatever came. With Paul he would shout, "Thanks be to God! He gives us the victory through our Lord Jesus Christ" (1 Corinthians 15: 57, NIV).

When was the last time you praised God in the midst of despair? Don't wait until you "feel like it" or you'll never do it. Do it, and then you'll feel like it!

September 10

LIFE ETERNAL AND INTERNAL

Thanks be to God for his indescribable gift! 2 Corinthians 9:15, NIV

MAN has two great spiritual needs. One is for forgiveness. The other is for goodness. Consciously or unconsciously, his inner being longs for both. There are times when man actually cries for them, even though in his restlessness, confusion, loneliness, fear, and pressures he may not know what he is crying for.

God heard the first cry for help, that cry for forgiveness, and answered it at Calvary. God sent His only Son into the world to die for our sins, so that we might be forgiven. This is a gift for us—God's gift of salvation. This gift is a permanent legacy for everyone who truly admits he has "fallen short" and sinned. It is for everyone who reaches out and accepts God's gift by receiving Jesus Christ as his Lord and Savior. Paul calls it God's "indescribable" gift.

But God also heard our second cry, that cry for goodness, and answered it at Pentecost. God does not want us to come to Christ by faith, and then lead a life of defeat, discouragement, and dissension. Rather, He wants to "fulfill every desire for goodness and the work of faith with power; in order that the name of our Lord Jesus may be glorified in you" (2 Thessalonians 1:11–12, NASB).

To the great gift of forgiveness God adds also the great gift of the Holy Spirit. He is the source of power who meets our need to escape from the miserable weakness that grips us. He gives us the power to be truly good.

If we are to live a life of sanity in our modern world, if we wish to be men and women who can live victoriously, we need this two-sided gift God has offered us: first, the work of the Son of God *for* us; second, the work of the Spirit of God *in* us. In this way God has answered mankind's two great cries: the cry for forgiveness and the cry for goodness.

As a friend of mine has said, "I need Jesus Christ for my eternal life, and the Holy Spirit of God for my internal life." He might have added, ". . . So I can live my external life to the fullest."

SALVATION IS FREE, NOT CHEAP

Three times I was beaten with rods, once I was stoned, three times I was shipwrecked, I spent a night and a day in the open sea, I have been constantly on the move. I have been in danger from rivers, in danger from bandits, in danger from my own countrymen, in danger from Gentiles; in danger in the city, in danger in the country, in danger at sea; and in danger from false brothers. I have labored and toiled and have often gone without sleep; I have known hunger and thirst and have often gone without food; I have been cold and naked. Besides everything else, I face daily the pressure of my concern for all the churches. Who is weak, and I do not feel weak? Who is led into sin, and I do not inwardly burn? If I must boast, I will boast of the things that show my weakness. 2 Corinthians 11:25–30, NIV

FOR Paul the Christian life was one of suffering. The same could be said of a multitude of Christ's followers, many of whom were killed for their faith. So when Christ said time after time that one must "deny himself and take up his cross and follow me," He was indicating that it is not easy to be His true follower. The apostle Paul warned, "Everyone who wants to live a godly life in Christ Jesus will be persecuted" (2 Timothy 3:12, NIV). He offers no cheap grace, no easy life. As someone has said, "Salvation is free but not cheap."

Charles T. Studd was a famous sportsman in England, captain of the Cambridge XI cricket team. A century ago he gave away his vast wealth to needy causes and led the "Cambridge Seven" to China. His slogan was, "If Jesus Christ be God and died for me, then no sacrifice can be too great for me to make for Him."

During the first decade of this century, Bill Borden left one of America's greatest family fortunes to be a missionary in

China. He only got as far as Egypt where, still in his twenties, he died of typhoid fever. Before his death he said, "No reserves, no retreats, no regrets!"

YOU CAN LEAP WALLS

And he [the Lord] said unto me, My grace is sufficient for thee: for my strength is made perfect in weakness. Most gladly therefore will I rather glory in my infirmities, that the power of Christ may rest upon me.
2 Corinthians 12:9

CONVERSION is that voluntary change in the mind of a sinner in which he turns on the one hand from sin and on the other hand to Christ. Conversion is the human side of the tremendous transformation that takes place in the divinely wrought "new birth," or "regeneration." It is simply man's turning from sin to Christ.

The Scripture teaches that God turns men to Himself, but men are also exhorted to turn themselves to God. God is represented as the author of the new heart and the new spirit, yet men are commanded to make for themselves a new heart and a new spirit. It is the old paradox of grace and free will.

No one can be converted except by the grace of God, for we are too weak to turn ourselves, unaided; and we turn only in response to some stimulus provided outside ourselves.

But no one can be converted except with the consent of his own free will, because God does not override human choice. We may not be free to choose, because sin weakens our power of moral choice; but we are free to refuse. We can refuse to be chosen.

Simon Peter could not become a disciple until Jesus called him and said, "Follow Me." But others heard the same call and refused it or put it off. One said, "Lord, let me first go and bury my father." Another one said, "Let me first say farewell to those at my home." These men refused Christ's call.

This combination of divine calling and the human responsibility of accepting or refusing God's grace runs throughout the Bible and characterizes all God's dealings with men.

The Bible confronts us with man's moral independence within himself and his spiritual dependence upon God.

In the picturesque words of Psalm 18:29 (RSV), David says, "By my God I can leap over a wall." A man can jump over some barriers by his own will and effort, but some walls are so high that they need more than this.

The psalmist knew such walls. Those could be leaped only with the help of God. God does not lift a man over. God helps a man when he takes the leap.

September 13
....

OUR OMNIPOTENT HELPER

The grace of the Lord Jesus Christ, and the love of God,
and the communion of the Holy Ghost, be with you all.
2 Corinthians 13:14

GOD the Holy Spirit is equal with the Son and with the Father in every respect. The Bible teaches that He is co-equal with God the Father and co-equal with God the Son. The Bible also teaches that the Holy Spirit is a Person. He is never to be referred to as "it." He is not just an agent; He is not just an influence. He is a mighty Person, the Holy Spirit of God.

The Bible tells us that He is omnipotent. That means that He has all power.

The Bible tells us that He is omnipresent. That means that He is everywhere at the same time.

The Bible tells us that He is omniscient. That means that He has all knowledge. He knows everything that we do—He watches us. "His eye is on the sparrow," and if God the Spirit is watching the sparrow, how much more He is watching us every moment.

He sees the thoughts and intents of our hearts. He delves into our minds, into the things we think, into the intents of our souls. He knows all about us. He knows everything. The Bible says that everything we do He writes down in a book, and someday it shall be brought out as evidence at the great Judgment of God.

The Bible teaches that the Holy Spirit is eternal. The Bible tells us that He is holy. He is referred to in the New Testament alone one hundred times as the Holy Spirit— absolute holiness, absolute purity, absolute righteousness.

What should this mean to me? With the seventeenth century Anglican bishop Jeremy Taylor, I can say, "It is impossible for that man to despair who remembers that his Helper is omnipotent."

September 14

THIS PRESENT EVIL WORLD

[Jesus] who gave himself for our sins, that he might deliver us from this present evil world, according to the will of God and our Father. Galatians 1:4

IN Luke 18, Jesus told of the self-righteous Pharisee who said, "God, I thank you that I am not like all other men—robbers, evildoers, adulterers—or even like this tax collector" (verse 11). The Pharisee kidded himself into thinking he was something, when he was not. But the tax collector, whom the Pharisee looked upon with scorn, saw himself as he was, and said, "God, have mercy on me, a sinner" (verse 13). Jesus said, "I tell you that this man, rather than the other, went home justified before God. For everyone who exalts himself will be humbled, and he who humbles himself will be exalted" (Luke 18:14).

How can we get our values right? How can our warped judgment be straightened out? Some tell us that education is the answer to these questions. Prove to people that crime doesn't pay, that illicit sex is psychologically harmful, that excessive drinking is injurious to the body and brain. Programs of social and personal reform are launched continually. Are they the answer to evil?

Others say that science is the answer. Science, supposedly, can make a clean bomb or a harmless cigarette. It can cope with the problems of drugs. Science, they say, can tap the brain of man and alter his desires.

But the Bible, which has withstood the test of time, tells us a different story. It says that we are possessed of a sinful, fallen nature which wars against us, that seeks to destroy us. Paul said, "I find this law at work [in me]: When I want to do good, evil is right there with me" (Romans 7:21). Evil is present to cleverly disguise itself as good. Evil is present to control and deceive us. We are not at peace with ourselves or with God. That is what the Cross of Christ is all about: to reconcile us to God and to give us a new nature.

September 15

GOD CAME DOWN

I am crucified with Christ: nevertheless I live: yet not I, but Christ liveth in me: and the life which I now live in the flesh I live by faith of the Son of God, who loved me, and gave himself for me. Galatians 2:20

JESUS is not only the Christ, He is also "God, our Lord and Savior" (Titus 2:13). This is a staggering, almost incomprehensible truth: God Himself has come down on this planet in the Person of His only Son. The incarnation and the full Deity of Jesus are the cornerstones of the Christian faith. Jesus Christ was not just a great teacher or a holy religious leader. He was God Himself in human flesh—fully God and fully man.

Jesus Himself gave frequent witness to His uniqueness and divine nature. To His opponents He declared, "Before Abraham was, I am" (John 8:58). They immediately recognized this as a clear claim to divinity and tried to stone Him for blasphemy. On another occasion Jesus stated, "I and my Father are one" (John 10:30), and again His enemies tried to stone him "because that thou, being a man, makest thyself God" (John 10:33). Furthermore, He demonstrated the power to do things that only God can do, such as forgive sins (Mark 2:1–12). The charge brought against Him at His trial was that "he made himself the Son of God" (John 19:7); and when asked if He was the Son of God, He replied, "You are right in saying I am" (Luke 22:70, NIV).

Irenaeus said it well when he wrote, "The Word of God, Jesus Christ, on account of his great love for mankind, became what we are in order to make us what he is himself." What a sobering—and exhilarating—thought that should be!

September 16

GOD'S CHILDREN

For ye are all the children of God by faith in Christ Jesus.
Galatians 3:26

AS God's children, we are His dependents. The Bible says, "Like as a father pitieth his children, so the LORD pitieth them that fear him" (Psalm 103:13).

Dependent children spend little time worrying about

meals, clothing, and shelter. They assume, and they have a right to, that all will be provided by their parents.

Jesus said, "Take no thought, saying, What shall we eat? or, What shall we drink? or, Wherewithal shall we be clothed? . . . But seek ye first the kingdom of God . . . and all these things shall be added unto you" (Matthew 6:31, 33).

Because God is responsible for our welfare, we are told to cast all our care upon Him, for He cares for us (1 Peter 5:7). Because we are dependent upon God, Jesus said, "Let not your heart be troubled" (John 14:1). God says, "I'll take the burden—don't give it a thought—leave it to Me."

Children are not backward about asking for things. They would not be normal if they did not boldly make their needs known.

God has said to His children, "Therefore come boldly unto the throne of grace, that [you] may obtain mercy, and find grace to help in time of need" (Hebrews 4:16). God is keenly aware that we are dependent upon Him for life's necessities. It was for that reason that Jesus said, "Ask, and it shall be given you; seek, and ye shall find; knock, and it shall be opened unto you" (Matthew 7:7).

What is troubling you today? Is your heart burdened because of some problem which threatens to overcome you? Are you filled with anxiety and worry about some problem, wondering what will happen? Listen: As a child of God through faith in Christ, you can turn these over to Christ, knowing that He loves you and is able to help you.

September 17

SALVATION OF SOCIETY

We through the Spirit wait for the hope of righteousness by faith. Galatians 5:5

THE late C. S. Lewis, in his remarkable book *Christian Behavior,* said, "Hope is one of the theological virtues." This means that a continual looking forward to the eternal world is not, as some modern people think, a form of escapism or wishful thinking, but one of the things a Christian is meant to do. It does not mean that we are to leave the present world as it is. If you read history you will find that the Christians who did the most for the present world were those who thought the most of the next. It is only since Christians have largely ceased to think of the other world that they've become so ineffective in this one. "Aim at heaven," said C. S. Lewis, "and you will get earth thrown in. Aim at earth, and you will get neither."

In the midst of the pessimism, gloom, and frustration of the present hour there is one bright beacon light of hope—and that is the promise of Jesus Christ, "If I go and prepare a place for you, I will come again" (John 14:3).

The whole nature of individual salvation rests squarely on the person and work of the Lord Jesus Christ. The Scripture says, "For by grace are ye saved through faith; and that not of yourselves: it is the gift of God: not of works, lest any man should boast" (Ephesians 2:8–9).

But the Bible also teaches that the salvation of society—in the reordering of man's social injustice, war, poverty, and disease—will be taken out of man's hands someday. We're not going to achieve all this by education, evolution, politics, technology, military power, or science. Nor will it be achieved by a universal church that can influence legislation in the congresses and parliaments of nations so as to produce such benevolent acts of man that all hate, evil, and sin will be abolished.

The salvation of society will come about by the powers and forces released by the apocalyptic return of Jesus Christ. It will come through the Kingdom of God in its principles of righteousness. It will be the prophesied fulfillment of redemption applied to every phase of human life and national existence.

September 18

THE MARK OF A CHRISTIAN

All the law is fulfilled in one word, even in this; Thou shalt love thy neighbor as thyself. Galatians 5:14

WHEN men turn to God, God gives them *agape* love—and then they love their neighbor no matter what the color of his skin, no matter what his circumstances. This is the love that God gives as a gift, and it is produced in the heart by the Holy Spirit who lives there.

The Christian is to love fellow Christians. "By this shall all men know that ye are my disciples, if ye have love one to another." Do we have love one to another? Do you know what the apostle Paul said about it? He said in 1 Corinthians 13, "Though I speak with the tongues of men and of angels. . . ." Speak with the tongues of angels!

Think of being the greatest orator in all the universe! Speaking with a thousand tongues in a thousand languages with the eloquence of the greatest speakers of all time! Paul said unless we have love, *agape* love—the divine love that only God can give—we are only "sounding brass or a tinkling cymbal."

Suppose I understand the Bible, have the gift of preaching, the gift of prophecy, and am the greatest preacher who ever lived. Paul said unless I have love "it profiteth me nothing." Suppose I understand all mysteries and all knowledge, read the Bible every day, carry it under my arm every day, believe in all the creeds. Unless I have love, Paul said I am nothing.

Suppose I have such faith that I could remove mountains. You say what great faith that is! That's nothing, unless I love.

Suppose I give all the money that I have to charity. You would say I was a great man—a Christian man. But Paul said unless I have love it is nothing. Do you have this love? Without Jesus Christ in your heart, without the Holy Spirit in your heart, you can't have this love. You can't produce this love except with the power of the Holy Spirit. That's the reason why you must receive Christ, and when you do He gives you the power and the strength, through the Holy Spirit, to produce this love.

George Sweeting says, "Life minus love equals nothing!"

September 19

THE WALK OF THE WILLING

This I say then, Walk in the Spirit, and ye shall not fulfill the lust of the flesh.   Galatians 5:16

To paraphrase Galatians 5:16—"Walk by means of the Spirit." In Romans 8:14 Paul writes, "As many as are led by the Spirit of God, they are the sons of God."

To walk in the Spirit is a challenging and inspiring exercise, for it combines activity with relaxation. To walk means to place one foot in front of the other. If you stop doing this, you are no longer walking—you are standing still. Walking always implies movement, progress, and direction.

Living for Christ is a day-to-day going on with Him. It is a continuous dependence upon the Spirit of God. It is believing in His faithfulness. You cannot live the Christian life by yourself. The Holy Spirit must live in you and express Himself through you.

Sin will no longer rule or dominate you if you are allowing the Holy Spirit to live Christ's life through you. It is living by faith, living by trust, living in dependence upon God.

If we look to our own resources, our own strength, or our

own ability as Peter did when he walked on the water, we will fail.

The first key for usefulness and power for Christians today is humility. The second is the realization that sanctification is only in Christ. The third is reliance on the Holy Spirit.

Realize that God is in control. Habakkuk the prophet cried out to God and said, "O God, why are these terrible evils coming upon the world?" God said, "Habakkuk, don't be discouraged. I am working a work in your day; if I told you what it is, you would not believe it" (see Habakkuk 1:5).

God is at work in the midst of crisis. In the midst of the problems, pessimism, and frustrations of our day, God is doing His own work. Let us realize that there are certain things we cannot do. Let us be faithful in the things He has called us to do.

September 20

PEACE: THE FRUIT OF THE SPIRIT

The fruit of the Spirit is . . . peace. Galatians 5:22

PEACE carries with it the idea of unity, completeness, rest, ease, and security. In the Old Testament the word was *shalom*. Many times when I meet Jewish friends I greet them with "*Shalom.*" And often, when I greet my Arab friends I use a similar term that they use for peace, "*salam.*"

Recently as I watched the televised report of passengers disembarking from a hijacked plane, I saw terror, horror, and fear on their faces. But one woman had a little child in her arms, calmly sleeping through it all. Peace in the midst of turmoil.

Isaiah said, "Thou wilt keep him in perfect peace, whose mind is stayed on thee: because he trusteth in thee" (Isaiah 26:3). This is the picture of any Christian who stands alone on the battlefield, by faith garrisoned round about with God's holy weapons, and in command of the situation. Such a man is not troubled about the future, for he knows who holds the key to the future. He does not tremble on the rock, for he knows who made the rock. He does not doubt, for he knows the One who erases all doubt.

When you and I yield to worry, we deny our Guide the right to lead us in confidence and peace. Only the Holy Spirit can give us peace in the midst of the storms of restlessness and despair. We should not grieve our Guide by indulging in worry or paying undue attention to self.

What are you worried about? Why?

September 21

REALLY LIVING

The fruit of the Spirit is love, joy, peace, long-suffering, gentleness, goodness, faith, meekness, temperance. Galatians 5:22–23

THE moment you come to Christ, the Spirit of God brings the life of God into you and you begin to live. For the first time you begin to live with a capital "L." There's a spring in your step and a joy in your soul and a peace in your heart, and life has taken on a new outlook.

There's a whole new direction to your life because the Spirit of God has given to you the very life of God, and God is an eternal God—that means you'll live as long as God lives.

The Bible also teaches us that the Spirit of God produces the fruit of the Spirit. Now these nine clusters of fruit are to characterize the life of every Christ-born child of God. But what do we find? We find in the average so-called Christian today the very opposite.

Everyone before he comes to Christ is dominated by one nature—the "old man," which is called the flesh, the world, the devil—who controls your life. You're controlled by your ego, you're controlled by yourself. The moment you receive Christ as your Savior, that self is put down, and Christ is put on the throne in your life and the Spirit of God dominates your life.

However, self is still there—sometimes hidden, sometimes quiet, sometimes secondary—waiting his opportunity and his chance to attack the citadel of your soul and take control again.

As a Christian you have the willpower to yield either to the flesh and live a fleshly, carnal life; or you have the power to yield to the Spirit, to live a Spirit-filled life. Our life is an up-and-down experience. God never meant it to be that way. God meant the Christian life to be on the highest possible plane at all times, bearing the fruit of the Spirit.

September 22

BE ON SPEAKING TERMS WITH HIM

But God forbid that I should glory, save in the cross of our Lord Jesus Christ, by whom the world is crucified unto me and I unto the world. Galatians 6:14

THE Bible reveals that God has a plan for every life, and that if we live in constant fellowship with Him, He will direct and lead us in the fulfillment of this plan.

Many of us have God's plan second or third at best. However, if you have substituted the good for the best, do not despair. Wherever you are at this moment, yield your life unconditionally to God, and He can still make it a thing of beauty and an honor to His name.

Keep in mind that God's will is revealed only to born-again believers. The Bible says, "Be ye transformed . . . that ye may prove what is that good, and acceptable, and perfect, will of God" (Romans 12:2). God does not reveal His plan through fortune-tellers, soothsayers, and workers of hocus-pocus. His will is reserved for those who have trusted Christ for salvation. He shares His secrets only with those who are redeemed and transformed.

You cannot know the will of God for your life unless you first come to the Cross and confess that you are a sinner and receive Christ as Lord and Savior. If you want the perfect plan that God has for your life, you will have to go by way of Calvary to get it. It is only through Christ that we can be on speaking terms with God and know God's plan for our lives.

September 23

BLOOD FOR THE BATTLE

In whom we have redemption through his blood, the forgiveness of sins, according to the riches of his grace. Ephesians 1:7

WE are involved in a spiritual conflict. This is a battle between the forces of God and the forces of Satan. We must choose sides.

The Bible warns us about being taken in by the evil of this cosmos. Satan's lies are cleverly mixed with truth. When he tempted Christ, he was convincingly logical and even quoted Scripture. So the Bible proposes that Christians make a clean break with all the evils of the world and that we be separated from them. The apostle Paul said, "Wherefore come out from among them, and be ye separate, saith the Lord, and touch not the unclean thing; and I will receive you" (2 Corinthians 6:17).

Now Jesus ate with publicans and sinners (see Mark 2:16). Nearly everyone He associated with was an outcast. But His relationship with them was not purely social; it was redemptive.

Now we are not to get our worlds mixed up at this point. This is where the confusion lies. God meant that we are not to mingle with the world, but we are to witness to the world.

We are to love the world of men whom God loves. We are to weep with those who weep (see Romans 12:15), suffer with those who suffer, and identify ourselves with the poor, the sick, and the needy.

This then is our problem: to associate with and love those who are involved in the world without being contaminated, influenced, or swayed by them. This distinction can only be achieved by a close walk with Christ, by constant prayer, and by seeking the Holy Spirit's leadership every hour of the day. God has provided us the power to resist the world and be separated from it, and it is ours to appropriate that power every hour of our lives.

We are in the world, but the world is not to be in us. It is good for a ship to be in the sea, but bad when the sea gets into the ship. As our Lord prayed, "I pray not that thou shouldest take them out of the world, but that thou shouldest keep them from the evil" (John 17:15).

September 24

CHRISTIAN CONVERSION

For by grace are ye saved through faith; and that not of yourselves: it is the gift of God: not of works, lest any man should boast.
Ephesians 2:8–9

THE grace is God's: the faith is ours. God gave us the free will with which to choose. God gave us the capacity to believe and trust. Therefore within every conversion there is the working of the divine and the human; but their relation to each other remains a mystery.

It has been my privilege to see thousands converted to Christ, and I still do not understand the mystery of God's grace and man's faith. But I know that both are involved.

On the one hand, Jesus said, "Him who comes to me I will

not cast out" (John 6:37, RSV). And on the other hand He said, "No one can come to me unless the Father who sent me draws him" (John 6:44, RSV).

I am convinced that the Bible teaches the necessity of conversion. I am absolutely certain of my own conversion. I am equally convinced of the genuineness of the conversion of thousands of people in many parts of the world.

Saint Augustine described his own conversion in a famous passage in which he said, "I continued my miserable complaining. How long, how long shall I go on saying, 'Tomorrow,' and again, 'Tomorrow'? Why not now? Why not have an end of my uncleanness this very hour?

"Such things I said weeping in the most bitter sorrow of my heart, and suddenly I heard a voice from some nearby house, a boy's voice or a girl's voice I do not know, but it was a sort of singsong, repeated again and again: 'Take and read, take and read, take and read!' I arose, interpreting the incident as quite certainly a divine command to open my book of Scripture and read the passage at which I should open.

"I snatched it up and opened it and in silence read the passage [Romans 13:13–14] on which my eyes fell: 'Not in rioting and drunkenness, not in chambering and wantonness, not in strife and envying: but put ye on the Lord Jesus Christ, and make not provision for the flesh, to fulfill the lusts thereof.' I had no wish to read further, and no need; for in that instant, with the very ending of the sentence, it was as though a light of utter confidence shone in all my heart and all the darkness of uncertainty vanished away." In that hour Augustine was converted.

Before this moment, Augustine was one of the most wicked of men. In no sense could he be called a Christian. He was cultured and civilized, but nevertheless a pagan. As a result of this one experience he became one of the greatest Christian theologians of all time.

TRANSFORMATION, NOT REFORMATION

For we are his workmanship, created in Christ Jesus unto good works,
which God hath before ordained that we should walk in
them. Ephesians 2:10

THIS new birth is far more than reformation. Many persons make New Year's resolutions only to break them because they do not have the capacity to keep them. Man is ever reforming, but reformation at best is only temporary. Man's nature must be transformed.

A group of barbers at their annual convention decided to exhibit the value of their tonsorial art. They found a derelict on skid row, gave him a haircut, a shave, and a bath; and they dressed him in new clothes of the finest tailoring. They had demonstrated to their satisfaction the worth of tonsorial excellence, but three days later the man was in the gutter again. He had been outwardly transformed into a respectable-looking man, but the impulses and drives of his inner being had not been changed. He had been powdered and perfumed, but not changed.

You can scrub a pig, sprinkle Chanel No. 5 on him, put a ribbon around his neck, and take him into your living room. But when you turn him loose, he will jump into the first mud puddle he sees because his nature has never been changed. He is still a pig.

Through the new birth the Bible teaches that man enters a new world. There is a new dimension of living. The change that comes over a man is expressed in the Bible in various contrasts: lust and holiness, darkness and light, death and resurrection, a stranger to the kingdom of God and now a citizen. The man who has experienced the new birth is called a member of God's household. The Bible teaches that his will is changed, his objectives for living are changed, his disposition is changed, his affections are changed, and he now has purpose and meaning in his life.

September 26

CENTERING ON THE CROSS

But now in Christ Jesus you who once were far off have been brought near in the blood of Christ . . . [reconciling] us both to God in one body through the cross. . . . Ephesians 2:13, 16, RSV

THE fact of the death of Jesus Christ is the very heart of Christianity. The sacrificial Cross of Christ is the secret of Christianity's survival through all the ages and the hope of its victory in the ages to come.

The Cross is more than an example. It is more than a system of ethics. It is the mighty act of God's justice and love. God is saying to the whole world, "I love you. I am willing to forgive your sins." God is saying to all of those who are filled with guilt today, "Your sins are forgiven because of the Cross." God is saying to all those who are lonely today, "Behold, I am with you until the end of the age" (cf. Matthew 28:20). Every person reading these words is guilty of sin, and there is no way to remove that stain of guilt except by the sacrifice of Christ.

In Westminster Abbey there is a memorial tablet erected by the British government in memory of Major John Andre, with whom Benedict Arnold negotiated for the surrender of the fortress of West Point and who was hanged as a spy on October 2, 1780. It was a case where the man who ought to have been hung escaped and the man who was caught in a strange series of circumstances was hung.

Andre was still in his twenties. He was a gifted writer. Just before his execution he wrote a poem entitled, "Hail, Sovereign Love," in which the great truth of the atonement,

Christ's substitution for the sinner, was gloriously told. He describes in this poem how his own soul was for a time too proud to seek Christ. However, there came a time when Andre was convicted of his sin, and he went to the Cross and found a glorious and wonderful peace.

I read about a clergyman some time ago who was conducting a communion service. Because he no longer believed in the substitutionary death of Christ on the Cross for our sins, he distributed flowers to the congregation instead of the bread and the wine.

The idea of the atonement was repugnant to him, so he gave flowers as a substitute. But there is no substitute for Christ and Him crucified, no substitute for the rugged and bloodstained cross.

September 27

HE IS OUR PEACE

For he is our peace, who hath made both one, and hath broken down the middle wall of partition between us . . . to make in himself of twain one new man . . . that he might reconcile both unto God in one body by the cross, having slain the enmity thereby. Ephesians 2:14–16

OUTSIDE the work of the Cross, there is bitterness, intolerance, sedition, ill will, prejudice, lust, greed, and hatred. Within the efficacy of the Cross, there is love and fellowship, new life and new brotherhood. The only human hope for peace lies at the Cross of Christ, where all men, whatever their nationality or race, can become a new brotherhood.

Recently a university professor said, "There are two things that will never be solved—the problems of race and war." I say that these and all other problems can be solved, but only at the Cross. The Cross of Christ is not only the basis of our peace and hope; but it is also the means of our eternal salvation. The object of the Cross is not only a full and free pardon; it is also a changed life, lived in fellowship with God. No wonder Paul said two thousand years ago, "We preach Christ crucified." This is the message for the world today. This is the message of hope and peace and brotherhood. This is what the world calls foolishness but what God has been pleased to call wisdom.

The poet John Greenleaf Whittier put it well when he wrote:

> Drop Thy still dews of quietness,
>   Till all our strivings cease;
> Take from our soul the strain and stress,
> And let our ordered lives confess
>   The beauty of Thy peace.

He is our Peace!

September 28
....
THE LOVE THAT PASSES KNOWLEDGE

. . . That Christ may dwell in your hearts through faith; that you, being rooted and grounded in love, may . . . know the love of Christ which surpasses knowledge, that you may be filled with all the fullness of God. Ephesians 3:17–19, RSV

BEHIND the love of God lies His omniscience—His ability to "know and understand all." Omniscience is that quality of God which is His alone. God possesses infinite knowledge and an awareness which is uniquely His. At all times, even in the midst of any type of suffering, I can realize that He knows, loves, watches, understands, and, more than that, He has a purpose.

As a boy I grew up in the South. My idea of the ocean was so small that the first time I saw the Atlantic I couldn't comprehend that any little lake could be so big! The vastness of the ocean cannot be understood until it is seen. This is the same with God's love. It passes knowledge. Until you actually experience it, no one can describe its wonders to you.

A good illustration of this is a story my wife told me about a little boy in China who saw a man selling cherries; and when he saw the fruit, his eyes filled with longing. But he had no money with which to buy cherries.

The kindly seller asked the boy, "Do you want some cherries?" And the little boy said that he did.

The seller said, "Hold out your hands." But the little boy didn't hold out his hands. The seller said again, "Hold out your hands," but again the little boy would not. The kind seller reached down, took the child's hands, and filled them with two handfuls of cherries.

Later, the boy's grandmother heard of the incident and asked, "Why didn't you hold out your hands when he asked you to?" And the little boy answered, "His hands are bigger than mine!"

God's hands, also, are bigger than ours!

September 29

LEARNING FROM ADVERSITY

You did not so learn Christ! Ephesians 4:20, RSV

ALEXANDER MACLAREN, a distinguished Manchester preacher (1826–1910), wrote, "What disturbs us in this world is not trouble, but our opposition to trouble. The true source of all that frets and irritates and wears away our lives is not in external things but in the resistance of our wills to the will of God expressed by eternal things."

To resent and resist God's disciplining hand is to miss one of the greatest spiritual blessings we Christians can enjoy this side of heaven.

Whatever it is—aggravations, trouble, adversity, irritations, opposition—we haven't "learned Christ" until we have discovered that God's grace is sufficient for every test.

Though Job suffered as few men have, he never lost sight of God's presence with him in the midst of suffering. He emerged victorious on the other side of sorrow and testing because he never allowed resentment to cloud his relationship with God.

The attitude which can overcome resentment is expressed by the writer to the Hebrews: "No discipline seems pleasant at the time, but painful. Later on, however, it produces a harvest of righteousness and peace for those who have been trained by it" (12:11, NIV).

September 30

RENEWED, NOT JUST RELIGIOUS

. . . Be renewed in the spirit of your minds, and put on the new nature, created after the likeness of God in true righteousness and holiness. Ephesians 4:23–24, RSV

W E Christians are not to be conformed to the world *spiritually*. We are not to be conformed to the world's definition of what it means to be religious, but are to make sure that we have met God's requirements for discipleship.

No nation was ever more religious than Israel in Isaiah's day. The Temple was filled. The altar ran red with the blood of sacrifice. The religious festivals were strictly observed, and the voice of prayer was heard in the house of God. But there was a lack of depth and true devotion in Israel's worship. The nation was deteriorating morally, even though record crowds were attending the Temple. Speaking as God commanded, Isaiah said, "Bring no more vain oblations; incense is an abomination unto me; the new moons and sabbaths, the calling of assemblies, I cannot [endure]; it is iniquity, even the solemn meeting" (Isaiah 1:13).

Then Isaiah told them how to regain the favor of God. These people who were members of the church—these people who had been reared according to the formalities of their religious laws, but during the week were not living a righteous life—Isaiah warned of the judgment of God.

Then he told them how they could be cleansed from their sin. He said, "Wash you, make you clean, put away the evil of your doings from before mine eyes; cease to do evil. . . . Come now, and let us reason together, saith the LORD: though your sins be as scarlet, they shall be as white as snow; though they be red like crimson, they shall be as wool" (Isaiah 1:16, 18).

There are thousands of people who do not give themselves to Jesus Christ, because they have conformed to the world. They are afraid of being called fanatic, pious, puritanical, or religious. A true Christian is a nonconformist. He does not conform himself to the worldly concepts of religion. Instead, he is to become a true disciple, a "follower" of the Lord.

October

October 1

SUFFERING

And walk in love, as Christ also hath loved us, and hath given himself for us an offering and a sacrifice to God for a sweet-smelling savor. . . . Christ also loved the church, and gave himself for it.
Ephesians 5:2, 25

AT the heart of our universe is a God who suffers in redemptive love. We experience more of His love when we suffer within an evil world. Someone has said that if one suffers without succeeding, he can be sure that the success will come in someone else's life. If he succeeds without suffering, he can be equally sure that someone else has already suffered for him.

High up in the foothills of the Himalayas is a beautiful city called Kohima. It is in Nagaland, one of the states of India. We were there to help them celebrate a hundred years of Christianity. It was there that the Japanese were stopped in their thrust toward India during World War II. Buried in a cemetery are the bodies of hundreds of Indians, British, Americans, and those of other nationalities who made up the Allied force that halted the Japanese advance. At the entrance to the cemetery there is an engraved memorial which says, "They gave their tomorrow that you might have today."

After sixteen difficult years as a missionary on the continent of Africa, David Livingstone returned to his native Scotland to address the students at Glasgow University. His body was emaciated by the ravages of some twenty-seven fevers which had coursed through his veins during the years of his service. One arm hung useless at his side, the result of being mangled by a lion. The core of his message to those young people was, "Shall I tell you what sustained me amidst the toil, the hardship, and loneliness of my exile? It was Christ's promise,

'Lo, I am with you always, even unto the end.'"

We, like David Livingstone, may claim the same promise from our Savior and Lord. He *does* go with us through our sufferings, and He awaits us as we emerge on the other side of the tunnel of testing—into the light of His glorious presence to live with Him forever!

October 2

BEING FILLED WITH THE SPIRIT

Do not get drunk on wine. . . . Instead, be filled with the Spirit. Ephesians 5:18, NIV

I THINK it proper to say that anyone who is not Spirit-filled is a defective Christian. Paul's command to the Ephesian Christians, "Be filled with the Spirit," is binding on all of us Christians everywhere in every age. There are no exceptions. We must conclude that since we are ordered to be filled with the Spirit, we are sinning if we are not filled. And our failure to be filled with the Spirit constitutes one of the greatest sins against the Holy Spirit.

It is interesting to note that the command to "Be filled with the Spirit" actually has the idea of continuously being filled in the original Greek language which Paul used. We are not filled once for all, like a bucket. Instead, we are to be filled constantly. It might be translated, "Be filled and keep on being filled," or "Be being filled."

Ephesians 5:18 literally says, "Keep on being filled with the Spirit." Dr. Merrill C. Tenney has compared this to the situation of an old-time farmhouse kitchen. In one corner was a sink; above it was a pipe through which came a continuous stream of water from the spring outside. The water, by running constantly, kept the sink brimful of good water. In like manner the Christian is not to let himself be emptied of the Spirit that he may later become full again; rather he is constantly to accept the direction and energy of the Spirit so he is always overflowing.

October 3

SEEING GOD'S WILL

Giving thanks always for all things unto God and the Father in the name of our Lord Jesus Christ. Ephesians 5:20

ONE of the most thrilling things about studying the Bible is to know that the infinite God has been pleased to share some of the secrets of His universe with His redeemed children.

Sin has blinded men, so the unsaved man sees life in a false perspective. But the born-again Christian sees life not as a blurred, confused, meaningless mass, but as something planned and purposeful. His eyes have been opened to spiritual truth.

In Christ's first sermon at Nazareth He said that one of the reasons He had come to earth was to preach "recovering of sight to the blind" (Luke 4:18). The Gospel of Christ helps us to see our need and helplessness, and then shows us the redeeming grace which God has placed within reach of every man.

In the Bible we are called "the children of light, and the children of the day" (1 Thessalonians 5:5), because it pleased God to share His mysteries and secrets with us. We are no longer in the dark—we know where we came from, we know why we are here, and we know where we are going.

In Ephesians 1:9–10 we learn of one of God's mysteries which has been revealed: "Having made known unto us the mystery of his will, according to his good pleasure which he hath purposed in himself: that in the dispensation of the fulness of times he might gather together in one all things in Christ, both which are in heaven, and which are on earth."

It is God's will that sometime in the future, perhaps very soon, we shall all be together with Him.

And what is God's will for us today? Down through the ages it has been the heart's desire of devout men to know and to follow the will of God each day. David said, "Teach me to do thy will" (Psalm 143:10).

Teach and do. He has taught. Are you doing?

October 4

SHALL MAN LIVE AGAIN?

For me to live is Christ, and to die is gain.   Philippians 1:21

THE great question of the ages has been, "If a man die, shall he live again?" We know that the first part of that sentence is fulfilled every day. There is no "if" about it. "It is appointed unto men once to die" (Hebrews 9:27). The question is "Shall man live again?"

There are those who say that all there is to man is just bone, flesh, and blood. They say that when you are dead, when you die, nothing happens; you don't go anywhere. It is dust to dust and ashes to ashes.

Ask the scientist and he cannot give an answer. I have asked a number of scientists questions concerning life after death, and most of them say, "We just do not know." Science deals in formulas and test tubes. There is a spiritual world that science knows nothing about.

Because many do not believe in life after death, their writings are filled with tragedy and pessimism. The writings of William Faulkner, James Joyce, Ernest Hemingway, Eugene O'Neill, and many others are filled with pessimism, darkness, and tragedy.

How different from Jesus Christ who said, "I am the

resurrection, and the life: he that believeth in me, though he were dead, yet shall he live: and whosoever liveth and believeth in me shall never die" (John 11:25–26). Again he said, "Because I live, ye shall live also" (John 14:19). Our hope of immortality is based on Christ alone—not on any desires, longings, arguments, or any instincts of immortality. Yet the hope of immortality that is revealed in Christ agrees with all those great desires and instincts.

October 5

VICTORIOUS SUFFERING

For it has been granted to you that for the sake of Christ you should not only believe in him but also suffer for his sake.
Philippians 1:29, RSV

ONE person whose name is synonymous with "victorious suffering" is the courageous, gifted quadriplegic, Joni Eareckson Tada. As the result of a diving accident, she is confined to a wheelchair, unable to care for her simplest needs. And yet she is one of the most vibrant, beautiful human beings I have known.

She has shared the platform with us many times in our Crusades, and her testimony to what the Lord has done for her in and through her testing never ceases to amaze and humble me. Joni has emerged from the fire of her testing with an unbelievably broad and perceptive insight into not only the meaning of suffering, but also into all the great theological truths that bear on this subject. Joni has had her own small Armageddon.

Her ability to grasp the deepest truths and phrase them in simple terms awes and inspires me. I know of very few people, including some of our greatest theologians, who have such a practical and wide-ranging grasp of who God is and what He is doing in His world. Her service for God is many times greater than if she had never had that accident while diving into the Chesapeake Bay.

Most of us will never experience the kind of handicap Joni has faced. But we complain just the same.

If you are physically well, praise God and learn not to complain about comparably minor irritations. If you do suffer from a physical infirmity, remember that the Lord is your strength and that He will not only see you through this life, but He will give you a brand new body in the next life.

October 6

SUCCESS WITHOUT SUFFERING?

For unto you it is given in the behalf of Christ, not only to believe on him, but also to suffer for his sake. Philippians 1:29

W E can find comfort in the midst of mourning because *God can use our sufferings to teach us and make us better people.* Sometimes it takes suffering to make us realize the brevity of life, and the importance of living for Christ. Often God uses suffering to accomplish things in our lives that would otherwise never be achieved.

The Bible puts it succinctly: "Count it all joy, my brethren, when you meet various trials, for you know that the testing of your faith produces steadfastness. And let steadfastness have its full effect, that you may be perfect and complete, lacking in nothing" (James 1:2–4, RSV). Some of the godliest people I have ever known were men and women who had been called upon to endure great suffering—perhaps even grown bitter and resentful if they had faced such circumstances—and yet, because they knew Christ and walked in the joy of His presence every day, God had blessed them and turned them into people who reflected Christ. Often I have gone into a sickroom or hospital room to encourage someone and have left feeling I was the one who had been encouraged and helped, because God had used their trials to make them more like Christ.

Before the power of the atom was discovered, science had to devise a way to "smash" the atom. The secret of the atom's immeasurable and limitless power was in its being crushed.

Dr. Edward Judson, at the dedication of the Judson Memorial Church in New York City, said, "Suffering and success go together. If you are succeeding without suffering, it is because others before you have suffered; if you are suffering without succeeding, it is that others after you may succeed."

October 7

THE CHRISTIAN'S MINDSET

Let this mind be in you, which was also in
Christ Jesus. Philippians 2:5

WE Christians are not to be conformed to this world mentally. The world by its advertisements, its conversation, and its philosophy is engaged in a gigantic brainwashing task. Not always consciously but sometimes unconsciously, the Christian is beset by secular and worldly propaganda.

Ads which proclaim that "the man of distinction" prefers a certain brand of whisky, imply that abstainers are not people of distinction.

Tobacco ads loudly proclaiming that "thinking men" prefer a certain filter, imply that only fools would reject their brand.

Much entertainment, even on Sunday, is slanted to those who feed on violence, sex, and lawlessness. It would seem that some diabolic mastermind is running the affairs of this world and that his chief objective is to brainwash Christians and get them to conform to this world.

The world's sewage system threatens to contaminate the stream of Christian thought. Satan will contest every hour you spend in Bible reading or prayer.

However, above the din we can hear the voice of Scripture: "Let this mind be in you, which was also in Christ Jesus" (Philippians 2:5), and "Be ye transformed by the renewing of your mind, that ye may prove what is that good, and acceptable, and perfect, will of God" (Romans 12:2).

We Christians are not even to be conformed to the world's anxieties.

Many Christians are wringing their hands and saying, "What's the world coming to?"

The Bible has already told us that "the world and the lust thereof" are going to pass away. We have already been told in Scripture that the world is coming to a cataclysmic judgment.

We Christians are to be lights in the midst of darkness, and our lives should exemplify relaxation, peace, and joy in the midst of frustration, confusion, and despair.

Time yourself the next time you read the Bible and pray. Compare this amount of time to that you spend, say, watching television. Is God getting His share of your time and attention?

October 8

THE SUMMARY OF SALVATION

And being found in fashion as a man, he humbled himself, and became obedient unto death, even the death of the cross.   Philippians 2:8

THE heart of the Christian Gospel with its incarnation and atonement is in the Cross and the resurrection. Jesus was born to die. Jesus did for man what man cannot do for himself. He did it through the Cross and the resurrection.

Today we look for man-made philosophical panaceas. Discussions and debates go on in every center of learning in a search for ultimate wisdom and its resultant happiness. No solution has been found. We still wrestle with the same philosophical problems that concerned Plato and Aristotle.

We are searching for a way out of our dilemma, and the universal sign we see is "no exit." But the Cross presents itself in the midst of our dilemma as our only hope. Here we find the justice of God in perfect satisfaction—the mercy of God extended to the sinner—the love of God covering every need—the power of God for every emergency—the glory of God for every occasion. Here is power enough to transform human nature. Here is power enough to change the world.

Samuel Rutherford, the great Scottish theologian and pastor who died in 1661, put it well when he wrote, "The cross of Christ, on which He was extended, points, in the length of it, to heaven and earth, reconciling them together; and in the breadth of it, to former and following ages, as being equally salvation to both." The apostle Paul indeed gave us the summary of salvation when he wrote, "And being found in fashion as a man, he humbled himself, and became obedient unto death, even the death of the cross."

October 9

THE FELLOWSHIP OF HIS SUFFERINGS

. . . I count all things but loss for the excellency of the knowledge of Christ Jesus my Lord: for whom I have suffered the loss of all things, and do count them but dung, that I may win Christ, and be found in him, not having mine own righteousness, which is of the law, but that which is through the faith of Christ, the righteousness which is of God

by faith: that I may know him, and the power of his resurrection, and the fellowship of his sufferings, being made conformable unto his death. Philippians 3:8–10

NOWHERE does the Bible teach that Christians are to be exempt from the tribulations and natural disasters that come upon the world. It does teach that the Christian can face tribulation, crisis, calamity, and personal suffering with a supernatural power that is not available to the person outside of Christ. Christiana Tsai, the Christian daughter of a former governor of Kiangsu Province in China, wrote, "Throughout my many years of illness [53], I have never dared to ask God why He allowed me to suffer so long. I only ask what He wants me to do." St. Augustine wrote, "Better is he that suffereth evil than the jollity of him that doeth evil."

The eagle is the only bird that can lock its wings and wait for the right wind. He waits for the updraft and never has to *flap* his wings, *just soar.* So as we wait on God He will help us use the adversities and strong winds to benefit us! The Bible says, "They that wait upon the LORD . . . shall mount up with wings as eagles" (Isaiah 40:31).

Christians can rejoice in the midst of persecution because they have eternity's values in view. When the pressures are on, they look beyond their present predicament to the glories of heaven. The thought of the future life with its prerogatives and joys helps to make the trials of the present seem light and transient. ". . . For theirs is the kingdom of heaven."

October 10

INNER JOY AND OUTWARD VICTORY

Rejoice in the Lord always. I will say it again: Rejoice!
Philippians 4:4, NIV

WHEN our hearts are surrendered totally to the will of God, then we delight in seeing Him use us in any way He desires. Our plans and desires begin to agree with His, and we accept His direction in our lives. Our sense of joy, satisfaction, and fulfillment in life increases, no matter what the circumstances, if we are in the center of God's will.

Resentment or resignation are not the answer to the problem of suffering. And there is a step beyond mere acceptance. It is accepting with joy. We need to listen to the words of James: "Consider it pure joy, my brothers, whenever you face trials of many kinds, because you know that the testing of your faith develops perseverance. Perseverance must finish its work so that you may be mature and complete, not lacking anything" (1:2–4, NIV).

The Christian life is a joyful life. Christianity was never meant to be something to make people miserable. The ministry of Jesus Christ was one of joy. The Bible teaches that a life of inward rest and outward victory is a Christian's birthright.

"What a witness to the world Christians would be," wrote Amy Carmichael, "if only they were more evidently very happy people." Joy is one of the marks of a true believer. Miss Carmichael quotes Prebendary Webb-Peploe as having said, "Joy is not gush: joy is not jolliness. Joy is simply perfect acquiescence in God's will, because the soul delights itself in God Himself."

The ability to rejoice in any situation is a sign of spiritual maturity.

October 11

ANXIOUS IN NOTHING

Have no anxiety about anything, but in everything by prayer and supplication with thanksgiving let your requests be made known to God.

And the peace of God, which passes all understanding, will keep your hearts and your minds in Christ Jesus.   Philippians 4:6–7, RSV

HAPPY is the person who has learned the secret of coming to God daily in prayer. Fifteen minutes alone with God every morning before one starts the day can change our outlooks and recharge our batteries.

But all of this happiness and all of these unlimited benefits which flow from the storehouse of heaven are contingent upon our relationship to God. Absolute dependency and absolute yieldedness are the conditions of being His child. Only His children are entitled to receive those things that lend themselves to happiness; and in order to be His child, there must be the surrender of the will to Him.

We must admit we are poor before we can be made rich. We must admit we are destitute before we can become children by adoption.

When we realize that all our own goodness is as filthy rags in God's sight and become aware of the destructive power of our stubborn wills, when we realize our absolute dependence upon the grace of God through faith and nothing more, then we have started on the road to happiness.

We do not come to know God through works—we come to know Him by faith through grace. We cannot work our way toward happiness and heaven; we cannot moralize our way, we cannot reform our way, we cannot buy our way. Salvation comes as a gift of God through Christ.

October 12

THE PATH TO PEACE

And the peace of God, which passeth all understanding, shall keep your hearts and minds through Christ Jesus.   Philippians 4:7

THERE are no troubles that distress the mind and wear upon the nerves as do borrowed troubles. The psalmist said, "Fret not thyself . . ." (Psalm 37:1). The implication is that fretting, complaining, and distress of mind are often self-manufactured and can best be coped with by a change of attitude and transformation of thought. As someone has said, "Worry is an old man with bended head, carrying a load of feathers which he thinks is lead."

The psalmist also said, "I will both lay me down in peace, and sleep: for thou, LORD, only makest me dwell in safety" (Psalm 4:8). Job asks, "When he giveth quietness, who then can make trouble" (Job 34:29)?

Many of our troubles are caused by self-centeredness. The human mind is not meant to be limited to such a narrow scope. It is to be free to soar, to dream, to hope, and to trust. When our eyes are turned inward instead of upward, we suffer from spiritual nearsightedness.

Anticipation of trouble makes trifles appear unduly large, and the troubles that never come make up an imagined burden that will crush the spirit. They are haunting specters, as insubstantial as a bad dream, and we spend the strength that should be expended in constructive work and services in fighting problems that do not even exist.

Instead of "borrowing trouble" we should listen to the Lord when He says, "Peace I leave with you, my peace I give unto you: not as the world giveth, give I unto you. Let not your heart be troubled, neither let it be afraid" (John 14:27).

October 13

PAUL'S THORN IN THE FLESH

I can do all things through Christ which strengtheneth me. Philippians 4:13

THE apostle Paul, by firsthand experience, knew what it meant to suffer. As he was telling the people of Corinth about some of his personal experiences with the risen Lord, he confessed that he had a real physical problem: "To keep me from becoming conceited because of these surpassingly great revelations, there was given me a thorn in my flesh, a messenger of Satan, to torment me" (2 Corinthians 12:7).

We don't know exactly what that "thorn in the flesh" was, but it must have been a physical ailment. It may have been some type of eye disease or epilepsy; or, as Sir William Ramsay thought most likely, malarial fever. However, we do know how he handled his problem and what his subsequent attitude toward it was:

> Three times I pleaded with the Lord to take it away from me. But he said to me, "My grace is sufficient for you, for my power is made perfect in weakness." Therefore I will boast all the more gladly about my weaknesses, so that Christ's power may rest on me. That is why, for Christ's sake, I delight in weaknesses, in insults, in hardships, in persecutions, in difficulties. For when I am weak, then I am strong.
> (2 Corinthians 12:8–10, NIV)

Certainly Paul did not like that thorn in the flesh. But when he knew that it was not possible to get rid of it, he stopped groaning and began glorifying. He knew it was God's will and that the affliction was an opportunity for him to prove the power of Christ in his life.

Would you be able to live above your circumstances as Paul did? To withstand suffering as severe as his in our own power would be impossible. Yet with the apostle we can say, "I can do everything through him who gives me strength" (Philippians 4:13, NIV).

GOD WILL SUPPLY ALL OUR NEEDS

My God will meet all your needs according to his glorious riches in Christ Jesus. Philippians 4:19, NIV

WHAT a promise this is for the Christian! The source is God—"my God," the apostle calls Him. The supply is inexhaustible—"according to his glorious riches." And the Savior is the channel through whom these riches come to us. The equation is totally in my favor. My needs are balanced over against His riches. There is no way I could improve upon that arrangement. No matter what my need, He is more than able to meet it. We are not to treat God as the anonymous writer puts it: "Some people treat God like they do a lawyer; they go to Him only when they are in trouble."

I find that I need Christ just as much, and sometimes more, in my more exalted hours as I do in the times of difficulties, troubles, and adversity. Many times we make the mistake of thinking that Christ's help is needed only for sickrooms or in times of overwhelming sorrow and suffering. This is not true. Jesus wishes to enter into every mood and every moment of our lives. He went to the wedding at Cana as well as to the home of Mary and Martha when Lazarus died. He wept with those who wept and rejoiced with those who rejoiced. Someone has said, "There are just as many stars in the sky at noon as at midnight, although we cannot see them in the sun's glare."

I seriously doubt if we will ever understand our trials and adversities until we are safely in heaven. Then when we look back we are going to be absolutely amazed at how God took care of us and blessed us even in the storms of life. We face dangers every day of which we are not even aware. Often God intervenes in our behalf through the use of His marvelous angels. I do not believe that anything happens to an obedient Christian by accident. It is all in God's purpose. "We know that in all things God works for the good of those who love him, who have been called according to his purpose" (Romans 8:28, NIV).

October 15

GOD'S GREAT PLUS SIGN

For it pleased the Father that in him [Jesus] should all fulness dwell; and, having made peace through the blood of his cross, by him to reconcile all things unto himself. . . .
Colossians 1:19–20

THOUSANDS of people suffer from guilt complexes. Almost everyone senses that somehow they are wrong, like the little boy who said, "I guess I was just born wrong." God said from the Cross, "I love you."

He was also saying, "I can forgive you." The most glorious and thrilling word in any language is "forgiveness." God in Christ had a basis for forgiveness. Because Christ died, God can justify the sinner and still be just.

Christ's dying on the cross was more than the death of a martyr. It was more than His setting a good example by offering His life for His fellow man. His was the sacrifice that God had appointed and ordained to be the one and only sacrifice for sin. The Scripture says, "The LORD hath laid on him the iniquity of us all. . . . it pleased the LORD to bruise him; he hath put him to grief" (Isaiah 53:6, 10). Because God Himself has set forth Christ to be the covering for human guilt, then God cannot possibly reject the sinner who accepts Jesus Christ as Savior. "Whom God hath set forth to be a propitiation through faith in his blood" (Romans 3:25).

This is what the communion table in the church is all

about. Every time we eat the bread we are remembering the body of Christ nailed to the cross for us, and every time we drink the wine we are remembering the blood that was shed on the cross as a covering for our sins. A little girl, seeing a cross on the communion table, asked, "Mama, what is that plus sign doing on the table?" The cross is God's great plus sign of history.

October 16

THE CENTRALITY OF THE CROSS

For in him [Christ] all the fulness of God was pleased to dwell, and through him to reconcile to himself all things, whether on earth or in heaven, making peace by the blood of his cross.
Colossians 1:19–20, RSV

MY friend and associate Cliff Barrows told me this story about bearing punishment. He recalled the time when he took the punishment for his children when they had disobeyed. "They had done something I had forbidden them to do. I told them if they did the same thing again I would have to discipline them. When I returned from work and found that they hadn't minded me, the heart went out of me. I just couldn't discipline them."

Any loving father can understand Cliff's dilemma. Most of us have been in the same position. He continued with the story: "Bobby and Bettie Ruth were very small. I called them into my room, took off my belt and my shirt, and with a bare back, knelt down at the bed. I made them both strap me with the belt ten times each. You should have heard the crying! From them, I mean! They didn't want to do it. But I told them the penalty had to be paid and so through their sobs and tears they did what I told them."

Cliff smiled when he remembered the incident. "I must

admit I wasn't much of a hero. It hurt. I haven't offered to do that again, but I never had to spank them again, either, because they got the point. We kissed each other when it was over and prayed together."

In an infinite way that staggers our hearts and minds, we know that Christ paid the penalty for our sins, past, present, and future.

That is why He died on the cross.

October 17

A GLORIOUS HOPE

To them God has chosen to make known among the Gentiles the glorious riches of this mystery, which is Christ in you, the hope of glory. Colossians 1:27, NIV

ONE of the bonuses of being a Christian is the glorious hope that extends out beyond the grave into the glory of God's tomorrow.

The Bible opens with a tragedy and ends in a triumph.

In Genesis we see the devastation of sin and death, but in the Revelation we glimpse God's glorious victory over sin and death. Revelation 14:13 (NIV) says, "'Blessed are the dead who die in the Lord from now on.' 'Yes,' says the Spirit, 'they will rest from their labor, for their deeds will follow them.'"

But what is the basis of the Christian's hope of eternal life? Is our hope of life after death merely wishful thinking or blind optimism? Can we have any certainty that there is life after death and that someday those who know Christ will go to be with Him throughout eternity?

Yes! There is one great fact which gives the Christian assurance in the face of death: *the resurrection of Jesus Christ.* It is the physical, bodily resurrection of Christ that gives us confidence and hope. Because Christ rose from the dead, we know beyond doubt that death is not the end, but is merely the transition to eternal life.

Never forget that the resurrection of Christ is in many ways the central event of all history. Paul said, "If Christ has not been raised, your faith is futile; you are still in your sins. If only for this life we have hope in Christ, we are to be pitied more than all men. But Christ has indeed been raised from the dead" (1 Corinthians 15:17–20, NIV). The resurrection of Christ makes all the difference! Because He rose from the dead, we *know* that He was in fact the Son of God who came to save us through His death on the cross, as He claimed.

October 18

READY—OR SORRY?

For yourselves know perfectly that the day of the Lord so cometh as a thief in the night. 1 Thessalonians 5:2

WHEN the late President Eisenhower was vacationing in Denver many years ago, his attention was called to an open letter in a local newspaper, which told how six-year-old Paul Haley, dying of incurable cancer, had expressed a wish to see the president of the United States. Spontaneously, in one of those gracious gestures remembered long after a man's most carefully prepared speeches are forgotten, the president decided to grant the boy's request.

So one Sunday morning in August, a big limousine pulled up outside the Haley home, and out stepped the president. He walked up to the door and knocked.

Mr. Donald Haley opened the door, wearing blue jeans, an old shirt, and a day's growth of beard. Behind him was his little son, Paul. Their amazement at finding President Eisenhower on their doorstep can be imagined.

"Paul," said the president to the little boy, "I understand you want to see me. Glad to see you." Then he shook hands with the six-year-old, took him out to see the presidential limousine, shook hands again, and left.

The Haleys and their neighbors, and a lot of other people, will probably talk about this kind and thoughtful deed of a busy president for a long time to come. Only one person was not entirely happy about it—that was Mr. Haley. He can never forget how he was dressed when he opened the door. "Those jeans, the old shirt, the unshaven face—what a way to meet the president of the United States!" he said.

Of course, the visit was unannounced, and under the circumstances it wasn't to be expected that he would be all dressed up in his best clothes. But all his life he will wish he had gotten up a bit earlier that day, shaved a little sooner, and at least put on a clean shirt before the president arrived. Readiness and watchfulness are all urged upon Christians, lest Christ's coming, taking us by surprise, should find us unprepared.

October 19

PRAY WITHOUT CEASING

Pray without ceasing . . . and the very God of peace sanctify you wholly. . . . 1 Thessalonians 5:17, 23

REMEMBER that you can pray anytime, anywhere. Washing dishes, digging ditches, working in the office, in the shop, on the athletic field, even in prison—you can pray and know God hears! We have a friend on Death Row who prays for us every morning between four and six. How often this fact has encouraged and cheered us on.

Try to have a systematic method of prayer. Prayer combined with Bible study makes for a healthy Christian life.

The Bible says, "Pray without ceasing." If you have special prayer periods that you set aside during the day, your unconscious life will be saturated with prayer between the prayer periods. It is not enough for you to get out of bed in the morning and just bow your knee and repeat a few sentences. There should be stated periods in which you slip apart with God. For the overworked mother or one living under extremely busy circumstances, this may be impossible. But here is where "prayer without ceasing" comes in. We pray as we work. As we have said, we pray everywhere, anytime.

The devil will fight you every step of the way. He will cause the baby to cry, the telephone to ring, someone to knock at the door—there will be many interruptions, but keep at it! Don't be discouraged. Soon you will find that these periods of prayer are the greatest delight in your life. You will look forward to them with more anticipation than to anything else. Without constant, daily, systematic prayer, your life will seem barren, discouraging, and fruitless. Without constant prayer you never can know the inner peace that God wants to give you.

October 20

WHOLLY HOLY

And the very God of peace sanctify you wholly; and I pray God your whole spirit and soul and body be preserved blameless unto the coming of our Lord Jesus Christ. 1 Thessalonians 5:23

GOD is first of all concerned with what you *are*. What you *do* is the result of what you are. Quality of life is the purpose and intent of sanctification.

"Ye are a chosen generation, a royal priesthood, a holy nation, a peculiar people; that ye should show forth the praises of him who hath called you out of the darkness into his marvelous light" (1 Peter 2:9). "That ye might walk worthy of the Lord unto all pleasing, being fruitful in every good work, and increasing in the knowledge of God" (Colossians 1:10).

The Law required conformity to a set of rules, but the Law was a shadow of things to come. The Bible says, "By the law is the knowledge of sin" (Romans 3:20).

The New Testament, in contrast to the Law, says, "Christ in you, the hope of glory" (Colossians 1:27). There is no way that we, by ourselves, can generate sanctification. Our sanctification is Christ. There is no way we can be holy. Our holiness is Christ.

This caused Paul to write, "Not having mine own righteousness, which is of the law, but that which is through the faith of Christ, the righteousness which is of God by faith" (Philippians 3:9). It caused the hymn writer to say this:

> When He shall come with trumpet sound,
> O may I then in Him be found;
> Dressed in His righteousness alone,
> Faultless to stand before the throne!

D. L. Moody said, "Next to the might of God, the serene beauty of a holy life is the most powerful influence for good in the world."

October 21

GOD OWNS THE FUTURE

Grace to you and peace from God our Father and the Lord Jesus Christ . . . to give you who are troubled rest. . . .
2 Thessalonians 1:2, 7, NKJV

IN recent years we have been witnessing an increase of violence in the Western world. It has been said that our era will be known as "the age of violence." I don't know what it's going to be called, but I do know that the future belongs to God. To you who are troubled by the events you read about in your newspapers, to you who are disturbed about the things you see on your television screens, the apostle Paul says, "Rest with us." What he is saying is, "Relax."

There are three problems we have never been able to solve. The first is that of human iniquity. The city of Pittsburgh is the headquarters of over a hundred major corporations. The city has solved some great human problems through technology. It was in Pittsburgh that Dr. Jonas Salk isolated the polio vaccine. Here is a city that could teach the world a few lessons. But there's one problem none of our great cities has solved—the problem of human iniquity: lying, hate, lust, greed. When Christ comes back He's going to solve that problem.

There is another problem that has not been solved: the problem of human suffering. Modern civilized man is developing a high suicide rate. He may live in the finest home in town, and yet suffer from a broken heart, loneliness, boredom, physical or mental suffering. Christ at His return will take away suffering; He says He will wipe away all tears. There will be no more backaches or headaches; cancer and heart disease will be eliminated; mental illness will be no more. All the diseases of mankind will be cured when Christ comes back.

The greatest unsolved problem of all is the crisis of death, which each of us has to face. "It is appointed unto men once to die," says the Bible. But when Christ returns for His church, those redeemed ones who are alive will not die but will be caught up to meet Him in the air. For them, death will be ended.

When Christ comes, peace will come. Our greatest

statesmen and scholars are seeking a way for peace, but they are attempting to do it without the Prince of Peace. Man cannot bring enduring peace. Enduring peace will be brought only when the Prince of Peace comes and sets up His great and mighty Kingdom.

October 22

PERSECUTION OR POPULARITY?

. . . We ourselves glory in you in the churches of God for your patience and faith in all your persecutions and tribulations that ye endure. 2 Thessalonians 1:4

Popularity and adulation can be far more dangerous for the Christian than persecution. It is, unfortunately, easy when all goes well to lose our sense of balance and our perspective. We must learn like Paul "how to abound" and "how to be abased." We must learn in "whatsoever state" we are "therewith to be content" (Philippians 4:11).

As we have said elsewhere in this book, the important thing is to walk with Christ, to live for Christ, and to have one consuming passion to please Him. Then, whatever happens, we know that He has permitted it to teach us some priceless lesson and to perfect us for His service. He will enrich our circumstances, be they pleasant or disagreeable, by the fact of His presence with us. The tomorrows fill us with dread. John 10:4 says, "He putteth forth his own sheep." Whatever awaits us is *encountered* first by Him. Like the oriental shepherd always went ahead of his sheep—therefore any attack on sheep has to *deal first* with the shepherd—all the *tomorrows* of our lives have to pass Him before they get to us!

Three Hebrew children were cast into the burning fiery furnace, but the king said, "Lo, I see four men loose, walking in the midst of the fire, and they have no hurt; and the form of the fourth is like the Son of God" (Daniel 3:25). Our God is with us in the midst of persecution.

An apocryphal story tells of the first convert of a certain missionary who was tortured to death for his faith. Years later, the missionary died. In heaven he met that first convert and asked him how it felt to be tortured to death for his faith. "You know," the man replied with a shrug and looking a bit bewildered, "I can't even remember."

October 23

OUR FATHER

May our Lord Jesus Christ himself and God our Father, who loved us and by his grace gave us eternal encouragement and good hope, encourage your hearts and strengthen you in every good deed and word.
2 Thessalonians 2:16–17, NIV

WHEN we become Christians we can say, "Our Father," for those who receive Christ have the right to become children of God (John 1:12). So then we can look to God as our Father. We are to put our trust in Him and come to know Him in the close, intimate companionship of father and child. We can have a personal sense of His love for us and His interest in us, for He is concerned about us as a father is concerned for his children.

As Peter Marshall once put it, "God will not permit any troubles to come upon us, unless he has a specific plan by which great blessing can come out of the difficulty."

It is through the suffering, the tests and trials of life, that we can draw near to God. A. B. Simpson once heard a man say something he never forgot: "When God tests you, it is a good time for you to test Him by putting His promises to the proof, and claiming from Him just as much as your trials have rendered necessary."

There are two ways of getting out of a trial. One is to simply try to get rid of the trial, and be thankful when it is over. The other is to recognize the trial as a challenge from God to claim a larger blessing than we have ever had.

October 24

....

DEFENDED FROM SATAN

But the Lord is faithful, and he will strengthen and protect you from the evil one. 2 Thessalonians 3:3, NIV

THE Bible teaches that the demons are dedicated to controlling this planet for their master, Satan. Even Jesus called him "the prince of this world" (John 12:31). He is the master organizer and strategist. Many times throughout biblical history, and possibly even today, angels and demons engage in warfare. Many of the events of our times may very well be involved in this unseen struggle.

We are not left in doubt about who will ultimately triumph. Time after time Jesus has assured us that He and the angels would be victorious: "When the Son of man shall come in his glory, and all the holy angels with him, then shall he sit upon the throne of his glory" (Matthew 25:31). The apostle Paul wrote, "The Lord Jesus shall be revealed from heaven with his mighty angels, in flaming fire . . ." (2 Thessalonians 1:7–8).

Jesus also taught that "Whosoever shall confess me before men, him shall the Son of man also confess before the angels of God" (Luke 12:8). It is impossible to comprehend one's suffering of eternal loss when he learns that angels do not acknowledge him because he has been false in his claims to know Christ. But what a moment it is going to be for believers throughout all the ages, from every tribe, nation, and tongue, when they are presented in the Court of Heaven.

Scripture calls it "the marriage supper of the Lamb" (Revelation 19:9). This is the great event when Jesus Christ is crowned King of kings and Lord of lords. Both believers of all ages, and all the angelic hosts will join in bowing their knees and confessing that He is Lord.

October 25

THE FACT OF FAITH

I know whom I have believed, and am persuaded that he is able to keep that which I have committed unto him against that day.
2 Timothy 1:12

IF you are saved from sin, you are saved through a personal faith in the Gospel of Christ as defined in the Scriptures. Though it may at first seem dogmatic and narrow to you, the fact remains that there is no other way. The Bible says, "I declare unto you the gospel which I preached unto you . . . for I delivered unto you first of all that which I also received, how that Christ died for our sins according to the scriptures; and that he was buried, and that he rose again the third day according to the scriptures" (1 Corinthians 15:1, 3–4). The Bible says that we are saved when our faith is in this objective fact. The work of Christ is a fact, His Cross is a fact, His tomb is a fact, His resurrection is a fact.

It is impossible to believe anything into existence. The Gospel did not come into being because men believed it. The tomb was not emptied of Christ's body that first Easter because some faithful persons believed it. The fact preceded the faith. We are psychologically incapable of believing without an object of our faith.

You are not called upon to believe something that is not credible, but to believe in the *fact* of history that in reality transcends all history. We call upon you to believe that this work of Christ for sinners is effective in all who will risk their souls with Him. Trusting in Him for your eternal salvation is trusting, not in a figment of someone's imagination, but in a fact.

October 26

NO PRAYER, NO PEACE

I will therefore that men pray every where, lifting up holy hands, without wrath and doubting.   1 Timothy 2:8

DOWN through our history our nation's leaders have carried their plans and hopes to God in prayer. Yet today we have come to a place where we regard prayer in our national life simply as a venerated tradition. We have no sense of coming earnestly to God; we simply use prayer as a formality.

If this nation was born in a meeting based on prayer, some of its most important decisions being made only after careful prayer to God, how can we go on unless there is a renewed emphasis on prayer today?

One of the reasons the United Nations has become so ineffective in handling world situations is that there is no prayer, no recognition of God. At the first meeting of the United Nations in San Francisco, no prayer was lifted to God for guidance and blessing. We were afraid that the atheistic Communists would not like it, so we yielded in deference to them.

I predict that unless the leaders of the nations turn to God in prayer, their best plans will fail, just as did the plans of those who built the tower of Babel.

There are thousands of people who say prayers only in times of great stress, danger, or uncertainty. I have flown through bad storms, when all around me people who never before thought to pray were praying. It is instinctive for man to pray in a time of trouble.

Christ instructed His followers to pray, both by teaching and by example. So fervent and so direct were His prayers that one time when He had finished praying, His followers turned to Him and said, "Lord, teach us to pray" (Luke 11:1). They knew that Jesus had been in touch with God, and they wanted to have such an experience.

Never before in history have we stood in greater need of prayer. Will we be people of prayer for such a time as this?

October 27

POSITIVE THOUGHTS ON PERSECUTION

We . . . suffer reproach, because we trust in the living God . . . but be thou an example of the believers, in word, in conversation, in charity, in spirit, in faith, in purity. 1 Timothy 4:10, 12

THE reproach we experience is the natural resentment in the hearts of men toward all that is godly and righteous. This is the cross we are to bear. This is why Christians are often persecuted. Paul made this clear in these comments to Timothy.

Let us not forget that there is happiness and blessing in persecution. As George MacDonald puts it, we become "hearty through hardship." Our Lord instructs the persecuted to be happy. "Rejoice," He said, "and be exceeding glad: for great is your reward in heaven: for so persecuted they the prophets which were before you" (Matthew 5:12).

The word "joy" has all but disappeared from our current Christian vocabulary. One of the reasons is that we have thought that joy and happiness were found in comfort, ease, and luxury. James did not say, "Count it all joy when you fall into an easy chair," but he said, "Count it all joy when you fall into divers temptations" (James 1:2).

The persecuted are happy because they are being processed for heaven. Persecution is one of the natural consequences of living the Christian life. It is to the Christian what "growing pains" are to the growing child. No pain, no development. No suffering, no glory. No struggle, no victory. No persecution, no reward! Jesus predicted that if they persecuted Him, they would persecute you who follow Him, too.

The Bible says, "The God of all grace, who hath called us unto his eternal glory by Christ Jesus, after that ye have suffered a while, make you perfect, establish, strengthen, settle you" (1 Peter 5:10). It is so easy to forget that "all things work together for good to them that love God" (Romans 8:28).

October 28

MONEY CAN BE DANGEROUS

For the love of money is the root of all evils; it is through this craving that some have wandered away from the faith. . . .
1 Timothy 6:10, RSV

THE Bible does not condemn money or material possessions. Some of the great people of the Bible were very rich. Abraham, Isaac, and Solomon were perhaps the richest men of their day. God's quarrel is not with material goods but with material gods. Materialism has become the god of too many of us. It is that state in which material possessions are elevated to the central place in life and receive the attention due to God alone.

The Bible teaches that preoccupation with material possessions is a form of idolatry. And God hates idolatry. It poisons every other phase of our life, including our family life.

The Bible declares that "the love of money is the root of all evil" (1 Timothy 6:10), not money but the *love* of money. This Scripture is being verified in our national life today, and we are reaping what we have sown for several generations. We are, at least in part, suffering the consequences of our selfish preoccupation with material things, especially since World War II, to the neglect of moral and spiritual values.

We thought that man had come of age and that God, if there was one, could be relegated to the sidelines. But Jesus told the story of the man who had his barn full, and he had all of his possessions, and he said, "Soul, take your ease, eat and drink and be merry" (Luke 12:19). He left God out, and that night he died—possibly of a heart attack. And there was a voice heard from heaven that said, "You fool" (Luke 12:20).

"What shall it profit a man, if he . . . gain the whole world, and lose his own soul" (Mark 8:36)? There is a day of reckoning ahead. The handwriting is on the wall. What does it say?

October 29

LIFE'S NEW DIMENSION

I know whom I have believed. 2 Timothy 1:12

DOES it work when a man comes, repenting of his sins, to receive Christ by faith? I can only tell you that it worked in my own life. Something did happen to me. I didn't become perfect, but the direction of my life was changed.

I was reared on a farm in North Carolina and did not have the best of education. During the Depression period my parents were unable to give me the advantages that young people have today. I grew up in a Christian home, but by the time I was fifteen, I was in full revolt against all religion—against God, the Bible, the church. To make a long story short, one day I decided to commit my life to Jesus Christ. Not to be a clergyman but, in whatever I was to be, to seek the Kingdom of God first.

As a result, I found a new dimension to life. I found a new capacity to love that I had never known before. Just in the matter of race, my attitude toward people of other backgrounds changed remarkably. All of our difficulties are not solved the moment we are converted to Christ, but conversion does mean that we can approach our problems with a new attitude and in a new strength.

I was a poor student until that time, but immediately my grades picked up. I am not suggesting that you should come to Christ in order to get better grades, but I am telling you that the life in Christ works. I have seen it work all over the world. I have seen those converted whom I might classify as intellectuals; but they have to come as children. We say to our children, "Act like grown-ups," but Jesus said to the grown-ups, "Be like children." You are not to come to the Cross as a doctor of philosophy, nor as a doctor of law, but simply as a human being; and your life can be changed.

October 30

HOPE HANGS A HALO

Wherein I suffer trouble, as an evildoer, even unto bonds; but the word of God is not bound. Therefore I endure all things for the elect's sake, that they may also obtain salvation which is in Christ Jesus with eternal glory. If we suffer, we shall also reign with him: if we deny him, he also will deny us. 2 Timothy 2:9–10, 12

IN a sense, Christ is a King in exile, and we who are His followers are often looked upon with derision. To be identified with Him here and now quite naturally entails some "loss of face," some persecution; but someday, we are told, we shall be "kings and priests" and shall be active participators in His Kingdom.

Paul must have had this fact in mind when he said, "For I

reckon that the sufferings of this present time are not worthy to be compared with the glory which shall be revealed in us. For the earnest expectation of the creature waiteth for the manifestation of the sons of God" (Romans 8:18–19).

If we should be called upon to suffer all our lives, it would not be long compared to eternity. We are in the position of heirs to a large estate who gladly endure a few days of suffering and privation with the hope that we shall soon come into our fabulous inheritance. Such a glorious hope hangs a halo over the drab existence of the here and now.

Life cannot lose its zest when down underneath our present discomfort is the knowledge that we are children of a King. Complaining becomes foolish; behaving in the manner of the world is unworthy; and love, gentleness, and meekness become the hallmark of God's nobility. "All things" are taken in stride; burdens become blessings in disguise; every wound, like good surgery, is for our good; and etched in every cross is the symbol of a crown.

October 31

THE SEAL, THE PLEDGE, AND THE WITNESS

Nevertheless, God's solid foundation stands firm, sealed with this inscription: "The Lord knows those who are his."
2 Timothy 2:19, NIV

JOHN WESLEY, the founder of the Methodist church, once observed, "It is hard to find words in the language of men, to explain the deep things of God. Indeed, there are none that will adequately express what the Spirit of God works in His children. But . . . by the testimony of the Spirit, I mean, an inward impression on the soul, whereby the Spirit of God immediately and directly witnesses to my spirit, that I am a child of God; that Jesus Christ hath loved me, and given Himself for me; that all my sins are blotted out, and I, even I, am reconciled to God."

We can see then that God places a *seal* on us when we receive Christ. And that seal is a person—the Holy Spirit. By the Spirit's presence God gives us security and establishes His ownership over us.

The Spirit is also God's *pledge*. He not only seals the arrangement, but He represents God's voluntary obligation to see us through. And fellowship with the Spirit is a sample of what we can expect when we come into our inheritance in heaven.

Finally, the Spirit *witnesses* to us by His Word and within our hearts that Christ died for us, and by faith in Him we have become God's children. What a wonderful thing to know the Holy Spirit has been given to us as a seal—a pledge—and a witness! May each of these give us new assurance of God's love for us, and give us confidence as we seek to live for Christ. And with the apostle Paul may we say, "Thanks be to God for His indescribable gift!" (2 Corinthians 9:15, NKJV).

November

GENTLE JESUS

And the Lord's servant must not be quarrelsome but kindly to every one,
an apt teacher, forbearing, correcting his opponents with gentleness.
2 Timothy 2:24–25, RSV

JESUS was a gentle person. When He came into the world, there were few institutions of mercy. There were few hospitals or mental institutions, few places of refuge for the poor, few homes for orphans, few havens for the forsaken. In comparison to today, it was a cruel world. Christ changed that. Wherever true Christianity has gone, His followers have performed acts of gentleness and kindness.

The word "gentleness" occurs only a few times in our English Bible. It is spoken of in connection with the three Persons of the Trinity. In Psalm 18:35, it is the gentleness of God; in 2 Corinthians 10:1, the gentleness of Christ; and in Galatians 5:23, the gentleness of the Holy Spirit.

Charles Allen points out, "In one's disdain of sin, one can be harsh and unkind toward a sinner. . . . Some people seem to have such a passion for righteousness that they have no room left for compassion for those who have failed."

From some unknown poet comes these meaningful lines:

> Just to be tender, just to be true,
> Just to be glad the whole day through,
> Just to be merciful, just to be mild,
> Just to be trustful as a child:
> Just to be gentle and kind and sweet,
> Just to be helpful with willing feet,
> Just to be cheery when things go wrong,
> Just to drive sadness away with song,
> Whether the hour is dark or bright,

Just to be loyal to God and right,
Just to believe that God knows best,
Just in His promise ever rest,
Just to let love be our daily key,
That is God's will for you and me.

November 2

RIGHT-SIDE-UP IN AN UPSIDE-DOWN WORLD

All that will live godly in Christ Jesus shall suffer persecution.
2 Timothy 3:12

THIS is a spiritual law which is as unchangeable as the law of gravity. We must get this fact firmly fixed in our minds: We live in an upside-down world. People hate when they should love; they quarrel when they should be friendly; they fight when they should be peaceful; they wound when they should heal; they steal when they should share; they do wrong when they should do right.

I once saw a toy clown with a weight in its head. No matter how it was placed, it invariably assumed an upside-down position. It could be placed on its feet or on its side, and when let go it flipped back on its head.

In our unregenerate state we are just like that! Regardless of the circumstances, we always revert to an upside-down position. From childhood to maturity we are always prone to do what we should not do and to refrain from doing what we ought to do. That is our nature. We have too much weight in the head and not enough ballast in our hearts, so we flip upside down when left alone.

That is why the disciples seemed to be misfits to the world. To an upside-down man, a right-side-up man seems upside down. To the nonbeliever, the true Christian is an oddity and an abnormality. A Christian's goodness is a rebuke to another's wickedness; his being right-side-up is a reflection upon the worldling's inverted position. So the conflict is a natural one. And persecution is inevitable.

EFFECTUAL PRAYER

The effectual fervent prayer of a righteous man availeth much.
James 5:16

FROM one end of the Bible to the other, there is the record of those whose prayers have been answered—men who turned the tide of history by prayer; men who fervently prayed, and God answered.

Hezekiah prayed when his city was threatened by the invading army of the Assyrians under the leadership of Sennacherib, and the entire army of Sennacherib was destroyed, and the nation was spared for another generation—because the king prayed (2 Chronicles 32).

The problems of the world will never be settled unless our national leaders go to God in prayer. If only they would discover the power and wisdom that there is in reliance upon God, we could soon see the solution to the grave problems that face the world.

How wonderful it would be if the vice president of the United States would ask the Senate, at the beginning of each session, to get on its knees before God! What a tremendous change there would be in all the affairs of government!

Elijah prayed, and God sent fire from heaven to consume the offering on the altar he had built in the presence of God's enemies. Elisha prayed, and the son of the Shunammite woman was raised from the dead.

Daniel prayed, and the secret of God was made known to him for the saving of his and his companions' lives, and the changing of the course of history.

Paul prayed, and hundreds of churches were born in Asia Minor and Europe. Peter prayed, and Dorcas was raised to life, to have added years of service for Jesus Christ.

As the seventeenth century theologian, John Owen, said, "He who prays as he ought, will endeavor to live as he prays."

November 4

ANGELS ARE WATCHING US

For the grace of God that bringeth salvation hath appeared to all men. Teaching us that, denying ungodliness and worldly lusts, we should live soberly, righteously, and godly, in this present world. Titus 2:11–12

THE charge to live righteously in this present world sobers us when we realize that the walk and warfare of Christians is the primary concern of heaven and its angelic hosts. Paul said, "I solemnly charge you in the presence of God and of Christ Jesus and of the chosen angels, that you guard and keep [these rules] . . ." (1 Timothy 5:21, AB). Paul was stirring up Timothy to remember that the elect angels were constantly watching how he served the Savior and lived the Christian life. What fact could provide a greater motivation to righteous living than that? I must say to myself, "Careful, angels are watching!"

It must give the angels great satisfaction to watch the Church of Jesus Christ minister the unsearchable riches of Christ to lost men everywhere. If the angels rejoice over one sinner who repents (Luke 15:10), then the angel hosts are numbered among the spectators in the heavenly grandstands. They are included among those who are referred to as "so great a cloud of witnesses" (Hebrews 12:1); and they never miss any of the details of our earthly pilgrimage. Yet they do not jeer as did the Greek crowds of Paul's day. Rather, as we declare the Gospel and see our friends saved, they rejoice with us.

In his book *Though I Walk Through the Valley*, Dr. Vance Havner tells of an old preacher who worked into the night on a sermon for his small congregation. His wife inquired why he spent so much time on a message that he would give to so few. To this the minister replied, "You forget, my dear, how large my audience will be!" Dr. Havner adds that "Nothing is trivial here if heaven looks on. We shall play a better game if, 'seeing we are encompassed,' we remember who is in the grandstand!"

Our valleys may be filled with foes and tears, but we can lift our eyes to the hills to see God and the angels, heaven's spectators, who support us according to God's infinite wisdom as they prepare our welcome home.

November 5

DEFEATING DISCOURAGEMENT

Looking for that blessed hope, and the glorious appearing of the great God and our Savior Jesus Christ. Titus 2:13

ONE of the best ways to get rid of discouragement is to remember that Christ is coming again. The most thrilling, glorious truth in all the world is the Second Coming of Jesus Christ. When we look about today and see pessimism on every side, we should remember the Bible is the only book in the world that predicts the future. The Bible is more modern than tomorrow morning's newspaper. The Bible accurately foretells the future, and it says that the consummation of all things shall be the coming again of Jesus Christ to this earth.

In John 14 Christ says, "Let not your heart be troubled: ye believe in God, believe also in me . . . I go to prepare a place for you. And if I go and prepare a place for you, I will come again, and receive you unto myself; that where I am, there ye may be also."

In Colossians 3:4 we read, "When Christ, who is our life, shall appear, then shall ye also appear with him in glory."

And in 1 John 3:2 we have a great promise to all believers: "Now are we the sons of God, and it doth not yet appear what we shall be: but we know that, when he shall appear, we shall be like him; for we shall see him as he is."

And finally, we trust in the promise in 1 Thessalonians 4:16–17: "For the Lord himself shall descend from heaven with a shout, with the voice of the archangel, and with the trump of God: and the dead in Christ shall rise first. Then we which are alive and remain shall be caught up together with them in the clouds, to meet the Lord in the air: and so shall we ever be with the Lord."

The sunlight of His love can still shine into the darkest part of your life. Jesus said, "I am the light of the world: he that followeth me shall not walk in darkness, but shall have the light of life" (John 8:12).

Are you watching and waiting for Christ's return with eager anticipation? Or do you take Him for granted?

November 6

THE HOPE OF HIS COMING

Awaiting our blessed hope, the appearing of the glory of our great God and Savior Jesus Christ. Titus 2:13, RSV

THE promised coming of the Lord has been the great hope of true believers down through the centuries. Emil Brunner once said, "What oxygen is to the lungs, such is hope to the meaning of life." Some years ago in a discussion by satellite, Lord Montgomery asked General Eisenhower, "Can you give any hope?" Mr. Eisenhower prescribed a way out, "which if man misses," he said, "would lead to Armageddon." Winston Churchill's favorite American song was, "The Battle Hymn of the Republic," which begins with the stirring phrase, "Mine eyes have seen the glory of the coming of the Lord."

The great creeds of the church teach that Christ is coming back. The Nicene Creed states that "He shall come again with glory to judge both the living and the dead." Charles Wesley wrote 7,000 hymns, and in 5,000 he mentioned the coming of Christ. When Queen Elizabeth II was crowned by the Archbishop of Canterbury, he laid the crown on her head with the sure pronouncement, "I give thee, O sovereign lady, this crown to wear until He who reserves the right to wear it shall return."

But till that time, one of America's best-known columnists summed it up when he said, "For us all, the world is disorderly and dangerous; ungoverned, and apparently ungovernable." The question arises: Who will restore order? Who can counter the danger of the nuclear holocaust? Who alone can govern the world? The only answer is Jesus Christ!

November 7

THE GRACE OF GOD

That being justified by his grace, we should be made heirs according to the hope of eternal life. Titus 3:7

HIS glorious appearing is more than an incident of the past, it is the hope of the Christian future. There beats in the heart of every child of God the glorious hope of Christ's return.

This hope is a stimulant toward righteous living and conduct and makes Christ more than a figure of history. This hope gives Him the living breath of reality. The expectancy of

His coming again makes Christ a vibrant living being who even now prepares Himself as the bridegroom to meet His bride, the Church.

The fourth letter in the word "grace" is "C" which stands for Christ who gave Himself for us. The *motive* of grace is the infinite, compassionate love of a merciful God, but the *work* of grace was the death of Christ on the cross.

Unless we view the grace of God through the suffering of the Lord Jesus Christ on the cross, we cannot comprehend its true meaning and significance. When I see Christ hanging there, the spikes in His hands, the crown of thorns on His brow, the blood being shed for our sins, I see the picture of God's grace toward men. I know then that man cannot work his own way to heaven, and that nothing can equal God's infinite love for sinful men.

Only as we bow in contrition, confession, and repentance at the foot of the Cross, can we find forgiveness. There is the grace of God! We don't deserve it! A man said some time ago, "When I get to the judgment of God, all that I will ask for is justice."

My beloved friend, if you get justice, then you will go to hell. You don't want justice. What you want is mercy—the mercy of God, the grace of God as it was in Christ Jesus who died for us and rose again.

November 8

AWARE OF ANGELS

Are they [angels] not all ministering spirits sent forth to serve, for the sake of those who are to obtain salvation? Hebrews 1:14, RSV

ANGELS are messengers of God who serve men as ministering spirits (Hebrews 1:14). So far as I know, no Scripture says that the Holy Spirit ever manifested Himself in human form to men. Jesus did this in the incarnation. The glorious Holy Spirit can be everywhere at the same time, but no angel can be in more than one place at any given moment. We know the Holy Spirit as spirit, not flesh, but we can know angels not as spirits alone but sometimes also in visible form.

At the same time, both angels and the Holy Spirit are at work in our world to accomplish God's perfect will. Frankly, we may not always know the agent or means God is using—the Holy Spirit or the angels—when we discern God's hand at work. We can be sure, however, that there is no contradiction or competition between the Holy Spirit and God's command of the angelic hosts. God Himself is in control to accomplish His will—and in that we can rejoice!

God uses angels to work out the destinies of men and nations. He has altered the courses of the busy political and social arenas of our society and directed the destinies of men by angelic visitation many times over. We must be aware that angels keep in close and vital contact with all that is happening on the earth. Their knowledge of earthly matters exceeds that of men. We must attest to their invisible presence and unceasing labors. Let us believe that they are here among us. They may not laugh or cry with us, but we do know they delight with us over every victory in our lives.

November 9

GOD IS OUR COMFORT

Because he [Jesus] himself suffered when he was tempted, he is able to help those who are being tempted. Hebrews 2:18, NIV

ONCE when I was in my latter teens I was in love with a girl. It might have been puppy love, but it was real to me, the "puppy." We became tentatively engaged to be married, even though we were both much too young. However, she was torn in her heart and felt that the Lord was leading her to another young man who was one of my best friends, and who was already an experienced young clergyman. I suffered a broken heart, and I remember going to a clergyman friend of mine to seek his help. He turned me to 2 Corinthians 1:3, 4–6:

> Praise be to the God and Father of our Lord Jesus Christ, the Father of compassion and the God of all comfort, who comforts us in all our troubles, so that we can comfort those in any trouble with the comfort we ourselves have received from God. . . . if we are comforted, it is for your comfort, which produces in you patient endurance of the same sufferings we suffer.

From those words of the apostle I gained comfort for myself in my personal trouble, just as many others have also done. But there is more to it than that. This passage from Paul suggests a new insight into suffering. Briefly put, it is this: Not only are we comforted in our trials, but our trials can equip us to comfort others.

It is an undeniable fact that usually it is those who have suffered most who are best able to comfort others who are passing through suffering. I know of pastors whose ministries have been enriched by suffering. Through their trials they have learned to "live through" the difficulties of the people in their parish. They are able to empathize as well as sympathize with the afflictions of others because of what they have experienced in their own lives.

Our sufferings may be rough and hard to bear, but they teach us lessons which in turn equip and enable us to help others. Our attitude toward suffering should not be, "Grit your teeth and bear it," hoping it will pass as quickly as possible. Rather, our goal should be to learn all we can from what we are called upon to endure, so that we can fulfill a ministry of comfort—as Jesus did. "Because he himself suffered when he was tempted, he is able to help those who are being tempted" (Hebrews 2:18, NIV). The sufferer becomes the comforter or helper in the service of the Lord.

By the way, by "enduring" suffering, God led me to my wonderful wife, Ruth, who was His intended one for me.

November 10

THE POWER OF PRAYER

Let us therefore come boldly unto the throne of grace, that we may obtain mercy, and find grace to help in time of need. Hebrews 4:16

WE are not the masters of our fate either as individuals or as a nation. How can people boast that they control their own destiny, when they cannot control a virus, invisible even under powerful microscopes?

One such virus, causing hepatitis, can lay low thousands of people.

How can the people of this nation, in spite of our military might, our tremendous wealth, and our foreign alliances, insist that we are the masters of our own fate, when history testifies that God shaped this nation's course?

Our nation was founded by people who believed in prayer. When our government was in the process of being formed, Benjamin Franklin addressed the chairman of the Constitutional Convention, meeting at Philadelphia in 1787, saying, "I have lived, sir, a long time, and the longer I live the more convincing proofs I see of this truth: that God governs in the affairs of men. And if a sparrow cannot fall to the ground without His notice, it is probable that an empire cannot rise without His aid."

Today the world is being carried on a rushing torrent of

history that is sweeping out of control. There is but one power available to redeem the course of events, and that is the power of prayer by God-fearing, Christ-believing people.

Abraham Lincoln, beloved and legendary president during the tumultuous days of the Civil War, said, "I have been driven many times to my knees by the overwhelming conviction that I had nowhere else to go. My own wisdom, and that of all about me, seemed insufficient for the day." Would that our leadership were as humble today!

November 11

THE ONE AND ONLY WAY

And being made perfect, he became the author of eternal salvation unto all them that obey him. Hebrews 5:9

A MAN in a car stopped to ask a pedestrian the way to a certain street. When the man told him the way, the driver asked doubtfully, "Is that the best way?" The man replied, "That is the *only* way."

There is only one way of salvation. Jesus said, "I am the way, the truth, and the life: no man cometh unto the Father, but by me" (John 14:6). The last invitation of the Bible says, "And the Spirit and the bride say, Come. And let him that heareth say, Come. And let him that is athirst come. And whosoever will, let him take of the water of life freely" (Revelation 22:17).

This is still an age of grace. God's offer of forgiveness and a new life still stands. However, the door will one day be closed. Someday it will be too late. That is why the Bible continually warns and challenges, "Now is the accepted time" (2 Corinthians 6:2). We're proclaiming the Gospel, asking people to come to a knowledge of the grace of the Lord Jesus Christ, because it is still a day of grace, and the door of salvation is still open. When the flood came, Noah was safe and secure in the ark. He trusted God and took Him at His Word. You too can be safe and secure in the world in which we live by believing and accepting what the world calls "foolish"—the fact that Christ died on the cross for our sins and rose for our justification. But to those of us who are saved, it is the power of God unto salvation.

This may make very little sense to this dying world. But to those of us who know Christ, it is a tremendous power and a great and glorious peace. Do you know this peace that only Christ can give? You can know it today by repenting of your sins and receiving Christ as your Lord, Master, and Savior. And you can do it right now wherever you are, anywhere in the world.

November 12

AN ENDLESS HOPE

We have this hope as an anchor of the soul, firm and secure. Hebrews 6:19, NIV

AN unbeliever only sees a hopeless end to life. But the Christian sees an endless hope. In a network television program Malcolm Muggeridge reflected that a true Christian "is longing for the termination of life in time as one longs for the end of a long and arduous three-week sea voyage when one is in the last three days. I look forward to the time when my life will partake of eternity with near irrepressible eagerness."

Perhaps these words of Malcolm Muggeridge do not describe your feelings about death. Perhaps you are afraid of death and don't relate to the quiet confidence this famous British journalist and TV personality feels. The torturing, tormenting fear of death is a condition that is perfectly normal for any who have never come to Christ. Death is an experience from which people instinctively shrink. Yet for the Christian the fear is removed. He has the assurance that the sins for which he would be judged at death have been dealt with, whereas the non-Christian has no such assurance. I do not look forward to the prospect of dying—but I do look forward to death itself. It will be a glorious release. It will be the fulfillment of everything I have ever longed for. The Scripture says, "In thy presence is fullness of joy; at thy right hand there are pleasures for evermore" (Psalm 16:11).

November 13
....

FAITH IS A FACT

Let us draw near with a true heart in full assurance of faith. Hebrew 10:22

DISREGARD feelings. You're not saved by feeling, and you may or may not feel the Spirit. Accept Him by faith as a fact. He lives within you right now to help you live the Christian life. He is living in you in order to magnify, glorify, and exalt Christ in you so that you can live a happy, victorious, radiant, Christ-honoring life.

The Bible commands, "Be filled with the Spirit" (Ephesians 5:18). If you are filled with the Spirit, then you are going to produce the fruit of the Spirit, which is "love, joy, peace, long-suffering, gentleness, goodness, faith, meekness, temperance" (Galatians 5:22–23). To be filled with the Spirit is not optional. It is a command to be obeyed—a duty to be done.

How do you know that you are filled? And how can you be filled? Is it some emotional experience through which you must pass? Not necessarily. When you give all you know of yourself to all that you know of Him, then you can accept by faith that you are filled with the Spirit of God. That means that He can have all of you. Commitment actually is surrender—total, absolute, unconditional, irreversible surrender. "I beseech you therefore, brethren, by the mercies of God, that ye present your bodies a living sacrifice, holy, acceptable unto God, which is your reasonable service" (Romans 12:1).

It is only the consecrated, Spirit-filled Christian who can have victory over the world, the flesh, and the devil. It is the Holy Spirit who will do the fighting for you. "We wrestle not against flesh and blood, but against the rulers of darkness" (Ephesians 6:12). This is a spiritual warfare. You cannot fight against these three enemies with normal weapons. Only as we become channels and let the Holy Spirit do the fighting through us are we going to get complete victory. Don't hold back anything from Christ. Let Him be completely the Lord and Master of your life. He said, "Ye call me Master and Lord: and ye say well; for so I am" (John 13:13).

November 14

WATCHING OUR WALK

But recall the former days when, after you were enlightened, you endured a hard struggle with sufferings, sometimes being publicly exposed to abuse and affliction, and sometimes being partners with those so treated. Hebrews 10:32–33, RSV

AS God's angels have watched the drama of this age unfolding, they have seen the Christian Church established and expanded around the world. They miss nothing as they watch the movements of time, "To the intent that now unto the principalities and powers in heavenly places might be known by the church the manifold wisdom of God"

(Ephesians 3:10). Dr. Joppie reminds us that the word "now" actually covers the vast expanse of this Church age. Angel hosts have witnessed the formation of the Church of Christ Jesus, and have watched the walk of each believer as the Lord worked His grace, love, and power into each life. The angels were observing firsthand the building of the body of the true Church in all places of His dominion this very hour.

But what are they thinking as we live in the world today? Do they observe us as we stand fast in the faith and walk in righteousness? Or may they be wondering at our lack of commitment? These two possibilities seem evident from Ephesians 3:10: "[The purpose is] that through the church the complicated, many-sided wisdom of God in all its infinite variety and innumerable aspects might now be made known to the angelic rulers and authorities [principalities and powers] in the heavenly sphere" (AB).

Our certainty that angels right now witness how we are walking through life should mightily influence the decisions we make. God is watching, and His angels are interested spectators, too. The Amplified Bible expresses 1 Corinthians 4:9 this way: "God has made an exhibit of us . . . a show in the world's amphitheater—with both men and angels [as spectators]." We know they are watching, but in the heat of the battle, I have thought how wonderful it would be if we could hear them cheering.

What kind of exhibit are you?

November 15

A HOME AND A HOPE

You yourselves had [in heaven] a better and lasting possession. Hebrews 10.34, AB

THANKS be unto God, we believers in Christ have the

assurance that we are going to a home where all is happiness, joy, and peace. This blessed hope fortifies us to bear our hardships. We will not insist on our wants here and fight over our rights, but we will be willing to suffer the loss of all things for the sake of those things which are yet to come. Earthly possessions will not vitally concern us. The quality here may be poor, but the Bible teaches that the quality there is far better. The possessions here will pass away; the possessions there are enduring.

No one can have real peace who does not have the assurance of a permanent and happy home which will not be subject to earthly casualty.

Some time ago two old friends were dying. The one was rich, and the other poor. The rich man was outside of Christ, and he was talking to another of his friends. "When I die," he said, "I shall have to leave my riches. When he dies, he will go to his riches."

Thus in a word he summed up the two radically different principles which govern the world and the Christian.

Peace is not arbitrary. It must be based upon definite facts. God has all the facts on His side; the world does not. Therefore God, and not the world, can give peace. It is honorable, right, and praiseworthy that our leaders should seek and promote national and world peace; but they must recognize its limitations without Christ, the Prince of Peace.

The Bible teaches that the world will never come to this place of tranquillity and permanent peace until Christ, the Prince of Peace, comes back to this earth. When He comes to reign and rule, man shall know war no more.

SERVING IN HEAVEN

Ye have in heaven a better and an enduring substance.
Hebrews 10:34

THE Father's house will be a happy home because there will be work to do there. Certainly this is true in every well-ordered home on earth. Some people are so overworked that their greatest longing is for rest. The Bible verse that most appeals to them is, "There remaineth therefore a rest to the people of God" (Hebrews 4:9).

But the time will come when they will be rested and will become weary of doing nothing. I can think of no more terrible fate than to be condemned to sit forever and ever in idleness.

John wrote in Revelation 22:3, "His servants shall serve him." Each one will be given exactly the task that suits his powers, his tastes, and his abilities. Perhaps God will give us new worlds to conquer. Perhaps He will send us to explore some distant planet or star, there to preach His message of everlasting love. Whatever we do, the Bible says we will serve Him.

And the Father's house will be a happy home because friends will be there. Have you ever been to a strange place and had the joy of seeing a familiar face? Not one of us who enters the Father's house will feel lonely or strange, for our friends will be there.

Alexander MacLaren described heaven in this way: "The joys of heaven are not the joys of passive contemplation, of dreamy remembrance, of perfect repose; but they are described thus, 'They rest not night or day,' and 'His servants serve him and see his face.'"

THE ARK OF SAFETY

By faith Noah, being warned by God concerning events as yet unseen, took heed and constructed an ark for the saving of his household; by this he condemned the world and became an heir of the righteousness which comes by faith. Hebrews 11:7, RSV

THE Bible warned the people of Noah's day, "My spirit shall not always strive with man" (Genesis 6:3). You cannot come to Jesus Christ unless the Spirit of God brings you and unless you yield to the prompting and urging of the Holy Spirit. I beg of you to come to Christ while there is yet time.

Outside the ark men and women were struggling for their lives, clutching at pieces of driftwood, until the pitiless hand of death reached up and drew them down beneath those cruel and relentless waves. All were lost. Every soul outside the ark perished. They had had their chance but tossed it away. There were hundreds that day who were close to the ark, and yet lost.

This fearful scene from the Bible is a type and shadow of that day of judgment that lies before our world. The Bible says, "It is appointed unto men once to die, but after this the judgment" (Hebrews 9:27).

The ark is a type of Jesus Christ. In this day when the clouds of judgment are beginning to gather, Christ is the refuge. Each of us must cross the threshold and pass into the ark.

Are you in? You may be close, but are you inside? The universal and terrible storm is coming. The days of Noah may be soon upon us. Are you ready for the day of judgment?

Even if the world does not end in your lifetime in a cataclysmic judgment, the moment you die will be the end of the world for you. The world that you live in will die with you. Are you ready for death? Are you ready for the judgment that is to come the moment you step out into eternity?

History repeats itself. What happened thousands of years ago will happen again. There is a possibility it could happen in this century or even in this decade. However, while there is life, there is hope. The Spirit of God is knocking faithfully at the door. If we repent, mend our ways, throw off our sins, we can yet be used of God to bring healing and help to a dying civilization.

November 18

THE FAITH OF A FRIEND

By faith Abraham, when called to go to a place he would later receive as his inheritance, obeyed and went, even though he did not know where he was going. By faith he made his home in the promised land like a stranger in a foreign country; he lived in tents, as did Isaac and Jacob, who were heirs with him of the same promise. For he was looking forward to the city with foundations, whose architect and builder is God. By faith Abraham, even though he was past age—and Sarah herself was barren—was enabled to become a father because he considered him faithful who had made the promise.
Hebrews 11:8–11, NIV

ABRAHAM walked with God and was called a friend of God (Isaiah 41:8; James 2:23). Walk with God as Noah did; when the flood came, Noah was saved. Walk with God as Moses did in the solitude of the desert; when the hour of judgment fell upon Egypt, Moses was prepared to lead his people to victory. Walk with God as David did as a shepherd boy; when he was called to rule his people he was prepared for the task of kingship. Daniel and his three young friends walked with God in Babylon, and when trouble came, God was beside them—whether it was in the lions' den or in the fiery furnace.

However, the Bible teaches that God does not always

deliver His saints from adversity. A careful reading of Hebrews 11 shows that "others" were just as faithful as Abraham, Moses, Daniel, or David; they, too, walked with God—but they perished. God has not promised to deliver us *from* trouble, but He has promised to go *with us through* the trouble.

Stephen was a young man "full of faith and of the Holy Spirit" (Acts 6:5, NIV). They stoned him to death, but his was a triumphal entry into heaven. If you are not strengthening the inner man now by daily walking with God, when a crisis comes you will quake with fear and give in, having no strength to stand up for Christ.

November 19

FAITH IN THE FOG

And all these, though well attested by their faith, did not receive what was promised, since God had foreseen something better for us, that apart from us they should not be made perfect.   Hebrews 11:39–40, RSV

THEY wandered about in goatskins, being destitute, afflicted, and tormented. Time after time they must have called on God to send His mighty angels to help. No delivering angel came. They suffered and endured almost as though there were no God.

Why? We find a clue when our Lord faced Calvary as He prayed, "If it be possible, let this cup pass from me" (Matthew 26:39) but then He added, "Nevertheless not my will, but thine be done" (Luke 22:42). In the sufferings and death of these great saints not physically delivered, God had a mysterious plan, and was performing His will. Knowing this, they suffered and died *by faith*. The latter part of Hebrews 11 indicates that those who received no visible help in answer to prayer will have a far greater heavenly reward because they endured by "faith" alone. But having died, they did enjoy the ministry of angels who then escorted their immortal souls to the throne of God. If the first part of Hebrews 11 is called "God's Hall of Fame," the second should be called, "God's Winners of the Medal of Honor."

Once when I was going through a dark period I prayed and prayed, but the heavens seemed to be brass. I felt as though God had disappeared and that I was all alone with my trial and burden. It was a dark night for my soul. I wrote my mother about the experience and will never forget her reply: "Son, there are many times when God withdraws to test your faith. He wants you to trust Him in the darkness. Now, Son, reach up by faith in the fog and you will find that His hand will be there." In tears I knelt by my bed and experienced an overwhelming sense of God's presence. Whether or not we sense and feel the presence of the Holy Spirit or one of the holy angels, by faith we are certain God will never leave us nor forsake us.

November 20

ANGELS UNAWARES

Be not forgetful to entertain strangers: for thereby some have entertained angels unawares. Hebrews 13:2

THE incident occurred in 1942, after the Japanese had won control of certain areas of China. One morning around nine o'clock, a Japanese truck stopped outside the bookroom. It was carrying five marines and was half-filled with books. The Christian Chinese shop assistant, who was alone at the time, realized with dismay that they had come to seize the stock. By nature timid, he felt this was more than he could endure.

Jumping from the truck, the marines made for the shop door; but before they could enter, a neatly dressed Chinese gentleman entered the shop ahead of them. Though the shop assistant knew practically all the Chinese customers who traded there, this man was a complete stranger. For some unknown reason the soldiers seemed unable to follow him, and loitered about, looking in at the four large windows, but not entering. For two hours they stood around, until after eleven, but never set foot inside the door. The stranger asked what the men wanted, and the Chinese shop assistant explained that the Japanese were seizing stocks from many of the bookshops in the city, and now this store's turn had come. The two prayed together, the stranger encouraging him, and so the two hours passed. At last the soldiers climbed into their truck and drove away. The stranger also left, without making a single purchase or even inquiring about any items in the shop.

Later that day the shop owner, Mr. Christopher Willis (whose Chinese name was Lee), returned. The shop assistant said to him, "Mr. Lee, do you believe in angels?"

"I do," said Mr. Willis.

"So do I, Mr. Lee," said the clerk. Could the stranger have been one of God's protecting angels? Dr. Bell, my wife's father, always thought so.

November 21

SURROUNDED BY ANGELS

The angel of the LORD encampeth round about them that fear him, and delivereth them. Psalm 34:7

CORRIE TEN BOOM writes of a remarkable experience at the terrible Nazi Ravensbruck prison camp:

Together we entered the terrifying building. At a table were women who took away all our possessions. Everyone had to undress completely and then go to a room where her hair was checked.

I asked a woman who was busy checking the possessions of the new arrivals if I might use the toilet. She pointed to a door, and I discovered that the convenience was nothing more than a hole in the shower-room floor. Betsie stayed close beside me all the time. Suddenly I had an inspiration, "Quick, take off your woolen underwear," I whispered to her. I rolled it up with mine and laid the bundle in a corner with my little Bible. The spot was alive with cockroaches, but I didn't worry about that. I felt wonderfully relieved and happy. "The Lord is busy answering our prayers, Betsie," I whispered. "We shall not have to make the sacrifice of all our clothes."

We hurried back to the row of women waiting to be undressed. A little later, after we had had our showers and put on our shirts and shabby dresses, I hid the roll of underwear and my Bible under my dress. It did bulge out obviously through my dress; but I prayed, "Lord, cause now Thine angels to surround me; and let them not be transparent today, for the guards must not see me." I felt perfectly at ease. Calmly I passed the guards. Everyone was checked, from the front, the sides, the back. Not a bulge escaped the eyes of the guard. The woman just in front of me had hidden a woolen vest under her dress; it was taken from her. They let me pass, for they did not see me. Betsie, right behind me, was searched.

But outside awaited another danger. On each side of the door were women who looked everyone over for a second time. They felt over the body of each one who passed. I knew they would not see me, for the angels were still surrounding me. I was not even surprised when they passed me by; but within me rose the jubilant cry, "O Lord, if Thou dost so answer prayer, I can face even Ravensbruck unafraid."

Every true believer in Christ should be encouraged and strengthened! Angels are watching; they mark our path. They superintend the events of our lives and protect the interest of the Lord God, always working to promote His plans and to bring about His highest will for us. Angels are interested spectators and mark all we do, "for we are made a spectacle unto the world, and to angels, and to men" (1 Corinthians 4:9). God assigns angelic powers to watch over us.

November 22

DEALING WITH DEATH

For here we do not have an enduring city, but we are looking for the city that is to come. Hebrews 13:14, NIV

DEATH will ultimately be abolished. The power of death has been broken and death's fear has been removed. Now we can say with the psalmist, "Yea, though I walk through the valley of the shadow of death, I will fear no evil: for thou art with me; thy rod and thy staff they comfort me" (Psalm 23:4).

Paul looked forward to death with great anticipation as a result of the resurrection of Christ. He said, "For to me to live is Christ, and to die is gain" (Philippians 1:21). As Velma Barfield on Death Row in North Carolina said: "I love Him so much I can hardly wait to see Him."

Without the resurrection of Christ there could be no hope for the future. The Bible promises that someday we are going to stand face to face with the resurrected Christ, and we are going to have bodies like unto His own body.

> Face to face with Christ my Savior,
> Face to face, what will it be?
> When with rapture I behold Him,
> Jesus Christ who died for me?
>
> Face to face I shall behold Him,
> Far beyond the starry sky;

Face to face in all His glory
I shall see Him by and by.

Carrie E. Breck

November 23

GOD CONTROLS THE CLOCK

. . . There is laid up for me a crown of righteousness, which the Lord, the righteous judge, shall give me at that day: and not to me only, but unto all them also that love his appearing. 2 Timothy 4:8

MANY people are asking, "Where is history heading?" A careful student of the Bible will be led to see that God controls the clock of destiny. Amidst the world's confusion, God's omnipotent hand moves, working out His unchanging plan and purpose; and the kingdoms of this world shall become the Kingdom of the Lord Jesus Christ, "For he must reign, till he hath put all enemies under his feet" (1 Corinthians 15:25).

The Communists say that time and history are on their side. But they ignore the fact that Jesus Christ is coming to earth again. He is in control, and He will determine the outcome. If the Bible is clear at any point, it is this: "Unto them that look for him shall he appear the second time" (Hebrews 9:28).

What is to be the attitude of the Christian toward the fact of Christ's coming? One man said to me recently, "Well, the Lord is coming soon; so what is there to do anything about?" Such a fatalistic attitude is not the one taught by the Lord Jesus Christ. When He told His disciples of his return to earth, He said, "Occupy till I come" (Luke 19:13), and "Blessed is that servant, whom his lord when he cometh shall find so doing" (Matthew 24:46).

Dwight L. Moody once said, "I look upon this world as a wrecked vessel. Its ruin is getting nearer and nearer. God said to me, 'Moody, here's a lifeboat. Go out and rescue as many as you can before the ship sinks.'" If the end seemed about to come in Moody's day, how much closer must we be to the climax of history?

If there was ever a time when we should man the lifeboats and go out and rescue as many as we can, it is now. That is why we are proclaiming the Gospel in the strategic centers of the world wherever we can.

We believe this is a day of glorious opportunity to proclaim the saving grace and power of Christ, and to declare the Gospel against the opposition of every false ideology.

George Whitefield, the great English evangelist, said, "I am daily waiting for the coming of the Son of God." But he did not sit down and do nothing. He burned out his life in proclaiming the Gospel of Christ. Can we do less?

November 24

THANKSGIVING AND THE PATH TO PEACE

My brethren, count it all joy when ye fall into divers
temptations. James 1:2

GOD promises no easy life or days without troubles, trials, difficulties, and temptations. He never promises that life will be perfect. He does not call His children to a playground, but to a battleground.

Some people have a warped idea of living the Christian life. Seeing talented, brilliant Christians, they attempt to imitate them. For them, the grass on the other side of the fence is always greener. When they discover that their own contributions are more modest or perhaps invisible, they collapse in discouragement and overlook genuine opportunities that are open to them.

Be like the apostle Paul and say, "None of these things move me." Few men suffered as Paul did, yet he learned how to abound and how to be abased. He learned to live above his circumstances—even in a prison cell. You can do the same. Refuse to permit circumstances to get you down. In the midst of your difficulties, there will be a deep joy. "For the joy of the Lord is your strength," says the Bible.

Believe it or not, this is the path to peace. Paul said, "Troubled on every side, yet not distressed; we are perplexed, but not in despair; persecuted, but not forsaken; cast down, but not destroyed" (2 Corinthians 4:8). All these qualities are characteristic of true Christians. They can be yours, giving you the ultimate victory. They are part of your birthright. Claim them!

As a child of God, you need never suffer spiritual defeat. Your days of defeat are over. From now on, you will want to live every minute to its fullest. Certainly, you will welcome each day as another twenty-four hours to devote to Christ. Every new day will be filled with opportunities to serve others. You will spend many moments with God, and you will know that your sins are forgiven and that you are on the way to heaven.

Taking this "servant" attitude of thankfulness in all of life's circumstances will help you react as old Matthew Henry did when he was mugged. He wrote in his diary, "Let me be thankful first because I was never robbed before; second, although they took my purse, they did not take my life; third, because although they took my all, it was not much; and fourth, because it was I who was robbed, not I who robbed."

I wonder if I could be that thankful. Could you?

November 25

Blessed is the man who endures trial, for when he has stood the test he will receive the crown of life which God has promised to those who love him. James 1:12, RSV

TO the Christian, death is said in the Bible to be a coronation. The picture here is that of a regal prince who, after his struggles and conquests in an alien land, comes to his native country and court to be crowned and honored for his deeds.

The Bible says we are pilgrims and strangers in a foreign land. This world is not our home; our citizenship is in heaven. To him who is faithful, Christ will give a crown of life. Paul said, "Henceforth there is laid up for me a crown of righteousness, which the Lord, the righteous judge, shall give me at that day: and not to me only, but unto all them also that love his appearing" (2 Timothy 4:8).

When D. L. Moody was dying, he looked up to heaven and said, "Earth is receding, heaven is opening, this is my coronation day." Yes, death is the Christian's coronation, the end of conflict, and the beginning of glory and triumph in heaven.

November 26

PATIENCE AND PERFECTION

. . . The testing of your faith produces patience. But let patience have its perfect work, that you may be perfect and complete, lacking nothing. James 1:3–4, NKJV

WRITING to Christians who were suffering for their faith, James said, "Be *patient*, then, brothers, until the Lord's coming.

See how the farmer waits for the land to yield its valuable crop and how patient he is for the autumn and spring rains. You, too, be patient and stand firm, because the Lord's coming is near" (James 5:7–8 NIV, italics mine).

Patience is not simply a "teeth-clenched," complacent endurance of a particular situation. It is an attitude of expectation. The farmer was able to stare at his seemingly barren ground with patience because he was assured that there would be results of his labors. He could have patience in his labors because there would be products of his labor.

And so it is in the spiritual realm. God can produce valuable qualities in our lives through the hurts and suffering we experience. We can suffer patiently, for our suffering will yield a spiritual harvest.

And we can suffer during this life patiently, for we know that in God's perfect time His Son will return as the greatest reward for the waiting and working believer.

"He that is slow to anger is better than the mighty; and he that ruleth his spirit than he that taketh a city" (Proverbs 16:32).

November 27

TUNE IN!

My dear brothers, take note of this: Everyone should be quick to listen, slow to speak and slow to become angry. . . . Do not merely listen to the word, and so deceive yourselves. Do what it says. Anyone who listens to the word but does not do what it says is like a man who looks at his face in a mirror and, after looking at himself, goes away and immediately forgets what he looks like. But the man who looks intently into the perfect law that gives freedom, and continues to do this . . . he will be blessed in what he does. James 1:19, 22–25, NIV

REVELATION is a means of communication. It means "to

make known" or "to unveil." Revelation requires a "revealer," who in this case is God, and it also requires a "hearer." God's hearers were the chosen prophets and apostles who recorded God's revelation. Thus it is a line of communication, at one end of which is God, and at the other end, man.

When I was a boy, radio was just coming of age. We would gather around a crude homemade set and twist the three tuning dials in an effort to establish contact with the transmitter. Often all the sound that came out of the amplifier was the squeak and squawk of static, but we knew that somewhere out there was the unseen transmitter and if contact was established and the dials were in adjustment, we could hear a voice loud and clear. After a long time of laborious tuning, the far distant voice would suddenly break through and a smile of triumph would illuminate the faces of all in the room. At last we were tuned in!

In the revelation that God established between Himself and us, we can find a new life and a new dimension of living, but we must "tune in." There are higher levels of living to which we have never attained. There is peace, satisfaction, and joy that we have never experienced. God is trying to break through to us. The heavens are calling. God is speaking! Let man hear.

November 28
....
WORKLESS FAITH?

What does it profit, my brethren, if a man says he has faith but has not works? Can his faith save him? If a brother or sister is ill-clad and in lack of daily food, and one of you says to them, "Go in peace, be warmed and filled," without giving them the things needed for the body, what does it profit? So faith by itself, if it has no works, is dead. But someone will say, "You have faith and I have works." Show me your

faith apart from your works, and I by my works will show you my
faith. . . . Was not Abraham our father justified by works, when he
offered his son Isaac upon the altar? You see that faith was active along
with his works, and faith was completed by works, and the scripture
was fulfilled which says, "Abraham believed God, and it was reckoned to
him as righteousness"; and he was called the friend of God. You see that
a man is justified by works and not by faith alone.
James 2:14–18, 21–24, RSV

CHARLES HADDON SPURGEON, the great London preacher, was once the guest of a man who made his virtues the chief topic of conversation; but his virtues were all of the negative kind, consisting of the bad things he had not done.

Disgusted with the man's self-righteousness, Spurgeon said, "Why, man, you are simply a bundle of negatives. You don't drink, you don't gamble, you don't swear. What in the name of goodness do you do?"

We know that, fundamentally, salvation is not of works. But in stressing this phase of the Gospel, too many have neglected to emphasize the fact that we will be judged more according to the good we have left undone than for the evil we have done.

Good works are not a means of salvation because we are saved by grace through faith. We are saved only on the grounds of the death and resurrection of Jesus Christ.

But, our good works are an evidence of salvation; and if we fail to do all the good we can, to all the people we can, at any time we can, by any means we can, we will be condemned at the judgment bar of God. Make no mistake about that.

THE DISCIPLINES OF LIFE

. . . As the body without the spirit is dead, so faith without works is dead also. James 2:26

THE Scriptures teach that a Christian is one who trusts Christ to save him and obeys Him as Lord. Trust gets him into the Kingdom, but obedience and love to God are the badges of citizenship. The Christian life is a happy blending of trust and toil, wrestling and striving, receiving and doing. There is that which God does, and there is that which we must do for ourselves. It is in a sense like a farmer's wheat harvest—it is a gift of God, but the appropriation of that gift requires hard work and strenuous effort. God may give a person the gift of music, but it takes much practice and discipline to make that gift come to life.

Salvation is indeed a gift of God, but there is a sense in which we work out our own salvation with fear and trembling. His creative action takes place through our obedient action, and He is able to work when we work. We receive the new life as a free gift, but we must practice the gift if we are to live a victorious Christian life in a period of crisis. Therefore it is impossible to live a victorious life without careful discipline.

There are many verbs used in the New Testament that describe this type of life. We are told that as Christians we are to fight, wrestle, run, strive, suffer, endure, resist, agonize, and mortify. These New Testament verbs clearly denote strenuous effort and vigorous action.

When I see a person who claims to be a Christian, believes all the creeds, and calls himself an evangelical Christian, but he does not live the Christian life—his life is not characterized by brokenness, tenderness, and love—I remember the words

of Jesus when He said, "By their fruits ye shall know them."
After being born again we are to demonstrate our faith by our
works. As James said, "Faith without works is dead."

November 30

GOD'S PRESENCE IS PROMISED

Come near to God and he will come near to you. James 4:8, NIV

WHAT a blessed promise and provision this is! It means that
each of us can come close to God, with the assurance that He
will come close to us—so close that we become conscious of
an intimate, personal relationship with Him.

This is the greatest experience we can know, to have this
sense of a personal relationship between God and ourselves.
The conception is filled with rich meaning.

Every Christian life is closely bound up with the life of
God because in Him we live and move and have our being.
He breathed into us the breath of life. He has put something
within us that is like unto Himself, something capable of
developing into the rich quality of Christlike character.

Because God is the giver and source of our life, He has a
legitimate claim upon our lives. He is our Father, and He has
the right to expect us to be loyal and loving children. Because
I am His child, He longs to have a fellowship with me.

The story of the prodigal son is a revelation of God's
desire for human fellowship. He yearns over His children who
have wandered far from Him and longs for them to come
home and be near to Him.

All through the Bible we see God's patience and
perseverance as He pursues misguided and obstinate men and
women—men and women who were born to a high destiny as
His sons and daughters, but who strayed from His side. From
Genesis to Revelation God is constantly saying to such,

"Return to me, and I will return to you."

Incredible as it may seem, God wants our companionship. He wants to have us close to Him. He wants to be a father to us, to shield us, to protect us, to counsel us, and to guide us in our way through life.

December

December 1

THE TIME IS NOW

Go to now, ye that say, Today or tomorrow we will go into such a city, and continue there a year, and buy and sell, and get gain: Whereas ye know not what shall be on the morrow. . . . James 4:13–14

I ONCE read about a sundial on which was inscribed the cryptic message, "It is later than you think." Travelers would often pause to meditate on the meaning of that phrase. We Christians have a sundial—the Word of God. From Genesis to Revelation it bears its warning, "It is later than you think." Writing to the Christians of his day Paul said, "It is already the hour for you to awaken from sleep; for now salvation is nearer to us than when we believed. The night is almost gone, and the day is at hand. Let us therefore lay aside the deeds of darkness and put on the armor of light" (Romans 13:11–12, NASB).

Billy Bray, a godly clergyman of another generation, sat by the bedside of a dying Christian who had been very shy about his testimony for Christ during his life. The dying man said, "If I had the power I'd shout glory to God." Billy Bray answered, "It's a pity you didn't shout glory when you had the power." I wonder how many of us will look back over a lifetime of wasted opportunities and ineffective witness and weep because we did not allow God to use us as He wanted. "Night is coming, when no man can work" (John 9:4, NASB).

If ever we are to study the Scriptures, if ever we are to spend time in prayer, if ever we are to win souls for Christ, if ever we are to invest our finances for His Kingdom—it must be now.

December 2

COMING AGAIN!

Be ye also patient; establish your hearts: for the coming of the Lord draweth nigh. James 5:8

JESUS CHRIST is absolute truth. Matthew 24 and 25 are entirely given over to statements about His coming again. For example, Matthew 24:27 says, "For as the lightning cometh out of the east, and shineth even unto the west; so shall also the coming of the Son of man be." The Bible again says in Matthew 25:31–32, "When the Son of man shall come in his glory, and all the holy angels with him, then shall he sit upon the throne of his glory: and before him shall be gathered all nations. . . ." This prophecy has yet to be fulfilled, but He said it, and I believe it will be.

Jesus didn't lie to us. He said, "I go to prepare a place for you. And if I go and prepare a place for you, I will come again, and receive you unto myself; that where I am, there ye may be also" (John 14:2–3). He's going to come back in person. The Lord Jesus is coming back Himself! That's how much He loves us. The plan of salvation is not only to satisfy us in this world and give us a new life here, but He has a great plan for the future. For eternity!

The Bible says we are going to reign with Him. We're joint heirs with the Lord Jesus Christ, and we're going to spend eternity with Him! What is He doing now? He's preparing a home for us! It's been nearly two thousand years. What a home it must be! Eye cannot see nor ear hear, nor hath entered into the heart of man, what God has prepared for those who love Him! In Revelation John wrote, ". . . the Lord God giveth them light: and they shall reign for ever and ever. . . . Behold, I come quickly!" (22:5, 7). Even so, come, Lord Jesus!

....

REDEEMED BY THE BLOOD

*You know that it was not with perishable things such as silver or gold
that you were redeemed from the empty way of life handed down to you
from your forefathers, but with the precious blood of Christ, a lamb
without blemish or defect.* 1 Peter 1:18–19, NIV

THE word "redeem" means to "buy back"—to recover by
paying a price. Not only the first man, but every man since
then has plunged headlong into Satan's trap of sin. Man had
to be recovered, delivered, and bought back.

The word "redeemed" can be illustrated by the position of
a slave who had been captured or enticed into serving one
who was not his legal master, but whose real master, intent on
recovering the slave's love and service, buys him back at great
personal cost. That is what God did for us.

Captured by Satan and enticed into his service, mankind in
his disobedience and unfaithfulness did not dismay God nor
diminish His love for us. Instead, on the cross, He paid the
price for our deliverance, a price unthinkably greater than our
true value. He did this because He loved us. We were
redeemed, recovered, restored, not with corruptible things of
silver and gold, but with the precious blood of Christ.

A loving mother once saved her little girl from a burning
house, but suffered severe burns on her hands and arms.
When the girl grew up, not knowing how her mother's arms
became so seared, she was ashamed of the scarred, gnarled
hands and always insisted that her mother wear long gloves to
cover up that ugliness.

But one day the daughter asked her mother how her hands
became so scarred. For the first time the mother told her the
story of how she had saved her life with those hands. The
daughter wept tears of gratitude and said, "Oh Mother,

those are beautiful hands, the most beautiful in the world. Don't ever hide them again."

The blood of Christ may seem to be a grim and repulsive subject to those who do not realize its true significance, but to those who have accepted His redemption and have been set free from the slavery of sin, the blood of Christ is precious. The freed slave never forgets the overwhelming cost of his liberty and freedom.

December 4

ADAPTED OR ADOPTED?

He was chosen before the creation of the world, but was revealed in these last times for your sake. Through him you believe in God, who raised him from the dead and glorified him, and so your faith and hope are in God. 1 Peter 1:20–21, NIV

TODAY, as world leaders struggle with seemingly insurmountable problems, as storm clouds gather around the globe, this darkening and menacing situation simply accentuates the brightness of the One who proclaimed, "I am the light of the world: he that followeth me shall not walk in darkness, but shall have the light of life" (John 8:12). He is "the Lamb of God, which taketh away the sin of the world!" (John 1:29). He is the promised Messiah of ancient Israel. He is the hope of the hopeless, helpless Gentiles—which includes most of the population of the world, whether they be African, Asian, American, or European.

In all my evangelistic ministry I have never felt a need to "adapt" Jesus to the many and varied nationalities, cultures, tribes, or ethnic groups to whom I have preached. I believe in contextualization. I try to adapt illustrations or emphasize certain truths that will help a particular audience understand the Gospel more clearly in light of their cultural background.

But the essential truths of the Gospel do not change. All things were created by Him and He sustains all creation, so the message of His saving grace is applicable to all. The facts concerning His virgin birth, His sinless life, His sacrificial and substitutionary death, His resurrection and ascension to the right hand of the Father, and the glorious hope of His return must not be diluted or distorted in any way.

December 5

SPIRITUAL FOOD

Desire the sincere milk of the word, that ye may grow thereby.
1 Peter 2:2

OUR spiritual lives need food. What kind of food? Spiritual food. Where do we find this spiritual food? In the Bible, the Word of God. The Bible reveals Christ, the Bread of Life, for our hungry souls, and the Water of Life for our thirsty hearts. If we fail to partake of daily spiritual nourishment, we will starve and lose our spiritual vitality.

Some parts of our world do not enjoy the freedom we have to read the Bible and study it together with fellow Christians. In most of the world, in fact, there's a veritable famine for the Word of God! I recall the story of a Chinese musician in the People's Republic of China. He was converted and strengthened spiritually through the reading of individual pages of the Scripture torn from a Bible and slipped to him by an unknown friend. There are other stories of prisoners who survived twenty to thirty years at hard labor—and sometimes terrible torture—and came out with their minds intact, totally lacking in bitterness toward their captors.

We should not be content to skim through a chapter merely to satisfy our conscience. Rather, we should hide the Word of God in our hearts. A little portion well digested is of greater spiritual value than a lengthy portion scanned hurriedly. . . .

A good place to start is the gospel of John. As you read, the Holy Spirit will enlighten the passages for you. He will illuminate the difficult words and make obscure meanings clear. Even though you cannot remember all you have read, or understand it all, go on reading. The very practice of reading in itself will have a purifying effect upon your mind and heart. Let nothing take the place of this daily exercise.

Scripture memorized can come to mind when you do not have your Bible with you—on sleepless nights, when driving a car, traveling, when having to make an instantaneous important decision. It comforts, guides, corrects, encourages—all we need is there. Memorize as much as you can.

December 6

OUR PURPOSE—HIS PRAISE

But ye are a chosen generation, a royal priesthood, a holy nation, a peculiar people; that ye should show forth the praises of him who hath called you out of darkness into his marvelous light: which in time past were not a people, but are now the people of God: which had not obtained mercy, but now have obtained mercy. Dearly beloved, I beseech you as strangers and pilgrims. . . . 1 Peter 2:9–11

ALIENS are rarely shown the "welcome mat." They are often accepted only with a tongue-in-cheek attitude. Being aliens, with our citizenship not in the world but in heaven, we as Christ's followers will frequently be treated as "peculiar people" and as strangers.

Our life is not of this world. "Our conversation is in heaven" (Philippians 3:20). Our interests, primarily, are not in this world. Jesus said: "Lay up for yourselves treasures in heaven . . . for where your treasure is, there will your heart be also" (Matthew 6:20–21). Our hope is not in this world. The Bible says, "We look for the Savior, the Lord Jesus Christ: who shall change our vile body, that it may be fashioned like unto his glorious body, according to the working whereby he is able even to subdue all things unto himself" (Philippians 3:20–21).

Hence, in every sense we are an enigma to the world. Like a few right-handed persons among a host of left-handed persons, we comprise a threat to their status quo. We cramp their style. We are labeled as "wet blankets," as kill-joys, and as prudes. Like the enemies of Jesus, the world still inquires contemptuously, "Art not thou also one of his disciples?" (John 18:25). We are not to let persecution distract us from our purpose—"to show forth" His praises!

December 7

THE NEED FOR SUNSHINE AND SHADOW

If ye suffer for righteousness' sake, happy are ye. . . . For it is better, if the will of God be so, that ye suffer for well doing, than for evil doing. 1 Peter 3:14, 17

ALL the masterpieces of art contain both light and shadow. A happy life is not one filled only with sunshine, but one which uses both light and shadow to produce beauty. Persecution can become a blessing because it forms a dark backdrop for the radiance of the Christian life. The greatest musicians as a rule are those who know how to bring song out of sadness. Fanny Crosby, her spirit aglow with faith in Christ, saw more with her sightless eyes than most of us do with normal vision. She has given us some of the great gospel songs which cheer our hearts and lives. She wrote some two thousand hymns of which sixty are still in common use.

Paul and Silas sang their song of praise at midnight in a rat-infested jail in Philippi, their feet in stocks, their backs raw from the jailer's whip. But their patience in suffering and persecution led to the conversion of the heathen prison warden. The blood of the martyrs is mixed well into the mortar which holds the stones of civilization together.

In the words of Thornton Wilder: "Without your wounds, where would your power be? . . . The very angels of God in heaven cannot persuade the wretched and blundering children of earth as can one human being broken on the wheels of living. In love's service only wounded soldiers will do."

When was the last time you *really* suffered for righteousness' sake? For the cause of Christ?

December 8

POWERFUL PROOFS

Who is gone into heaven, and is on the right hand of God; angels and authorities and powers being made subject unto him. 1 Peter 3:22

WHAT proofs did Jesus offer that He was truly God come in human form?

First, there was the proof of His perfect life. He could ask, "Which of you convinceth me of sin?" (John 8:46)—and no one could answer, because His life was perfect. . . . He was able to confront the full fury of Satan's temptations and yet not yield to sin; He "was in all points tempted like as we are, yet without sin" (Hebrews 4:15).

Second, there was the evidence of His power. His power was the power of God almighty—the power only God has. . . . He could quiet the storms on the sea of Galilee. . . . He raised the dead, healed the sick, restored sight to the blind, and made the lame walk. His miracles were a witness to the fact that He is Lord of all nature: "For by him were all things created. . . . And he is before all things, and by him all things consist" (Colossians 1:16–17).

Third, there was the evidence of fulfilled prophecy. Hundreds of years before His birth the prophets of the Old Testament spoke precisely of the place where He would be born (Micah 5:2) and of the manner of His death and burial (Psalm 22; Isaiah 53). Uncounted details of His life were foretold by the prophets, and in every instance these prophecies were fulfilled.

Fourth, there was the evidence of His resurrection from the dead. Jesus Christ was "declared to be the Son of God with power, according to the spirit of holiness, by the resurrection from the dead" (Romans 1:4). The founders of the various non-Christian religions of the world have lived, died, and been buried; in some instances it is still possible to visit their graves. But Christ is alive! His resurrection is a fact! His tomb is empty—and this is a compelling and central proof of His unique divine nature as God in human flesh.

Fifth, there is the proof of changed lives. History vividly illustrates what the Bible clearly affirms: "The heart is deceitful above all things, and desperately wicked: who can know it?" (Jeremiah 17:9). Education and discipline can do no more than rub off the rough edges of human selfishness—but Christ alone, the divine Son of God, has power to change the human heart. And He does. Christ can take the most sin-laden, selfish, evil person and bring forgiveness and new life.

These are only five of the proofs on which I base my belief in the divinity of Christ.

PEACE

For he is our peace. . . .   Ephesians 2:14

FOR as long as I can remember there have been conferences and studies, plans, and supposedly innovative ideas for bringing peace to this earth. Organizations have been created, much money and time have been spent, books have been written . . . all in an effort to find a formula that would bring peace on earth and good will to men.

World War I was called "the war to end all wars," but it wasn't—not for the United States and not for most of the rest of the world. As I write, there are fifty wars occurring somewhere in the world. Whether men shoot and fight one another or not, there is "warfare" in the home; warfare between husband and wife, between parents and children, between brothers and sisters, between neighbors, between boss and employee.

Why? What can be done to bring peace in all of these situations? The reason for war is that we have rejected God's provision for peace. Jesus said, "My peace I give unto you: not as the world giveth, give I unto you. . . ." So, peace is not man's to give. It comes from Christ. We war with one another because of sin, which is a declared state of war against God.

Only Christ can cancel sin and create a peace treaty with God and then between men. When the angel pronounced peace on earth, good will to men, it was a universal pronouncement for any who would accept this Bethlehem baby as his or her Savior and for no one else.

Do you know this peace? It can be yours today simply by asking for it. God's gifts are free, but He is waiting to be asked.

RICH REWARDS

But rejoice that you participate in the sufferings of Christ, so that you
may be overjoyed when his glory is revealed. 1 Peter 4:13, NIV

IN these days of spiritual darkness and political upheaval, the
forward-looking Christian remains optimistic and joyful,
knowing that Christ must reign, and "if we endure, we will
also reign with him" (2 Timothy 2:12, NIV).

For every man, woman, and child throughout the world
who is suffering, our Lord has these words from the Sermon
on the Mount: "Blessed are you when people insult you,
persecute you and falsely say all kinds of evil against you
because of me. Rejoice and be glad, because great is your
reward in heaven, for in the same way they persecuted the
prophets who were before you" (Matthew 5:11–12, NIV).

Perhaps in your particular circumstances you are
undergoing psychological suffering, which is just as real as
physical suffering. It may be a suffering that you cannot
express, even to your dearest friend—an inward, heartrending,
heartbreaking suffering. In the midst of it all, there is the
promise of victory. Christ has overcome the world, and you,
by faith, can overcome the world through our Lord
Jesus Christ (1 John 5:5).

There is a joy to be discovered in the midst of suffering.
Sometimes we encounter it in our earthly pilgrimage. Once
we acknowledge that possibility, we will be astounded at how
possible it is to be "surprised by joy," as C. S. Lewis put it so
effectively in his book by the same title.

CLEANSED CONSCIENCES AND CHANGED LIVES

If we walk in the light, as he is in the light, we have fellowship one with another, and the blood of Jesus Christ his Son cleanseth us from all sin. 1 John 1:7

THE blood of Christ cleanses our consciences: "How much more, then, will the blood of Christ, who through the eternal Spirit offered himself unblemished to God, cleanse our consciences from acts that lead to death, so that we may serve the living God!" (Hebrews 9:14, NIV).

Each of us has a conscience which sits as a judge over our every thought, word, and deed. It speaks with a silent voice, accusing or excusing, condemning or acquitting. It can be sensitive, crude, undeveloped, or distorted, depending upon the way we have used or abused it.

The human conscience is defiled by sin, says the Bible. All of us have experienced the backlash of guilt after a transgression. We know the haunting of the heart, the self-reproach of the mind which conscience can bring, the internal suffering that can come from being out of fellowship with God. Sin's effect may be erased from the body, but it leaves its permanent scar on the conscience. Our consciences are seared and defiled by sin.

The conscience of man is often beyond the reach of the psychiatrist. With all of his psychological techniques, he cannot sound its depravity and depth. Man himself is helpless to detach himself from the gnawing guilt of a heart weighed down with the guilt of sin. But where man has failed, God has succeeded. The Bible says that the blood of Christ has power to cleanse the conscience from dead works to serve the living God. This is not mere theory; it is a fact of Christian experience.

CONFESSION IS GOOD FOR THE SOUL

If we confess our sins, he is faithful and just, and will forgive our sins
and cleanse us from all unrighteousness.   1 John 1:9, RSV

THERE is a well-known story of some men in Scotland who
had spent the day fishing. That evening they were having tea
in a little inn. One of the fishermen, in a characteristic
gesture to describe the size of the fish that got away, flung
out his hands just as the little waitress was getting ready to
set the cup of tea at his place. The hand and the teacup
collided, dashing the tea against the white-washed walls.
Immediately an ugly brown stain began to spread over the
wall. The man who did it was very embarrassed and
apologized profusely, but one of the other guests jumped up
and said, "Never mind." Pulling a pen from his pocket, he
began to sketch around the ugly brown stain. Soon there
emerged a picture of a magnificent royal stag with his antlers
spread. That artist was Sir Edwin Landsee, England's
foremost painter of animals.

This story has always beautifully illustrated to me the fact
that if we confess not only our sins but our mistakes to God,
He can make out of them something for our good and for
His glory. Somehow it's harder to commit our mistakes and
stupidities to God than it is our sins. Mistakes and stupidities
seem so dumb, whereas sin seems more or less to be an
outcropping of our human nature. But Romans 8:28 tells us
that if they are committed to God He can make
circumstances work "for good with these who love Him, who
are called according to His purpose."

When you bake a cake, you put in raw flour, baking
powder, soda, bitter chocolate, shortening, etc., none of
which taste very good by themselves, but which work together

to make a delicious cake. And so with our sins and our mistakes—although they are not good by themselves, if we commit them in honest, simple faith to the Lord, He will work them out His own way and in His own time make something of them for our good and His glory.

December 13

WHEN WORRY BECOMES WORLDLY

Love not the world, neither the things that are in the world.
1 John 2:15

WORLDLINESS has been vastly misunderstood by many Christians. There are certain elements of daily life which are not sinful in themselves but that lead to sin if they are abused. Abuse literally means "overuse" or "extreme use" of things lawful which then become sin. Pleasure is lawful in its use, but unlawful in its overuse. Ambition is an essential part of true character, but it must be fixed on lawful objects and exercised in proper proportion.

Our daily occupation, reading, dress, friendships, and other similar phases of life are all legitimate and necessary but can easily become illegitimate, unnecessary, and harmful. Thought about the necessities of life is absolutely essential, but this can easily degenerate into anxiety.

The making of money is necessary for daily living, but moneymaking is apt to degenerate into money-loving, and then the deceitfulness of riches enters in and spoils our spiritual lives.

Worldliness is not confined to any particular rank, walk, or circumstance of life. But worldliness is a spirit, an atmosphere, an influence, permeating the whole of life in human society, and it needs to be guarded against constantly and strenuously. The Bible says, "Love not the world, neither the things that are in the world." It also warns that "the world passeth away, and the lust thereof; but he that doeth the will of God abideth for ever" (1 John 2:17).

We must make an out-and-out stand for Christ. It does not mean that in society we are snobs or have a superiority complex, lest we be in danger of spiritual pride (which would be far worse than worldliness). But today there are so many professing Christians who are walking hand in hand with the world that it is difficult to tell the difference between the Christian and the sinner. Our lives must make it plain whose we are and whom we serve!

December 14

GOD'S FOREVER KINGDOM

Beloved, now are we the sons of God, and it doth not yet appear what we shall be: but we know that, when he shall appear, we shall be like him; for we shall see him as he is. 1 John 3:2

THE government in God's kingdom is unique. It is not a democracy where the people govern, but a Christocracy where Christ is the supreme Authority. In a government of unredeemed men, democracy is the only fair and equitable system. But no democracy can ever be better than the people who make it up. When men are selfishly motivated, the government will be inequitable. When men are dishonest, the government will be the same. When everyone wants his own way, someone is going to get hurt.

But in God's Kingdom, Christ is King. He is compassionate, fair, merciful, and just. When He is sovereign in men's hearts, anguish turns to peace, hatred is transformed into love, and misunderstanding into understanding.

Not only this, but God's Kingdom is lasting. The history of man has been a continuous series of half successes and total failures. Prosperity exists for a time, only to be followed by war and depression. Twenty-six civilizations have come and gone, and man still battles with the same problems, over and over again.

But the Kingdom of God will abide forever. The fluctuations of time, the swinging of the pendulum from war to peace, from starvation to plenty, from chaos to order, will end forever. The Bible says, "And of his kingdom there shall be no end" (Luke 1:33).

December 15

THE SUPREME SUFFERER

Hereby perceive we the love of God, because he laid down his life for us. 1 John 3:16

THROUGHOUT His earthly life, Jesus was constantly exposed to personal violence. At the beginning of His ministry, His own townsfolk at Nazareth tried to hurl Him down from the brow of the hill (Luke 4:29). The religious and political leaders often conspired to seize Him and kill Him. At length He was arrested and brought to trial before Pilate and Herod. Even though He was guiltless of the accusations, He was denounced as an enemy of God and man, and not worthy to live.

The sufferings of Jesus also included the *fierce temptations of the devil*: "Then Jesus was led by the Spirit into the desert to be tempted by the devil" (Matthew 4:1).

Remember, too, that *He knew in advance what was coming*, and this enhanced His suffering. He knew the contents of the cup He had to drink; He knew the path of suffering He should tread. He could distinctly foresee the baptism of blood that awaited Him. He spoke plainly to His disciples of His coming death by crucifixion.

Jesus, the supreme sufferer, *came to suffer for our sins.* As a result of His sufferings, our redemption was secured.

What does the divine sufferer demand from us? Only our faith, our love, our grateful praise, our consecrated hearts and lives. Is that too much to ask?

Christ living in us will enable us to live above our circumstances, however painful they are. Perhaps you who read these words find yourself almost crushed by the circumstances which you are now facing. You wonder how much more you can stand. But don't despair! God's grace is sufficient for you and will enable you to rise above your trials. Let this be your confidence:

> Who shall separate us from the love of Christ? Shall trouble or hardship or persecution or famine or nakedness or danger or sword? . . . No, in all these things we are more than conquerors through him who loved us (Romans 8:35, 37).

December 16

SPIRIT-FILLED LIVING

Hereby we know that he abideth in us, by the Spirit which he hath given us. 1 John 3:24

THE Holy Spirit is already in every Christian heart, and He intends to produce His fruit. However, there must be a displacement. A boat does not sink when it is in the water, but it does sink when the water comes into the boat. We do not fail to enjoy the fruit of the Spirit because we live in a sea of corruption; we fail to do so because the sea of corruption is in us.

The internal combustion engine's worst enemy is the deadly carbon that builds up in the cylinder chamber. It reduces the power and causes the motor to lose efficiency. Oil will improve the engine's performance, but it will not remove the carbon so that the motor can run more efficiently. Mechanical surgery must be performed to remove the carbon so that the oil can do its best work and the motor perform as it was designed to do. Similarly, we must eliminate the works of the flesh from our inner lives so that deadly carbon and grit do not impair the effectiveness of our spiritual performance. This is possible only as we yield our lives to the control of the Holy Spirit. We must let the laser beam of God's Word scan us to detect the abiding sins and fruitless qualities which impair our personal growth and fruitfulness.

The story is told of a man who glanced at the obituary column in his local newspaper. To his surprise he saw his own name, indicating that he had just died. At first he laughed about it. But soon the telephone began to ring. Stunned friends and acquaintances called to inquire and to offer their sympathy. Finally, in irritation, he called the newspaper editor and angrily reported that even though he had been reported dead in the obituary column he was very much alive. The editor was apologetic and embarrassed. Then in a flash of inspiration, he said, "Do not worry, sir, I will make it all right, for tomorrow I will put your name in the births column."

This may sound like merely a humorous incident, but it is actually a spiritual parable. Not until we have allowed our old selves to be crucified with Christ can our new selves emerge to display the marvelous fruit that is characteristic of the life of Jesus Christ. And only the Holy Spirit can make possible the out-living of the in-living Christ.

GOD IS LOVE

He who does not love does not know God for God is love. In this the
love of God was made manifest among us, that God sent his only Son
into the world, so that we might live through him.
1 John 4:8–9, RSV

FROM Genesis to Revelation, from earth's greatest tragedy to earth's greatest triumph, the dramatic story of man's lowest depths and God's highest heights can be couched in twenty-five beautiful words: "For God so loved the world, that he gave his only begotten Son, that whosoever believeth in him should not perish, but have everlasting life" (John 3:16).

Many people misunderstand the attribute of God's nature which is love. "God is love" does not mean that everything is sweet, beautiful, and happy, and that God's love could not possibly allow punishment for sin.

God's holiness demands that all sin be punished, but God's love provided a plan of redemption and salvation for sinful man. God's love provided the Cross of Jesus Christ by which man can have forgiveness and cleansing. It was the love of God that sent Jesus Christ to that cross.

Who can describe or measure the love of God? The Bible is a revelation of the fact that God is love. When we preach justice, it is justice tempered with love. When we preach righteousness, it is righteousness founded on love.

When we preach atonement, it is atonement planned by love, provided by love, given by love, finished by love, necessitated because of love. When we preach the resurrection of Christ, we are preaching the miracle of love. When we preach the return of Christ, we are preaching the fulfillment of love.

December 18

FAITH THAT FINISHES

For whatever is born of God overcomes the world; and this is the victory that overcomes the world, our faith. 1 John 5:4, RSV

BECAUSE all the powers of the evil world system seem to be preying on the minds of people already disturbed and frustrated in our generation, I believe the time has come to focus on the positives of the Christian faith. John the apostle also said, "Greater is he that is in you, than he that is in the world" (1 John 4:4). Satan is indeed capable of doing supernatural things—but he acts only by the permissive will of God; he is on a leash. It is God who is all powerful. It is God who is omnipotent. God has provided Christians with both offensive and defensive weapons. We are not to be fearful; we are not to be distressed; we are not to be deceived; nor are we to be intimidated.

Rather, we are to be on our guard, calm, and alert "lest Satan should get an advantage of us: for we are not ignorant of his devices" (2 Corinthians 2:11).

One of Satan's sly devices is to divert our minds from the help God offers us in our struggles against the forces of evil. However, the Bible testifies that God has provided assistance for us in our spiritual conflicts. We are not alone in this world! The Bible teaches us that God's Holy Spirit has been given to empower us and guide us. In addition, the Bible—in nearly three hundred different places—also teaches that God has countless angels at His command. Furthermore, God has commissioned these angels to aid His children in their struggles against Satan. The Bible does not give as much information about them as we might like, but what it does say should be a source of comfort and strength for us in every circumstance.

I am convinced that these heavenly beings exist and that they provide unseen aid on our behalf. I believe in angels because the Bible says there are angels; and I believe the Bible to be the true Word of God. I also believe in angels because I have sensed their presence in my life on special occasions.

Spiritual forces and resources are available to all Christians. Because our resources are unlimited, Christians will be winners. Millions of angels are at God's command and at our service. The hosts of heaven stand at attention as we make our way from earth to glory, and Satan's BB guns are no match for God's heavy artillery.

December 19

THE PLEDGE

Now it is God who makes both us and you stand firm in Christ. He anointed us, set his seal of ownership on us, and put his Spirit in our hearts as a deposit, guaranteeing what is to come.
2 Corinthians 1:21–22, NIV

AS we trust in Christ, God gives us the Spirit not only as a seal. He is also our pledge, or, as some translations read, "earnest" or "guarantee," according to such passages as 2 Corinthians 1:22 and Ephesians 1:14.

"Now He who establishes us with you in Christ and has anointed us is God, who also has sealed us and given us the Spirit in our hearts as a guarantee [pledge]" (2 Corinthians 1:21–22, NKJV).

In the apostle Paul's day, businessmen considered a pledge to do three things: It was a down payment that sealed a bargain, it represented an obligation to buy, and it was a sample of what was to come.

Suppose you were to decide to buy a car. The pledge would first be a down payment sealing the transaction. It would also represent your promise to pay the rest of the purchase price. This is what the Holy Spirit promises when we receive the "earnest of our inheritance" (Ephesians 1:14).

As the great missionary statesman Adoniram Hudson once said, "The prospect is as bright as the promises of God."

December 20

SOUL FOOD

Beloved, I pray that all may go well with you and that you may be in health; I know that it is well with your soul. 3 John 2, RSV

THE Bible teaches that a person is more than just a body—each of us is actually a living soul! Our souls are created in the image of God. Just as our bodies have certain characteristics and appetites, so do our souls. The characteristics of the soul are intelligence, emotions, and will. The human soul or spirit longs for peace, contentment, and happiness. Most of all, the soul has an appetite for God—a yearning to be reconciled to its Creator and to have fellowship with Him forever.

In our world, we give most attention to satisfying the appetites of the body and practically none to the soul. Consequently we are one-sided. We become fat physically and materially, while spiritually we are lean, weak, and anemic. Or we spend enormous amounts of time and money on fad diets, expensive exercise machines, and health clubs. For many people, these things only demonstrate their preoccupation with the physical side of life. To be sure, our bodies have been given to us by God, and we are to take care of them in every way possible. But even more important is taking care of our souls. The apostle Paul told Timothy, "Train yourself in godliness; for while bodily training is of some value, godliness is of value in every way, as it holds promise for the present life and also the life to come" (1 Timothy 4:7–8, RSV).

The soul actually demands as much attention as the body. It demands fellowship and communion with God. It demands worship, quietness, and meditation. Nothing but God ever completely satisfies, because the soul was made for God, and without God it is restless and in secret torment.

December 21

LED BY THE LAMB

For the Lamb which is in the midst of the throne shall feed them, and shall lead them unto living fountains of waters: and God shall wipe away all tears from their eyes. Revelation 7:17

THIS is the supreme reality of heaven. There will be an intimate relationship between Christ and His Church throughout eternity. He will be "the Lamb which is in the midst of the throne," and He shall feed His own and shall lead them to fountains of living waters.

With this great certainty and assurance, the future holds no terrors we cannot face. Beyond the crisis lies heaven and the utopia of our dreams. Thus the Christian should never be filled with fear, discouragement, or despondency.

If you do not know Christ as Savior, the future is bleak and dark and pessimistic indeed. Surrender your life to the Lord Jesus Christ. Let Him come to your heart and transform you and change you.

Courage, faith, and fortitude come from the cross where Christ emptied Himself and humbled Himself, even to the death of the cross. Jesus said, "In the world you will have troubles; but be of good courage, I have overcome the world."

Oliver Goldsmith, the Irish poet and playwright, penned these insightful words:

Hope, like a gleaming taper's light,
  Adorns and cheers our way;
And still, as darker grows the night,
  Emits a brighter ray.

You and I as Christians know the source of that "brighter ray."

December 22

THE CHRISTMAS SACRIFICE

He [Jesus] was delivered over to death for our sins and was raised to life for our justification. Romans 4:25, NIV

She [Mary] will give birth to a son, and you are to give him the name Jesus, because he will save his people from their sins. Matthew 1:21, NIV

DO we look at ourselves, our trials, our problems, when we are suffering? Do we live under the circumstances, instead of above the circumstances? Or do we look at the One who knew more suffering than we are able to conceive?

In *Table Talk* Martin Luther said, "Our suffering is not worthy the name of suffering. When I consider my crosses, tribulations, and temptations, I shame myself almost to death, thinking what are they in comparison to the sufferings of my blessed Saviour Jesus Christ."

There are several things about the life of Christ that reveal His role as the "suffering servant" Messiah. We cannot begin to trace every aspect of this search through His life, but consider these truths:

In Isaiah 53 the sufferings of the Savior are so minutely pictured that one might well read it as the record of an eyewitness, rather than the prediction of a man who wrote eight hundred years before the event.

Observe that Jesus' life began in the midst of persecution and peril. He came on a mission of love and mercy, sent by the Father. An angel announced His conception and gave Him His name. The heavenly host sang a glorious anthem at His birth. By the extraordinary star, the very heavens indicated His coming. In Himself He was the most illustrious child ever born—the holy child of Mary, the divine Son of God. Yet no sooner did He enter our world than Herod decreed His death and labored to accomplish it.

Notice, too, that He assumed a role of deep abasement. The Son of the eternal Father, He became the infant of days and was made in the likeness of man. He assumed our human nature with all its infirmities, and weakness, and capacity for suffering. He came as a child of the poorest parents. His entire life was one voluntary humiliation. He came to be a servant and to minister rather than to be ministered unto.

December 23

THE ANGEL'S ANNOUNCEMENT

And the angel said unto them, Fear not for, behold, I bring you good tidings of great joy, which shall be to all people. Luke 2:10

DOES it not seem mysterious that God brought the first message of the birth of Jesus to ordinary people rather than to princes and kings? In this instance, God spoke through His holy angel to the shepherds who were keeping sheep in the fields. This was a lowly occupation, so shepherds were not well educated. But Mary in her song, the Magnificat, tells us the true story: "He hath put down the mighty from their seats, and exalted them of low degree. He hath filled the hungry with good things, and the rich he hath sent empty away" (Luke 1:52–53). What a word for our generation!

What was the message of the angel to the shepherds? First,

he told them not to be afraid. Over and over again the presence of angels was frightening to those to whom they came. But unless they came in judgment, the angels spoke a word of reassurance. They calmed the people to whom they came. This tells us that the appearance of angels is awe-inspiring, something about them awakening fear in the human heart. They represent a presence that has greatness and sends a chill down the spine. But when the angel had quieted the fears of the shepherds, he brought this message, one forever to be connected with the evangel: "For, behold, I bring you good tidings of great joy, which shall be to all people. For unto you is born this day in the city of David a Saviour, which is Christ the Lord" (Luke 2:10–11).

I could preach a dozen sermons on those two verses for they contain so many important theological themes. But note that the angel does not preach the Gospel. Rather, he witnesses to it and demonstrates again the overwhelming concern angels have for it.

The good tidings were that the Savior had come. The people needed somebody who could bring them back into fellowship with God, because the blood of bulls and goats could not do this in any permanent way. But the blood of the Savior could. The angel message was that God had come, redemption was possible, the Lord had visited His people with salvation. What a testimony to the evangel this was!

December 24

THE DEMANDS OF FAITH

I can do all things through Christ which strengtheneth me. Philippians 4:13

A NUMBER of years ago I spent Christmas Eve on the battlefields of Korea. It was a beautiful evening; a half moon was in the sky; snow was several inches deep. Picking our way along in a small helicopter, we finally landed at a base hospital right behind the front lines. We could see the glow of the artillery over the side of the mountain.

In the hospital were several men who had just been carried back from their patrol post. One casualty, an ex-football player from one of our southern universities, was a battle-hardened marine. His doctor whispered to me, "Part of his spine has been shot out and he'll never walk again."

Because of his injury he was forced to lie face downward. He said, "Mr. Graham, we have been looking forward to your coming, and I'd like to see your face."

I got on my back on the floor and looked up into the face of that tough marine.

"I know that I'm in bad shape," he said, "but I want you to tell people when you get back to America that I'd gladly die for my country."

Would you give the same dedication to Jesus Christ? He gave no less for you, and He demands no less from you.

December 25

THE MEANING OF CHRISTMAS

Wherefore God also hath highly exalted him, and given him a name which is above every name: that at the name of Jesus every knee should bow, of things in heaven, and things in earth, and things under the earth; and that every tongue should confess that Jesus Christ is Lord, to the glory of God the Father. Philippians 2:9–11

GOD speaks to us in the person of His Son Jesus Christ. "God . . . hath in these last days spoken unto us by his Son" (Hebrews 1:1–2). The idea that God would someday visit this planet is an ancient truth that is no doubt an oral remnant of the original revelation God gave to Adam of a promised salvation (Genesis 3:15). We find crude references to it in most religions of the world, indicating that man at some time had heard or sensed that God would visit the earth. However, it was not until the "fulness of the time" when all the conditions were right, when all the prophetic considerations were fulfilled, that God "sent forth his Son, made of a woman" (Galatians 4:4).

On that first Christmas night in Bethlehem, "God was manifest in the flesh" (1 Timothy 3:16). This manifestation was in the person of Jesus Christ. The Scripture says concerning Christ, "In him dwelleth all the fullness of the Godhead bodily" (Colossians 2:9). This manifestation of God is by far the most complete revelation God ever gave to the world. If you want to know what God is like, then take a long look at Jesus Christ. In Him were displayed not only the perfections that had been exhibited in the creation—such as wisdom, power, and majesty—but also such perfections as justice, mercy, grace, and love. "The *logos* [Word] was made flesh and dwelt among us" (John 1:14).

To His disciples Jesus said, "Ye believe in God, believe also in me" (John 14:1). This sequence of faith is inevitable. If we believe in what God made and what God said, we will believe in the One whom God sent.

December 26

THE CROWN OF LIFE

Be thou faithful unto death and I will give thee a crown of life. Revelation 2:10

THE Bible has much to say about the brevity of life and the necessity of preparing for eternity. We need a new awareness of the fact that death is rapidly approaching for all of us, and that the Bible has many warnings for us to prepare to meet God. The rich with all their wealth cannot buy a reprieve from the death sentence that hangs over every man. The poor cannot beg one extra day of life from the "grim reaper" who pursues every man from the cradle to the grave.

The Scripture says, "What is your life? It is even a vapor, that appeareth for a little time, and then vanisheth away" (James 4:14). Even the cynical and secular at times think deeply about life and eternity. I am convinced that if people gave more thought to death, eternity, and judgment, there would be more holy living and a greater consciousness of God.

Too many Christians try to put off the thought of death and of the fact that all children of God will one day stand before the judgment seat of Christ to give an account of how they spent their time here on earth.

Job says that his days are "swifter than a weaver's shuttle." In North Carolina I have visited the textile mills and have watched the giant looms which turn out cloth for the nation. The shuttles move with the speed of lightning, scarcely visible to the naked eye. The Bible says this is the chronology of eternity. Though you live to be seventy, eighty, or ninety years old, that is but a snap of the finger compared to eternity. Put your hand on your heart and feel it beat. It is saying, "Quick! Quick! Quick!" We have only a few brief years at the most. Let's live them for the Lord.

December 27

JESUS IS VICTOR!

The kingdoms of this world are become the kingdoms of our Lord, and of his Christ; and he shall reign for ever and ever. Revelation 11:15

WE Christians need to rely constantly on the Holy Spirit. We need to remember that Christ dwells in us through the

Holy Spirit. Our bodies are the dwelling place of the Third Person of the Trinity. We should not ask Him to help us as we would a servant.

We should ask Him to come in and do it all, to take over in our lives. We should tell Him how weak, helpless, unstable, and unreliable we are. It is important that we stand aside and let Him take over in all our choices and decisions. We know that the Holy Spirit prays for us (Romans 8), and what a comfort that should be to the weakest of us.

It is impossible for us to hold out in the Christian life—but He can hold us. It is very difficult for Him to hold us if we are struggling, fighting, and striving. We should just relax and rest in the Lord, letting go all those inner tensions and complexes. We should rely completely on Him. I should not fret and worry about important decisions—I should let Him make them for me. Do not worry about tomorrow—He is the God of tomorrow. He sees the end from the beginning. Do not worry about the necessities of life—He is there to supply and provide. A true victorious Christian is one who, in spite of worries, inner conflicts, and tensions, is confident that God is in control and will be victorious in the end. In reliance on the Holy Spirit, we will find that many of our physical and mental ailments will disappear along with many worries, inner conflicts, and tensions.

Whatever our difficulties, whatever our circumstances, we must remember, as Corrie ten Boom used to say, "Jesus is victor!"

December 28

A COVENANT FOR CHRISTIANS

And there shall be no more curse: but the throne of God and the Lamb shall be in it; and his servants shall serve him.   Revelation 22:3

IT all started in the Garden of Eden, a place located somewhere between the Tigris and the Euphrates rivers in the Middle East. It is significant that the nations prominent in early history are once again prominent: Israel, Egypt, Syria, Iran, and so on. In that Garden God gave a great promise: "And I will put enmity between thee and the woman, and between thy seed and her seed; it shall bruise thy head, and thou shalt bruise his heel" (Genesis 3:15). As we approach the end of the age, the head of Satan is being battered and bruised as the forces of God gain momentum. Under the command of God, Michael the archangel is now organizing his forces for the last battle—Armageddon. The last picture in the Bible is one of heaven.

Many years ago I was visiting the dining room of the United States Senate. As I was speaking to various people, one of the senators called me to his table. He said, "Billy, we're having a discussion about pessimism and optimism. Are you a pessimist or an optimist?" I smiled and said, "I'm an optimist." He asked, "Why?" I said, "I've read the last page of the Bible."

The Bible speaks about a city whose builder and maker is God, where those who have been redeemed will be superior to angels. It speaks of "a pure river of water of life, clear as crystal, proceeding out of the throne of God and of the Lamb" (Revelation 22:1). It says, "And they shall see his face; and his name shall be in their foreheads. And there shall be no night there; and they need no candle, neither light of the sun; for the Lord God giveth them light: and they shall reign for ever and ever" (verses 4–5).

The next verse has a thrilling last word to say about angels: "These sayings are faithful and true: and the Lord God of the holy prophets sent his angel to shew unto his servants the things which must shortly be done."

Christian and non-Christian alike should meditate on the

seventh verse where God says, "Behold I come quickly: blessed is he that keepeth the sayings of the prophecy of this book." Where do you fit in this prophetic picture?

December 29

·······························

THE DEVIL DEFEATED

He seized the dragon, that ancient serpent, who is the devil, or Satan, and bound him for a thousand years . . . [where he] will be tormented day and night for ever and ever. Revelation 20:2, 10, NIV

THE most powerful being in all the world today, outside of God Himself, is the devil. At the temptation he showed Jesus all the kingdoms of the world, and he said in effect, "I will give you all of these if you will bow down and worship me" (Matthew 4:9). Jesus did not dispute him. Satan had the power to give Jesus the cosmos, the world system of evil. But, thank God, our Lord quoted Scripture, and that's one thing the devil can't stand! The Scripture defeats him every time.

In 2 Corinthians 4:4 he's also called "the god of this age." That means that he's the director of false religions and philosophies of the world. The Bible says the whole cosmos (world) is under his control. What's going to transpire if something doesn't happen to Satan? Who's going to dispose of evil? Who's going to dispose of Satan? Humanity is helpless before him. Man is unable to chain him. The Church cannot dethrone him. Legislation is impotent. The United Nations does not know how to handle him. They don't even understand that they're dealing with a spiritual power—an enormous power of evil in the world today.

Let's not forget one fact, however. There is One who is more powerful than Satan! This One defeated him 2,000 years ago on the cross. The devil didn't want Jesus Christ to go to the cross, because he was afraid of what Christ would do on the cross. He knew that when Christ died on the cross, He was bearing the sins of the whole world. And God was saying to mankind from the cross, "I love you. I want to forgive you of all of your sins. I want you to be My child, and one day to join Me in heaven." And if Jesus had come down from the cross, we couldn't be saved. We couldn't go to heaven. That's why the devil didn't want Him on the cross. That's why they taunted Him, "If Thou be the Son of God, come down from the cross." Satan suffered his greatest defeat at the cross, and in the resurrection of the Lord Jesus Christ.

December 30

A GLIMPSE OF HEAVEN

And God shall wipe away all tears from their eyes; and there shall be no more death, neither sorrow, nor crying, neither shall there be any more pain: for the former things are passed away. Revelation 21:4

THE description of heaven and the holy city given in Revelation 21 and 22 is beyond understanding. The Bible talks about gates of pearl, streets of gold, a river of life, and a tree of life.

It is a place so beautiful that when John, the apostle, caught a glimpse of it, the only thing to which he could liken it was a young woman on the crowning day of her life: her wedding day. He said that the holy city was like "a bride adorned for her husband."

The Bible teaches that heaven will be a home which is happy. I know many beautiful homes that are not happy. They are homes made beautiful by everything that culture and wealth can do, yet there is something wrong, something lacking. They are homes that bring to mind the wise man's words, "Better is a dry morsel, and quietness therewith, than a house full of sacrifices with strife" (Proverbs 17:1).

God's house will be a happy home because there will be nothing in it to hinder happiness (Revelation 21:4). This world has in it much happiness for those who know how to find it.

Sooner or later, however, something interferes. No face is so perfect but that it has some blemish. Every rose has its thorn, every cup of sweet has its drop of gall, but in the Father's house there will be nothing to mar the happiness.

Think of a place where there will be no sin, no sorrow, no quarrels, no misunderstandings, no hurt feelings, no pain, no sickness, no death. That is heaven!

December 31

FOCUS ON THE FUTURE

For ever, O God, thy word is settled in heaven.   Psalm 119:89

A s the Christian with the Bible in his hand surveys the world scene, he is aware that we do not worship an absentee God. He is aware that God is in the shadows of history and that He has a plan. The Christian is not to be disturbed by the chaos, violence, strife, bloodshed, and threat of war that fill the pages of our daily newspapers. We know that these things are the consequences of man's sin and greed. If anything else were happening, we would doubt the Bible. Every day we see a thousand evidences of the fulfillment of biblical prophecy. Every day as I read my newspaper I say, "The Bible is true."

No matter how foreboding the future, the Christian knows the end of the story of history. We are heading toward a glorious climax. Every writer of the New Testament believes that "the best is yet to be."

As John Baillie has said, "The Bible indicates that the

future is in God's hands. If it were in our hands, we would make a mess of it. The future is not in the devil's hands, for then he would lead us to destruction. The future is not at the mercy of any historical determinism leading us blindly forward, for then life would be without meaning. But the future is in the hands of One who is preparing something better than eye hath seen, or ear heard, or has entered into the heart of man to conceive."

The psalmist said, "The Lord is my light and my salvation, whom shall I fear? The Lord is the strength of my life; of whom shall I be afraid?" (Psalm 27:1).